Military Reforms in India

Military Reforms in India

Capt. (Retd) Brahmdutt Vats

PRASHANT PUBLISHING HOUSE
DELHI-110094

Published by :
Prashant Publishing House
C-34, 28 Foota Road, Gali-3,
West Karwal Nagar, Delhi-110094
Phone : 011-22963970, Mob. : 9810396373
e-mail.: prashantpublishinghouse@gmail.com

Military Reforms in India

First Published 2019

ISBN 978-93-88526-10-4

PRINTED IN INDIA
Published by Mr. R.K. Jha M/s Prashant Publishing House and Published at H.S. Offset House Press, Delhi.

Contents

Preface

The defence reforms that were undertaken periodically were reactive in nature and, in many cases, responses to crises as well as being sporadic, piecemeal and often ad hoc. The most recent review of security challenges undertaken occurred close to two decades ago, in the aftermath of the Kargil conflict of 1999. This was the Kargil Review Committee, and a subsequent Group of Ministers committee was appointed to study its report and suggest urgent measures for implementation of its suggestions, especially focussing on intelligence reforms, internal security, border management, and defence management.

India's defence planning architecture underwent a significant change with the Narendra Modi government deciding to establish an overarching Defence Planning Committee (DPC) under the National Security Adviser. The aim is to leverage this cross-governmental body — comprising the Chairman of the Chiefs of Staff Committee, three Service Chiefs, the Defence, Expenditure and Foreign Secretaries — to enhance India's ability to do some long-term strategising.

In a major move, Defence Minister Nirmala Sitharaman has approved the first batch of reforms in the Army which include relocation of 229 officers from the Army headquarters, creation of a new post of Deputy Chief for Military Operations and Strategic Planning, and setting up new wings for vigilance and human rights issues.

The Modi administration recently revealed its interim budget for the calendar year 2019-2020 is one which has already generated controversy. From the extremely low pension of Rs 6,000 a year for low income farmers, another pension scheme for workers in the organised sector amounting to Rs 3,000 a month after the age of 60, and the income tax exemption bracket being increased to Rs 5 lakh are just some of the measures this government has seen fit to undertake to provide much needed relief to the lower sections of society. While these measures have been stated to be nothing more than vote-capturing tactics for the 2019 general elections, one of the major changes the Finance Minister was proud to announce was the increase in the defence budget, which officially crossed Rs 3,00,000 crore for the first time, "the highest in any year." While it is good news the Indian armed forces have seen an increase in their budget, it is still a budget which does not satisfy the minimum requirements of a modern day military.

India is now genuinely poised to shine. It cannot do so with a feeble military machine, which functions on ad hoc basis or on the glorious past. We need to revamp and restructure before we are actually faced with the challenges we have talked about. The need today is for a synergistic and visionary national approach for the strong, purposeful and modern India that is just over the horizon.

Defence planning is essentially a subset of overall national level planning in the political, economic and social spheres and has to be evolved in the context of global and proximate factors affecting the nation.. It has also to take into account the philosophy and ethos animating the national psyche; in other words the historical and cultural forces which have shaped the collective memory and outlook of the people over the centuries.

This is a reference book. All the matter is just compiled and edited in nature, taken from the various sources which are in public domain.

The book is an indispensable guide to practitioners, scholars and researchers working on the area of defence and military studies, strategic and security studies, India's defence and security policies as well as to the informed reader.

—*Editor*

1

Introduction

India's defence planning architecture underwent a significant change with the Narendra Modi government deciding to establish an overarching Defence Planning Committee (DPC) under the National Security Adviser. The aim is to leverage this cross-governmental body — comprising the Chairman of the Chiefs of Staff Committee, three Service Chiefs, the Defence, Expenditure and Foreign Secretaries — to enhance India's ability to do some long-term strategising.

The DPC has been tasked with drafting reports on "national security strategy, international defence engagement strategy, roadmap to build a defence manufacturing ecosystem, strategy to boost defence exports, and priority capability development plans." Four subcommittees have been created under the DPC to focus on policy and strategy, plans and capability development, defence diplomacy, and the defence manufacturing ecosystem. Appointment of two more Deputy National Security Advisers, as opposed to just one in the earlier structure, is part of a major restructuring.

It has also been reported that a National Security Strategy document has been finalised, though it is unlikely that it will be made public. Given the growing focus of Indian security policy on China, the MEA is now running the Centre for Contemporary China Studies, an in-house think-tank which is exclusively devoted to studying China. It has personnel from across various branches of the government and will aim to provide inputs to policymakers on managing China, both on a day-to-day and long-term basis.

While addressing the Combined Commanders Conference in December 2015, Prime Minister Narendra Modi had underlined "At a time when major powers are reducing their forces and rely more on technology, we are still constantly seeking to expand the size of our forces. Modernisation and expansion of forces at the same time is a difficult and unnecessary goal. We need forces that are agile, mobile and driven by technology, not just human valour." In line with this, certain steps have been taken.

In the first such exercise of its kind since Independence to be completed by the end of 2019, the Modi government is also moving ahead with major restructuring of the Indian Army with a view to enhance its combat capabilities, as well as streamline budgetary allocation. The Ministry of Defence had constituted a committee under Lt. Gen. D.B. Shekatkar to recommend measures for enhancing combat capability and rebalancing defence expenditure of the armed forces which had submitted its report in December 2016. Most of its recommendations (65 out of 99) have been accepted and are now at various stages of implementation.

The very nature of warfare is evolving rapidly and India's neighbours are undertaking their own restructuring. Indian armed forces cannot remain beholden to their past practices without an assessment of the rapid evolution in technological and socio-political forces. The 1.3-million strong Indian Army hardly has any funds for modernisation, burdened as it is by revenue expenditure and pensions. A planned Army restructuring, aimed at reducing its strength by 1.5 lakh men, is expected to save up to Rs 7,000 crore a year in revenue expenditure.

These decisions come at a time when Indian defence planning stands at a crossroads. The silo-driven approach to defence planning has resulted in the lack of an integrated view. The three Services as well as the civilian and defence agencies are often seen to be working at cross purposes. Such an ad hoc approach has meant that more often than not, issues like threat perception and force structure are not managed via a centralised and authoritative overview. Instead, individual Services tend to be driving the agenda at their own levels.

This lack of synchronisation is manifested in various ways. On the one hand, the Indian Army Chief has been talking of a two-front war. On the other, the Vice-Chief of Army Staff testified before the Parliamentary Standing Committee on Defence that the budget allocated to the defence forces was hardly enough to complete the committed payments for the emergency procurements already made, let alone for pursuing an ambitious defence modernisation plan.

The headlines on Indian defence policy often tend to be completely divorced from the ground reality. India's $250-billion military modernisation programme is often talked about. But even as New Delhi remains keen on acquiring significant weapons platforms, there have been persistent doubts about its ability to harness these resources in service of a long-term strategy. Indeed, the absence of an Indian "grand strategy" that sets out political objectives for Indian power projection — and then ensures military, economic, intelligence and educational development — coordinated toward these objectives, has been a perennial topic of discussion within Indian strategic circles.

India's defence reform campaign has existed nearly as long as the current system itself. This drive focuses on extending resource integration and coordination throughout defence policymaking. Moreover, it recommends a state infrastructure able to adequately implement political judgements and to combine state resources to meet these judgements. This is currently missing in India.

Since the very beginning, the defence reform drive has implicitly targeted the need for a sufficiently integrative and coordinative state structure — required for an operationally effective defence policy. But not much success has been achieved.

Reforming this system remains a core requirement for India to adequately manage its scarce resources and align these with political objectives.

Effective defence planning and force structuring is a function of an institutional framework that allows for a clear delineation of political goals, efficient mobilisation of resources and effective use of these resources for developing instrumentalities of state power. The Modi government seems to have finally acknowledged the need for new structures and processes, but time is not on India's side.

At a time when advances in technology are revolutionising warfare, India is still debating the need to move towards leaner force structures. India needs to cut the flab on an urgent basis as over half of the annual defence budget going to meet salary and pension requirements is clearly not sustainable. The priorities of India's "Make in India" initiative and cumbersome defence procurement process will also have to be brought in sync with each other. India's status as the world's largest arms importer hardly does justice to its ambitions to emerge as a defence manufacturing hub. The debate on integration, both among the Services headquarters, and between the Services and the Ministry of Defence, also continues unabated and should be concluded.

Effective defence planning tends to put a premium on assuring future strategic and operational adaptiveness. In the Indian context, a transformative shift in mindset, structures and processes is needed. Rapidly evolving security environment as well as a near permanent pressure on scarce resources underscores the need for strategic defence planning. The Modi government has made moves in the right direction. Hopefully, it will be able to take this process of strategic restructuring to its logical conclusion.

THE ROADMAP TO MILITARY REFORM

In the debate on reform in the Indian military, there is a need for clear policy-driven directives that meet India's national security needs and challenges.

A recent historical overview would indicate just how confused things are, which doesn't augur well for a 'leading power'. The initial flavour of the debate in the decades following the Group of Ministers' report, the Kargil Review Committee report, and the Naresh Chandra Committee report focussed on a restructuring of higher defence organisation as the first step. This was intended to improve synergy among different tools of statecraft (bureaucracy, military, research and development, intelligence, internal security mechanisms, and more). When very little traction was seen in converting this into structural changes within the Ministry of Defence, and sharing of expertise, the debate shifted to the second tier of reform in the operational realm. This has unfortunately pitted the three services against one another in a series of turf wars that have ranged from control over space to control over cyber and special forces.

Targeting the IAF

When these turf wars did not result in the proposed space, cyber and special forces commands that were to complement the Headquarters Integrated Defence Staff and the Andaman and Nicobar Command as stepping stones to integration, one more hat was thrown into the ring — that of standalone integrated theatre commands. Without considering any restructuring of higher defence organisation, creation of Chief of the Defence Staff, or debating whether these theatre commands would be accompanied by a dilution in the operational control of the respective service chiefs, the debate now largely targets the Indian Air Force (IAF) in a subtle manner as being the 'spoiler' in what is otherwise a largely consensual approach to integration.

It is important to reiterate some of the core arguments that the IAF has in opposition to any piecemeal integration initiative. If there is any service that is truly 'joint' in terms of participation in statecraft or military operations in tandem with other tools, particularly as first responders, it is the IAF. There has never been any recorded criticism or shortfalls in the contribution of the IAF reported by the Indian Army or Navy to the political executive at apex forums like the Combined Commanders' Conference. If the flying task of the IAF in terms of its distribution between joint and exclusive tasks is scrutinised, conservative figures would reveal more than 60% as being committed to the former. The IAF is cognisant of its pivotal role in determining the trajectory of any limited high-intensity conflict in any kind of terrain.

Capturing ground beyond a few kilometres or taking physical control of vast maritime spaces for prolonged durations are no longer sustainable operations of war as they arguably result in avoidable depletion of combat potential. This causes unacceptable attrition in limited but high-tempo operations. It is in this context that air power would offer a viable alternative by shaping 'battle spaces' adequately before the other services enter combat.

The creation of large Naval and Army aviation arms demonstrates the IAF's understanding that there is a need to complement its dwindling resources with air arms that could act as tactical responders at best till the IAF brings its cutting-edge skills into the area to act as a decisive sword-arm.

Apprehensions over reserves

With such a deep understanding of joint operations, it is impossible to imagine that the reservations expressed by the IAF leadership in supporting the creation of integrated theatre commands in isolation is tantamount to stonewalling. Dissection of the recently conducted exercise, Gaganshakti, would provide a quantitative analysis of this assertion. The main apprehensions of the IAF leadership not only revolve around how best to exploit its dwindling offensive resources if they are hived off to multiple theatre commands, but also how the limited availability of enabling equipment and platforms (AWACS, refuelers, electronic warfare platforms and more) could seriously jeopardise operations even in a single-adversary limited conflict. (This conflict could involve up to three of the proposed theatre commands, including the Indian Navy.) To explain the resource crunch, the U.S.'s Pacific Command (PACOM) and Central

Command (CENTCOM) have their own air assets that are first supplemented by reserve units from the U.S. in emergency situations; they are not pooled in from other theatre commands. So, where will our reserves come from when the mantra today in the IAF is 'to do more with less'?

It is not my mandate to argue why the Indian Army and Navy may be able to support the theatre command concept without much churning/ diversion of assets. I will only say this: please listen to the operational argument offered by the IAF and carry out an independent analysis of how India's combat capability will be distributed if a theatre concept is to be viable.

India's armed forces have little experience in training, staffing and exercising Joint Task Forces based on at least a division-sized land component.

Creation of three division-sized task forces for operations in varied terrain, including out-of-area contingency operations, could be mulled over. These would be commanded by an Army, Navy and Air Force three-star officer, respectively, reporting to the Chairman of the Chief of Staffs Committee. This could offer real lessons in integration.

The solution for reform

Along with these turf wars has been an out-of-the-box proposition that a bottom-up approach may be the answer to India's quest for integration. Historical evidence of military reform (in Prussia, the U.S., the U.K., France and now China) shows that successful reform has always been driven by either a multipronged and simultaneous approach at all levels, or a sequential one beginning at the top. Any other approach that leaves the bottom and the top unattended is fraught with risk.

National security reforms and restructuring are bound to have far-reaching consequences and call for political sagacity, wisdom and vision. Ideally speaking, a concurrent three-pronged approach to military reform would be ideal. Such an approach should respect the collective wisdom of past reports and take into account contemporary political and security considerations.

NEED FOR HOLISTIC RESTRUCTURING OF THE INDIAN MILITARY

In the over five decades since Independence, vast changes have occurred in the security environment within the country, in the region of immediate concern, and at the global level. The last two decades have been of special importance, on account of the ongoing Revolution in Military Affairs (RMA), the end of the Cold War, the global war on terrorism and the globalisation of the economy.

The defence forces of India, at over 1.3 million strong, are perhaps the fourth largest in the world, in terms of numbers, as well as in terms of some items of capital equipment. Since Independence in 1947, they have been engaged in active operations on a sustained basis, with only short periods of peace. These challenges have helped them to earn a formidable reputation of a force that delivers, usually against heavy odds.

Although the defence forces of India are highly professional, are they structurally, technologically and organisationally sufficiently modern to meet the challenges of the 21st century? They are no doubt large in numbers, but do they also carry the necessary punch?

Do they create the necessary synergy that flows from a high degree of jointness? Are they capable of meeting the future challenges, which the country is likely to confront in the next two decades or so? If not, what changes are needed to enhance their capabilities? Should this be achieved by incremental changes or by radical and fundamental reforms? These are a few questions that need to be answered.

Conventional wisdom is that the fighting potential of the defence forces of India has decreased over the last two decades. There are many reasons for this, including a lack of vision and knowledge of security-related issues amongst the political leadership, as also the bureaucracy; decreasing budgetary allocations; antiquated procurement procedures; a costly research department, whose output has been much below expectations and which has prevented the entry of private enterprise in the defence sector; antipathy to change; narrow parochial interests; hesitancy to take risks at the senior leadership level and a status-quo mentality amongst the decision-makers.

The result is that while accretions have taken place in the number of persons in uniform, in the number of additional units and formations, and in the quality and quantity of armaments, the overall structure of the defence forces and the methods of doing business continue to be much the same as they were nearly six decades back.

No person with even some knowledge of "matters military" will have a second opinion about the overwhelming importance of joint endeavours in wars and conflicts of today and even more so those of tomorrow. Besides many other facets, the obvious one of synergy is indisputable. Before initiating a discussion on the kind of jointmanship that needs to prevail, it would be a good idea to know where the Indian military stands in this respect today.

Force structures are never evolved in a vacuum. Many factors need to be considered while carrying out structural changes. Some of these are fairly obvious, while others need considerable thought. Factors which affect the security aspects of the global and regional environment are of great importance and need to be taken into account. Threats and challenges are of course perennial considerations, but at times we tend to forget that national aspirations are crucial to force structuring, as are the desired capabilities the nation wants from its defence forces. The changing security environment is another factor that needs to be taken into account. A consideration of all these factors should logically point towards the size and shape of defence forces the nation needs, as well as the manner in which a transformation is to be achieved. These are the major aspects I intend to cover in this paper. For obvious reasons, the analysis would be broad-based in nature, the details being left to the concerned ministries and departments, which are tasked for such ventures.

DEFENCE FORCES OF INDIA

Let us briefly recapitulate the current defence forces fielded by India. The strength of the defence forces of India on the active list is approximately 1.3 million, with the army dominating with nearly 1.1 million personnel. The air force has a strength of 140,000 and the navy fields approximately 55,000 personnel. There is a Territorial Army component of approximately 40,000.

The field force of the army comprises thirteen corps, three armoured divisions, four Reorganised Army plains Infantry Divisions (RAPID), eighteen infantry divisions and ten mountain divisions, a number of independent brigades, and requisite combat support and service support formations and units. The main combat and combat support units are sixty two armoured regiments and there are over three hundred and fifty infantry battalions and three hundred artillery regiments (including two Surface to Surface Missile (SSM) units). Amongst major armaments and equipment, there are nearly 4000 main battle tanks, 2000 armoured personnel carriers, 4300 artillery pieces and 200 light helicopters. Unlike most modern armies, the Indian Army fields only reconnaissance helicopters in its aviation corps, with the air force still clinging to attack and medium lift helicopters, which should have been transferred to the army a long time back.

The organisational structure of the army is generally on traditional lines, heavily influenced as it has been by the erstwhile colonial British military. The Indian Army is competent in conducting both conventional as well as low intensity conflict (LIC) operations.

The navy has 26 principal surface combatants, including one aircraft carrier; 49 patrol and coastal combatants and 16 submarines. The naval aviation has 35 combat aircraft and 97 helicopters. There is also a coast guard with 52 patrol craft of various types.

The air force fields approximately 680 combat aircraft, grouped in 32 fighter ground attack and six fighter squadrons; 40 armed helicopters grouped in three squadrons; 12 transport squadrons; 19 helicopter squadrons and miscellaneous squadrons covering tanker, maritime attack, electronic countermeasures, survey, VIP movement, training and so on.

The growth of the defence forces of India in the past has usually been as a reaction to contemporary crises. Resultantly, the defence forces have generally remained unchanged, both structurally and in doctrinal terms, except for incremental changes to meet challenges as they arose. In recent years, however, there is a discernable doctrinal shift from attrition to manoeuvre warfare. Since the late 1980's, availability of funds has been a major constraint, with allocations for defence being less than 2.5 per cent of the GDP.

The three services are organised for conducting largely conventional operations, although a very large component of the army is heavily involved in Low Intensity Conflict operations. In all the three services, there has been some infusion of state-of-the-art equipment and armament, but much less than what is needed.

India is a responsible nuclear weapon state, with an unblemished record of non-proliferation, which cannot be easily matched by even nuclear weapon states of long standing. Our nuclear policy has two main components – minimum deterrence and no first use.

Our higher defence structure is perhaps the weakest part of the defence forces of India. The defence forces are not part of the government of India, but are an attached "office". The implications of this formulation are obvious and need not be amplified, except to highlight that this arrangement effectively keeps them outside the policy formulation loop. No doubt, the service headquarters are consulted on security issues, but that is no substitute for being part of formulating policy. The highest policy formulation body in the country is the Cabinet Committee on Security (CCS). It gets its inputs from a variety of sources, viz. the National Security Council (NSC), the Cabinet Secretariat, different ministries, intelligence agencies and so on. The inputs from the services are channeled through the ministry of defence; neither the service chiefs nor the Chairman Chief's of Staff Committee are members of the CCS, although service chiefs may be called for consultations, like many others.

A National Security Council (NSC) was created in 1999. A National Security Advisor (NSA) was also appointed. We have had three incumbents so far for this appointment – two were retired diplomats and the third is a retired intelligence specialist. The NSA has a secretariat, which is headed by a Deputy NSA.

This appointment too has been held by retired diplomats so far. As far as the secretariat is concerned, officers of various ranks hold senior, middle level and junior staff appointments, but the military is represented only by a handful of junior officers. An ironical state of affairs, indeed!

Within the Ministry of Defence, there is neither integration, nor any methodology for analysing issues jointly.

The Ministry of Defence asks service headquarters individually or jointly to submit their views on issues, whether they are on operational, intelligence or administrative matters or relating to personnel, and thereafter the Ministry deliberates on them, despite having little or no competence to analyse such military matters.

A similar situation prevails within service headquarters, wherein the stance of a particular service on an issue is first finalised in-house, including by obtaining inputs from their respective commands. Thereafter, it is forwarded to the Chief of Staff Committee for consideration. The Committee comprises the three service chiefs, with the seniormost being the Chairman. Such a structure and such formulations cannot hope to deliberate on issues objectively, as service biases are foremost in each member's mind.

Since last year, the service headquarters have started calling themselves as Integrated Headquarters. It is a meaningless exercise in semantics, as there is hardly any integration of the three services, let alone with the ministry of defence. Even the establishment of the post of Chief of Defence Staff (CDS) continues to remain unimplemented.

Global and Regional Security Environment

The global security environment will continue to be influenced by the unilateralism of the sole super power, the USA; the growing potential of regional powers, particularly China; fundamentalism and terrorism; and the internal upheavals in many developing countries.

The 21st Century had opened with the global environment focused more on economic issues and multilateral and bilateral cooperation amongst nations. However, after the events of 11 September 2001 (9/11), security issues have re-emerged and taken centre-stage. In addition to terrorism, the world continues to be plagued with conventional military threats, as well as non-military threats.

This state of affairs is likely to continue in the next two decades. The South Asian region is historically a conflict prone region, comprising post-colonial states, which have certain endemic vulnerabilities. Some of these are:

Legacy of colonialism, the bloody Partition of India in 1947 and the break up of Pakistan in 1971.

- Tendency to dishonour treaties demarcating boundaries settled during the British Empire, and the use of military force to realign borders.
- The intolerant attitude of the super powers during the Cold War towards those states that sought to pursue independent policies.
- Discord amongst ethnic, religious and linguistic groups, resulting in internal turbulence.
- Uncontrolled population explosion, leading to poverty, illiteracy, disease, environmental degradation and unplanned urbanisation. This is compounded by demographic shifts, both within nations and across borders.
- Arms and drug trafficking, and a growing nexus between crime and politics.

The security environment in South Asia continues to be influenced by historical disputes; nuclearisation; paucity of energy sources; inadequate harnessing of the abundant water resources; the growing potential of China; the war on terrorism; the spread of fundamentalism; and the social upheaval in practically all countries, due to the rising expectations of their people. The scenario is further complicated by a rise in trans-border terrorism, sponsored ethnic strife, and low intensity conflicts.6 The impact of the unilateralism of the sole super power, the USA, over events and policies in Asia, must also be factored in. All this is against the backdrop of vastly increased economic activity, globalisation and the great potential of the information revolution, which is making steady inroads into every facet of life.

India and Pakistan are the two nuclear states in South Asia, in addition to China, an earlier nuclear weapons power. The risk of a nuclear war in the region stands greatly reduced, but the proliferation of nuclear weapons and missiles is of grave concern, particularly when the countries involved are those which are prone to be influenced by terrorist activities, or have a history of promoting terrorists, either as state policy, or by ignoring the rise of religious fundamentalism in their countries, for various reasons. The revelations of major proliferation activities by Pakistan and North Korea are now history. Iran's ambitions in the nuclear field are a major cause for concern. The obvious conclusions are that the nuclear non-proliferation treaty (NPT) has not worked and perhaps an entirely new dispensation is needed to control the spread of nuclear weapons. As long as blatant acts of major proliferation, like those of Pakistan and North Korea, are glossed over by the major powers, especially by the United States, on account of their short-term gains, many new aspirants will attempt to go nuclear.7

On the conventional plane, while limited conventional conflicts are still likely to occur, they are gradually giving way to conflicts at the lower end of the spectrum of conflict. However, the proliferation of conventional weaponry and the transfer of weapons and equipment by China to Pakistan, Bangladesh and Myanmar, as also other countries on India's periphery, have adversely affected the South Asian regional military balance.

Threats and Challenges

India's sphere of influence needs to encompass not just the South Asian Sub-continent, but also the northern Indian Ocean area, from the eastern seaboard of Africa in the west, to the Malacca Straits in the east, and must include Iran, Afghanistan, the Central Asian Republics (CARs), China and Myanmar. India's credibility, as a regional power will be contingent upon institutional stability, economic development and military strength, including nuclear deterrence.

The long stretches of disputed borders with China and Pakistan and sizeable areas under their illegal occupation continue to be major irritants, notwithstanding the peace processes currently underway with both countries. These are unlikely to be resolved in the short term and will continue to generate tensions and instability at periodic intervals. Our vast island territories also need to be guarded.

Many of India's external challenges are related to its extensive land and sea frontiers. The land frontiers exceed 15,000 km, covering seven neighbouring countries. The border in the state of Jammu and Kashmir is perpetually volatile, except when a mutually agreed cease-fire is in force, as it is at present. Pakistan is in adverse possession of large areas of this Indian State. An on-going peace process between India and Pakistan continues, and there are many positive fallouts of this process, but unless Pakistan stops the infiltration of insurgents and terrorists into Jammu & Kashmir, substantive improvement is unlikely.

India has a disputed border with China, too. China continues to be in adverse possession of 40,000 sq km of Indian Territory. A dialogue to resolve various issues between India and China is currently in progress, albeit at a slow pace. India-China relations have improved in recent years. A "Peace and Tranquillity" treaty is in place. The momentum towards confidence building and improved relations is continuing. There are no major disputes with India's other neighbours, but the borders are extensive and somewhat porous.

The long coastline (7683 km), the island territories off both coasts, and an Exclusive Economic Zone (EEZ) of over two million square kilometres all add up to various types of challenges. For example, the island territories to the east, i.e. the Andaman and Nicobar group of islands, are 1300 kilometres from the Indian mainland, but only 150 kilometres from Indonesia, 500 odd kilometres from Malaysia and Thailand, 250 kilometres from Myanmar and 400 kilometres from Bangladesh.

The time has come for India to look outwards. There are many tasks and contingencies outside our frontiers. These include coming to the assistance of our neighbours; rescuing or assisting Indian nationals abroad; safeguarding our vital economic or other interests; rendering aid during natural or other calamities; forming part of a multi-national force; and so on. For these challenges, we do need to have a state-of-the-art tri-service trans-national capability. This does not mean we have designs on other countries or that we are now becoming hegemons.

The escalating world oil prices have enhanced our energy crisis. Currently, India is the world's sixth largest energy consumer and in 2010 we will hit the fourth place. We have made heavy investments abroad in the oil sector.

These include long term contracts for oil and gas supply, on-going negotiations for participation in pipeline projects, as well as energy projects involving exploration, development, transportation and refining of hydrocarbons to meet our future needs. These investments, in locations as far a field as the Middle East, Africa, Central Asia and Southeast Asia, need to be safeguarded against any unforeseen eventualities.

The next security challenge is the state of our neighbours. The political and economic status of most of our neighbours is a cause of major concern, as any major upheavals will pose great security and economic challenges for us. In addition, the governing elite in these countries tend to blame India for all their ills. It is no doubt a political ploy that works domestically.

We need to take initiatives at many levels, including at the military level, to allay their imagined and real fears, so that our relations with our neighbours can be brought to an even keel.

As far as the maritime dimension is concerned, the littorals of the Indian Ocean and the island nations are both important. We cannot have any hostile or inimical powers threatening them. These countries need to be given assistance in terms of military hardware, training or technical assistance and sometimes assistance in policing their waters or airspace.

The on-going and future threats from terrorism, insurgencies and resorts to mindless violence to meet political ends are other major challenges. These may well be the most important and biggest security challenges of the future.

We are a responsible nuclear weapon state, which entails the efficient management of this deterrent capability. For deterrence to be successful, the adversary must be convinced of the severity of our retaliation. In addition, we must ensure that our second strike capability is not only well protected, but that it is also overwhelmingly devastating.

The last challenge is to transform the defence forces into a lean, technology intensive, networked and joint entity. It sounds simple, but considering our historical baggage and a penchant for the status quo, it would be a difficult proposition. We also need to function in a holistic manner, where security, foreign and economic policies must be integrated. At present, we are unfortunately functioning in separate compartments.

National Aspirations and Desired Capabilities

India's primary strategic priority and goal remains the rapid socio-economic development of its people. Our national objectives may be summarised as under:

- Develop as a fully secular, multi-cultural state, in which freedom of speech, thought and equal opportunity are available to all, regardless of race, religion, caste, community or sex.

- o Ensure a secure and stable environment conducive to unhindered economic growth.
- o Preserve and ensure the sovereignty, unity and territorial integrity of India.
- o Contribute our share in international affairs, consistent with our policies.

To attain the above objectives, India needs to ensure a secure external and internal security environment. The defence forces of India, as the ultimate instrument of the state, are responsible for safeguarding the core values and national interests from external aggression and internal subversion.

Our objectives also need to have an ideological component and reflect the inner urges of the people. Keeping all these aspects in mind, our national policy could be stated as: "To establish a strong, economically vibrant and united democratic India, free from internal and external threats, enjoying a prominent status in the region and having its rightful and honoured place in the world."

India aspires to be recognised as an economic and military power of some reckoning, with a permanent membership of the UN Security Council. To achieve these objectives, India needs to ensure a peaceful internal environment, security from external threats and capability to project power in the greater South Asian region. Such an aspiration requires India to modernise its defence forces and equip them with contemporary techno-equipment to meet the expanded roles they would need to perform, while ensuring sustained economic growth and development.

ENVIRONMENTAL CHANGES AFFECTING MILITARY OPERATIONS

Globalisation has had a profound effect in making the world smaller and more accessible, but it has also had a major effect on the security environment. While military force factors continue to retain their significance in international relations, economic, political, technological, ecological, information and energy factors are also playing an increasingly dominant role in the shaping of the security environment. The regional military environment in South Asia is affected by on-going conflicts; proliferation and transfer of weapons; advancements in military technology; and the changing nature of war. These are elaborated in succeeding paragraphs.

Conflicts have continued in varying intensities in South Asia. Most of these conflicts have a historical baggage, with solutions so intractable that they linger despite many changes in the regional and national environments. Like volcanoes, they erupt once in a while and then lie dormant, but festering within, till another catalyst causes yet another eruption.

The notable conflicts in South Asia are the India-Pakistan adversarial relationship; the India-China border stand-off; and internal conflicts generated by a section of the people, like the LTTE problem in Sri Lanka, the Maoists' continuing struggle for power in Nepal, insurgencies and rebellions in Pakistan and a number of insurgencies in India.

In the last two decades, China's export of high-grade steel, navigational guidance systems and missile technologies to Pakistan had enabled it to arm itself with nuclear weapons, with matching delivery capabilities. In turn, Pakistan used this clandestinely acquired capability to proliferate it to North Korea in return for missiles and missile technology, in some kind of a barter deal.

A similar situation obtains in the conventional arena. The accelerating recourse to conventional weapons proliferation in recent years has enabled many countries to possess high technology weapons at low costs. This has serious implications for regional security. Besides Pakistan, China has also provided conventional weaponry to Bangladesh, Myanmar, Sri Lanka and Nepal, to name only a few countries. These actions have tended to alter the regional military balance.

Rapid advancements in technology, in the fields of information, nuclear energy, biotechnology, aviation, space and underwater operations, are changing the concept of warfare.

Capabilities for all weather surveillance, night vision devices, and extensive use of satellites and multiplicity of sensors have also affected all types of operations. In the field of information technology (IT), digitisation, networked communications, electronic warfare, as well as information warfare (IW), have highlighted the importance of systems integration. This has led to the concept of system of systems, which is a complete architecture of detection, selection, display, targeting and attack.

RMA, which is manifested by high technology weapons, sensors, communications and information technology, will increasingly have an impact on all types of military operations. Warfare in the information age, irrespective of whether it is nuclear, conventional or low intensity in nature, will require highly complex planning and coordination, near real time and total situational awareness, decision support systems and massive data-base and information-exchange capabilities to tackle both friendly and inimical situations. Technology has made information more readily available, and it has now become a weapon of choice. The armed forces of India need to focus on IT and Information Warfare (IW) in a big way in the coming years and decades.

The continuing wave of technological change is different, in two ways, from even the IT revolution of the 1990s. First, it is a vastly more profound transformation, due to the synergy of three emerging technologies, viz. bioengineering, nano-engineering, and robotics and artificial intelligence. Secondly, it is a revolution that will occur at a speed never seen before. Observations of change over the past century indicate that technology is evolving exponentially, which means change is accelerating or the rate of change is increasing. The proliferation of all types of missiles; the versatility of modern aviation platforms; the precision guided and terminally guided munitions (PGMs and TGMs); and multi-dimensional manoeuvre vehicles are some of the breakthrough technologies which have changed the nature of warfare.

Missile Defence (MD), whether national missile defence (NMD) or theatre missile defence (TMD), is another technological advancement which will have a major effect on warfare in future. At present, in this region, only India in South Asia and China further afield, are examining it with some seriousness. MD is a strategic shift of major importance – from a doctrine of deterrence to that of interdictory interception. MD is already vehemently opposed by China, whose response may well be a further up-gradation of its strategic nuclear forces. This is likely to have a ripple effect in many parts of the world, including in South Asia, particularly India.

The proliferation of Nuclear Biological Chemical (NBC) weapons, smart weapons, imaginative employment of IT, more lethal and precise weapons, the fielding of many types of missiles and major up-gradation of aviation assets, all have made substantive changes to the concepts and methodologies of waging war. Asymmetric Warfare, for example, focuses on fighting a stronger enemy and still winning. In the same context, non-nuclear deterrence, which is aimed at deterring regional conflicts with only conventional weapons, continues to be important.

Operations in the future may not be easily divided into conventional and low intensity conflicts. The modern battlefield will be characterised by short, intense operations, against a nuclear backdrop. There will be a large number of short, swift, and lethal engagements, using precision weapons, with heavy attrition, but with minimum collateral damage. Wars will be fought in all six dimensions – space, cyber, air, land, sea and sub-surface. Increased use of various types of sensors will bring total transparency to the battlefield. This will affect the achievement of surprise, both strategic and tactical, and there would be an overload of information at the command posts.

In conventional operations, front, depth and rear areas would be engaged simultaneously with real time surveillance, integrated Command Control Communication Computers Intelligence Interoperability (C4 I2), target acquisition and highly lethal precision weapons systems. The battlefield will become more digitised, more transparent and would experience a major increase in deployment of electronic devices, signalling the growing primacy of the electromagnetic spectrum. Escalation will have to be carefully controlled to ensure that no nuclear red lines are crossed. Despite this constraint, sufficient space for conventional operations will continue to be available. The ability of ground forces will depend upon the speed with which they can move, concentrate and regroup rapidly over any type of terrain. Today, joint and combined operations are the norm. IT, in all its manifestations, affects decision-making. At the same time, IW, including the creation of a favourable public opinion, is a necessary adjunct to the higher direction of war. Military planners will need to give considerable thought to the likelihood of terrorist threats, along with fighting conventional operations. Resultantly, greater number of troops and equipment would be required to cope with such threats.

FUTURE ROLE: DEFENCE FORCES OF INDIA

In the coming decades, the role of the defence forces will continue to be "to preserve national interests and safeguard territorial integrity and unity of the country, against any external or internal threats, by deterrence or by waging a war".

The defence forces have to deal with both traditional missions of deterrence and war fighting, as well as non-traditional missions. They also play an important role in nation building. The missions of the defence forces can be listed as under:

- o Deterring hostile neighbours possessing NBC weapons and missiles.
- o Sub-national threats from hostile neighbours, including proxy war and terrorism.
- o Operating under the aegis of the UN, other groupings, or even independently, in roles like peacekeeping, peacemaking, humanitarian assistance, disaster relief, or national reconstruction.
- o Tackling overseas crises that threaten Indian citizens, property and interests.
- o Domestic emergencies that exceed the capacity of other agencies like state governments, police forces or central agencies.

Excessive involvement of the defence forces, particularly the army, in internal security duties adversely affects their combat potential. Continued deployment on such duties also tends to alienate the populace and tarnishes the image of the defence forces. These are difficult operations, as their resolution essentially lies in the political domain and the army has to operate under a number of constraints. Therefore, over-exposure in internal security duties is counter-productive, especially when their employment on such duties is for a prolonged period.

Although there has been an exponential growth of many types of police forces in our country, they are currently incapable, or unwilling, or both, to tackle insurgencies. Consequently, I foresee that the defence forces, primarily the Army, will continue to be called out to tackle insurgencies, terrorism, proxy wars and even high-grade internal security situations.

India's military strategy has to be effective across the entire spectrum of possible conflicts. Increased focus on information technology and information warfare is also essential. The army particularly needs to transit from manpower orientation to high technology, tempering it with the knowledge that sub-conventional operations are manpower intensive.

India's aspirations for peace and security require the modernisation of the defence forces, restructuring them and equipping them with contemporary technological equipment. The restructuring should be such that the military continues to remain professionally strong. Restructuring includes optimisation of doctrine and concepts, restructuring of the field force, efficient management of internal conflicts, upgrading human resources, streamlining logistics and modernising the training methodology of the military.

At the upper end of the conflict spectrum, only nuclear weapons deter nuclear weapons. However, at the conventional level, the need is to build a capability for small-size operations, which are executed swiftly. At the sub-conventional level, the approach should be multi-faceted, with the military part being pro-active. Special Forces would play an extremely important role in such operations.

In the coming decades of the 21st Century, our defence forces need to address the following:

- o The growing number of non-traditional threats will continue to increase, and I fear that the nation will continue to rely on the defence forces as the principal instrument to deal with them.
- o The defence forces, as presently structured, may not be able to meet all the potential challenges ahead, which could span the entire spectrum of conflict.
- o For meeting the challenges of the new century and adapt to the rapid development of new technologies, the defence forces have to change radically and become increasingly unified.
- o The enormous human potential in the Army, its judicious harnessing, moulding it to exacting standards, providing it with special skills and injecting a high level of motivation, are also essential. Combat power is not simply the sum of machine performance. Machines can assist, but warfare will continue to be an intensely human activity.
- o There is a definite need for better decision-making and the integration of all instruments of power (political, economic, military and informational) to tackle the multidimensional challenges ahead.

Jointmanship

Modern War cannot be fought with outdated structures, wherein the army, the navy and the air force conduct operations independently, with coordination only being achieved with organisations as old as nearly seven-eight decades back. War is a joint endeavour, wherein the entire nation has to gear up for fighting it. Today, this truism is even more relevant, because waging war today is a complex phenomenon. This complexity is likely to increase in the future. The reasons include high technology, the nature of modern war, new threats and challenges and the reality of nuclear weapons in the arsenal of our potential adversaries. Consequently, a joint force, which acts in an integrated manner, is not just desirable but an imperative. Gone are the days when individual services, like the army or navy, fought wars on their own.

Most professional militaries have adopted jointmanship, not merely in their organisations and structures, but in their very approach to tackling military problems, big or small. Unfortunately, the Indian military is an exception amongst the more professional militaries. While everyone who matters endorses the need for joint endeavours, it eventually turns out to be merely lip service. This must change, for if we continue in this mode, we will be unable to generate the necessary synergy, so essential for winning conflicts, battles and wars.

The Indian military had realised the importance of jointmanship soon after our Independence. This vision was translated into reality by the setting up of joint institutions like the National Defence Academy (NDA), the Defence Services Staff College (DSSC) and the National Defence College (NDC). These institutions, all joint, covered a wide canvas, from pre-commissioning training to the highest level of formal training an officer undergoes. Unfortunately, somewhere along the way, we lost our focus and drifted into separate entities, which became institutionalised over time.

The wars we fought since our Independence added to this "lone ranger" syndrome. Our first war, in Jammu & Kashmir in 1947-48, was essentially an army affair, with some support from the air force. The navy was not involved. In 1962, when China attacked us, the army again operated alone, as it was decided not to employ the air force. Once again there was no role for the navy. The next war, against Pakistan in 1965, saw all the three services fighting the enemy, but mostly independently, although the army and the air force did carry out coordination in specific operations.

It was only in the 1971 war that the three services were employed synergistically and won the war decisively. Synergy during this war was achieved largely because of the personalities of the dramatis personae and the nearly nine month long planning and preparation time available and not because of any structural or organisational changes. Unfortunately, the example of the 1971 war continues to be quoted by those opposed to greater jointmanship, on the specious plea that since the structures worked during 1971, there was no need for instituting reforms now! This is of course absurd logic, considering that nearly four decades have passed since then. The entire nature of war has changed now and there is no surety that the personal chemistry of the new actors would again work positively.

Besides the above mentioned conflicts, the army has also been involved, almost continuously, in fighting different types of insurgencies and terrorism in various parts of the country. The nature of these operations does not need the navy and the air force to step in. So essentially, it is again the army operating on its own. This had its repercussions during the Kargil conflict in 1999, when initially the air force refused to participate, on the plea that it would escalate the conflict. When they did come in later, it took time to build up the necessary synergy. It is apparent that our experiences post-Independence lulled us into a state of complacency and we made little effort to forge joint concepts, structures and institutions, thus obtaining less than optimal results.

A major recommendation of the Kargil Review Committee set up after the Kargil conflict to recommend reforms, including in the higher defence structure, was the need to set up joint structures at the earliest. The GoM eventually accepted the recommendations, after some changes and implementation instructions were issued in mid-2001. While an integrated defence headquarters and two joint commands have been formed, a key recommendation, i.e. the establishment of the post of Chief of Defence Staff (CDS), remains unimplemented. Resultantly, the integrated headquarters gets its directions from the ineffective Chiefs of Staff Committee, an organisation which has neither the teeth nor the inclination to take any strong and meaningful decisions, including in the realm of jointmanship. Unfortunately, this state of affairs suits the principal actors, viz. the political leadership which continues to be bugged by the non-existent spectre of a military takeover, however preposterous it may sound; the bureaucracy, who see the CDS as threatening their overlordship over of the service headquarters; and even the service headquarters, who are highly reluctant to part with any power which will dilute their fiefdoms.

The service headquarters may not want to dilute any of their powers, but at least two out of three used to speak in favour of jointness. Now, nearly six years after the GoM had given their directions, even that has changed. Apparently, none of them are now interested in the appointment of a CDS. There is no discernable change in the stance of the political leadership as well as the bureaucracy. So we flounder along, believing in our fatalistic fashion that everything will turn out right in the end and through some sleight of hand the Indian military will, for the umpteenth time, again pull the chestnuts out of the fire, as it always has when the chips are down! The moot question is, should policies of such great importance, relating to the security and indeed the very existence of our nation, continue to be sacrificed at the altar of expediency or sloth or indifference, or all three?

Transformation

There is a need to transform our military in a deliberate manner. The transformation must be major in scope. This can only be done if sufficient resources are made available. For this, the armed forces have to convince the political leadership, as well as the people, of the legitimacy of their needs. Defence allocations continue to be meagre, at less than 2.5 per cent of the GDP. Our decision-making systems and processes are also slow. These need to change.

The transformation should begin with the development of a realistic strategic direction. The national strategy must clearly spell out interests, goals, priorities, and resource allocations. From this, a national military strategy should be evolved. This, in turn, will enable the military to decide on the details of restructuring, hopefully without the influences of service bias or sentimentality. Some assets will have to be phased out over time, as new, innovative systems come on line through the process of transformation.

The process of change must be extensive and should also include a review of our personnel system. We need to produce junior leaders with broader and more sophisticated educational and service experience. Quality-of-life areas, compensation, benefits, personal development, challenging experiences, and personnel stability have to be major considerations in getting and keeping the best and brightest our society has to offer. The future military will be an even more complex institution and will require truly competent and dedicated members.

We must seriously address joint warfare. The Services must eliminate the inter-service bickering that continues to be the bane of the defence forces. At the apex level, our structures for the management of higher defence and the systems for providing military advice, as well as recommendations for national security policy, also need to be re-examined. The CDS must be appointed without any delay and additional joint commands must be set up. While the eventual structures we should aim at must be integrated commands, this should come about in an evolutionary manner. The appointing of a CDS and gradual addition of new joint commands will, over a period of time, suggest the numbers and types of joint commands we need. For the next few years, we may leave operational commands as they are at present, except that the jointness amongst them must be substantially increased. There are other areas like Special Forces, Space, Training, Communications, Logistics and so on, which lend themselves for restructuring into joint commands

Within the army, having two sets of forces, a small-sized traditional army for deterrence and waging war and a much larger, lightly equipped internal security force (ISF) for combating low intensity conflicts is perhaps one answer for restructuring. In the Navy, while the enhancing of blue water capability must continue, some focus will have to shift to counter terrorism and militancy at sea, including greater control of coastal waters and our EEZ. Till now, the role of the Air Force in counter-terrorist and counter-insurgency operations has been confined to air transportation. This would need to change. Future low intensity threats would require the fielding of air power. Whether this takes the form of restructuring a part of the air force or enhancing army aviation assets so that they can take on these roles, can be debated, but the latter has obvious operational advantages. Major reforms and restructuring would be required for this, which would be opposed by large numbers, both within and outside the services.

In sum, the force structure of the defence forces of India should be such that it is able to achieve the objectives the nation expects from it. We need to be regional players of eminence, as well as have a say in global strategic formulations. The capabilities of the armed forces, therefore, must include the following:

- o Nuclear: We need to refine our nuclear doctrine, which should continue to be primarily for deterrence, but for use in case we are forced to use the nuclear option. Our retaliatory capability must be potent, comprehensive and timely. This entails, besides a range of warheads, the requisite delivery and support systems. We need to build up our current missile capability substantially, so that the army is equipped with a full range of missiles, capable of reaching all possible targets. It is important for India to continue to work towards a triad capability in the nuclear field. The military interface needs to be enhanced as it is currently less than desirable.
- o Conventional: Credible conventional deterrence will continue to be important. The conventional capability of the defence forces must be comprehensive against our likely adversaries. The armed forces must maintain an effective superiority in conventional forces vis-à-vis Pakistan. They must also have the capability for punitive response to provocations short of war. The challenge China is expected to pose in the mid and long terms requires that our deterrence capability be upgraded, by adding a potent offensive capability to our current

posture. In the maritime arena, we should have the capability to effectively guard our sea lanes of communications in the northern Indian Ocean region and protect our interests in the nation's EEZ. The air force must be capable of creating a favourable air situation at least in specified corridors, which have a direct linkage to offensive operations of the ground forces. The air force must also create additional strategic lift capability for tasks within the country's area of interest.

- o Low Intensity Conflict (LIC): The LIC commitments of the defence forces, particularly the army, are likely to increase in the coming years, as there has been no improvement in the capabilities of the central police forces in tackling insurgency and terrorism, despite their increasing numerical strengths. The defence forces must be capable of fighting both internal insurgencies as well as those launched or supported by other countries or foreign entities. However, its conventional capability must not get diluted on account of excessive employment on counter-insurgency and counter-terrorism roles. The army, particularly, must have adequate capability to fight high-grade insurgency in any part of India, including in our border states, as it is currently doing in Jammu and Kashmir. As both state and non-state actors are likely to resort to low intensity conflicts as their preferred mode of waging war, major restructuring may be required amongst the armed forces to meet this challenge. This may well imply a separate force, which must be equipped, manned and trained specifically for this role.
- o Peacekeeping: The defence forces will have to play an enhanced role in peacekeeping operations, mostly under the aegis of the United Nations, but perhaps under other circumstances, too.
- o Joint Endeavours: In all the above types of roles and operations, there would need to be a high level of

jointness, otherwise the defence forces will not be able to achieve synergy and consequently the best results.

Conclusion

Today, the defence forces of India are at the crossroads of a revolutionary change, marked by nuclearisation of the subcontinent, asymmetric threats like the on-going proxy war in Kashmir, our rapidly increasing interests within the region, military aspects of globalisation and rapid technological changes. In this new milieu, the defence forces must not only retain a combat edge in conventional operations, but also handle sub-conventional challenges effectively.

Focus on LIC operations must not distract the defence forces from other roles. We need to look at the totality of roles, which the military would need to perform. Deterrence is an essential element in all the roles of the military, whether they are in the conventional, non-conventional or sub-conventional arenas.

Change is no doubt difficult, as we are highly conservative. The bureaucracy, both civil and military, and the political leadership with vested interests in preserving the status quo, will resist change or will support only marginal changes. This will further complicate implementation of the needed reforms.

India is now genuinely poised to shine. It cannot do so with a feeble military machine, which functions on ad hoc basis or on the glorious past. We need to revamp and restructure before we are actually faced with the challenges we have talked about. The need today is for a synergistic and visionary national approach for the strong, purposeful and modern India that is just over the horizon.

2

Mega Reforms for the Indian Army

The reforms are hoped to make the 1.3 million-strong force more agile, leaner, and meaner, as well as to enhance its combat capabilities. A day after UN rights chief Michelle Bachelet expressed concern over reports of increasing harassment and targeting of minorities including Muslims and Dalits in India, the Defence Ministry in a massive overhaul has announced the inclusion of a human rights wing for the Indian Army.

It is part of the first batch of major reforms for the reorganisation of the Army headquarters, based on recommendations by Army Chief General Vipin Rawat, and approved by Defence Minister Nirmala Sitharaman on Friday. The reforms are hoped to make the 1.3 million-strong force more agile, leaner, and meaner, as well as to enhance its combat capabilities.

Decades of research went into deciding what's best for our army

The Army headquarters had instituted four studies with an overall aim to enhance the operational and functional efficiency of the force, optimise budget expenditure, facilitate modernisation, and address aspirations. The first study on "re-organisation and right-sizing of the Indian Army" was focused on the operational structures to make the force efficient and future-ready by taking into account the operational situation on western and northern borders, the spokesperson said.

The second study was on re-organisation of the Army headquarters with an aim to bring in "integration and preclude the redundancies". The third study was on "cadre review of officers" and its focus was to recommend how to carry out reorganisation and restructuring to meet the aspirations of the officers' cadre.

The fourth study on "review of terms of engagement of rank and file" was aimed at harnessing the higher life expectancy and ensuring younger profile of key commands and motivation of the personnel. Besides the independent studies, the Defence Ministry had also ordered a separate study under Lt Gen DS Hooda on how to effectively restructure the force.

Details of the much-awaited upgrade

Finalised after 12 independent studies, this transformation exercise has been launched in keeping with the challenges of future warfare, so as to develop a more capability-based task force to tackle them.

According to news reports, the restructuring would involve the relocation of 229 officers to operational posts, and the creation of new wings and posts like that of the Deputy Chief of the Army Staff (DCoAS) to supervise the directorates of military intelligence, operational logistics, and strategic planning. This will make him the third deputy chief to report to the Army Chief, after the Director General of Military Operations and the Director General of Military Intelligence.

Sources informed NDTV that the government has approved merging of the separate verticals of planning and strategy and the Master General Ordnance (MGO) into a single office of Capability Development and Sustenance. This department will oversee the entire modernisation and revenue procurement of the Indian Army.

"Towards the Army's capability-based modernisation needs, this would synergise and coalesce all revenue and capital spending under one organisation and effectively prioritise competing requirements with an operational focus to get better value for funds allocated by the government," a senior army official told the news channel.

Timely, modern, and progressive solutions

The defence minister has also approved the creation of a new Information Warfare wing, to combat the realities of cyber, hybrid, and social media threats. It will be monitored by a Lieutenant General for the first time. A new wing devoted to vigilance and human rights issues will be set up under major-generals. The ADG (Vigilance), who will report back to the Chief of Army Staff, will also have a new Vigilance Investigation Unit under him, the sources said.

To look after the cases of corruption and ensure probity and transparency, a new officer of the Major Genral rank has also been appointed under the Army Chief. The reforms will also include restructuring the Army's officer cadre, making young officers eligible for key commands, arresting the rise in revenue expenditure, and "right-sizing" the force. Meanwhile, the relocation of 229 officers, which accounts for 20% of the total official strength posted in Delhi, would 'flatten' the Army headquarters. These officers will now be posted to field fighting formations along the borders with China and Pakistan, thus strengthening border security.

Why it matters

The need for it could not have been clearer since the Doklam encounter with Chinese forces over Tibet. Some of the recommendations made for the reform, that have been gathering dust for over four decades, have just now been cleared, a month before the general elections.

Demands for these newly-adopted reforms, stalled and pending for decades, have been the point of high debate, especially in the wake of the Pulwama attack.

These reforms will be implemented with a sense of urgency. The creation of the human rights wing is a progressive move as the Indian Amry has been raked over coals multiple times for the atrocities committed on civilians under the garb of the Armed Forces (Special Powers) Act (AFSPA), especially in Kashmir and the north-east.

Decried by international bodies because it allows the army "special powers" to arrest, rape, and kill people with relative impunity, the AFSPA has come under increasing scrutiny owing to Irom Sharmila's 16-year-long hunger strike, and the naked protests led by the elderly Meitei women against a heinous rape and murder. In fact, the Supreme Court is overseeing a CBI probe into the alleged extrajudicial killings by the Army, Assam Rifles, and the state police in insurgency-hit Manipur between 1985 and 2010.

A 2004 committee report proposed the repeal of AFSPA but it was buried under two successive governments who did not want to hold the army accountable for its actions. For the Army's new human rights wing to function effectively, it needs to first hold its officers and soldiers responsible for their actions. The reforms, however, don't address the monumental difference in the number of men and women in the Indian Army. A report released last year by Raksha Rajya Mantri Dr. Subhash Bhamre quotes 1,561 women officers, compared to 41,074 male officers. In other words, 96.2% of the Indian army is male.

In a contentious remark last year, Rawat had taken a remarkably medieval stance against filling more ranks in the Indian Army with women soldiers. His egregious comments triggered a debate when he said that accepting a woman commander could be hard for the *jawans,*and how women *jawans* would add to logistical and security issues, saying they require separate huts to sleep and change in.

He has even questioned their ability to lead troops, saying that granting maternity leaves while on commanding duty leads to a "ruckus," suggesting that women aren't ready for combat roles as they are destined for motherhood and must prioritise raising kids.

The army chief also believes excluding women from combat roles is a good way of avoiding having to deal with sexual harassment. The lack of an internal committee to look into complaints of sexual assault within the ranks is a gaping hole which the mega-reforms ought to have addressed.

DEFENCE FORCES OF INDIA

Let us briefly recapitulate the current defence forces fielded by India. The strength of the defence forces of India on the active list is approximately 1.3 million, with the Army dominating with nearly 1.1 million personnel. The Air Force has a strength of 140,000 and the Navy fields approximately 55,000 personnel. There is a Territorial Army component of approximately 40,000. The field force of the army comprises thirteen corps, three armoured divisions, four Reorganized Army Plains Infantry Divisions (RAPID), eighteen infantry divisions and ten mountain divisions, a number of independent brigades, and requisite combat support and service support formations and units.

The main combat and combat support units are sixty-two armoured regiments and there are over three hundred and fifty infantry battalions and three hundred artillery regiments (including two Surface to Surface Missile (SSM) units). Amongst major armaments and equipment, there are nearly 4,000 main battle tanks, 2,000 armoured personnel carriers, 4,300 artillery pieces and 200 light helicopters.

Unlike most modern armies, the Indian Army fields only reconnaissance helicopters in its aviation corps, with the air force still clinging to attack and medium lift helicopters, which should have been transferred to the army a long time back. The organizational structure of the army is generally on traditional lines, heavily influenced as it has been by the erstwhile colonial British military. The Indian Army is competent in conducting both conventional as well as low intensity conflict (LIC) operations. The navy has 26 principal surface combatants, including one aircraft carrier; 49 patrol and coastal combatants and 16 submarines. The naval aviation has 35 combat aircraft and 97 helicopters. There is also a coast guard with 52 patrol craft of various types. The air force fields approximately 680 combat aircraft, grouped in 32 fighter ground attack and six fighter squadrons; 40 armed helicopters grouped in three squadrons; 12 transport squadrons; 19 helicopter squadrons and miscellaneous squadrons covering tanker, maritime attack, electronic counter-measures, survey, VIP movement, training and so on.

The growth of the defence forces of India in the past has usually been as a reaction to contemporary crises. Resultantly, the defence forces have generally remained unchanged, both structurally and in doctrinal terms, except for incremental changes to meet challenges as they arose. In recent years, however, there is a discernable doctrinal shift from attrition to manoeuvre warfare. Since the late 1980s, availability of funds has been a major constraint, with allocations for defence being less than 2.5 per cent of the GDP.

The three services are organised for conducting largely conventional operations, although a very large component of the army is heavily involved in Low Intensity Conflict operations. In all the three services, there has been some infusion of state-of-the-art equipment and armament, but much less than what is needed. India is a responsible nuclear weapon state, with an unblemished record of non-proliferation, which cannot be easily matched by even nuclear weapon states of long standing.

Our nuclear policy has two main components—minimum deterrence and no first use. Our higher defence structure is perhaps the weakest part of the defence forces of India. The defence forces are not part of the government of India, but are an attached 'office'. The implications of this formulation are obvious and need not be amplified, except to highlight that this arrangement effectively keeps them outside the policy formulation loop. No doubt, the service headquarters are consulted on security issues, but that is no substitute for being part of formulating policy. The highest policy formulation body in the country is the Cabinet Committee on Security (CCS). It gets its inputs from a variety of sources, viz., the National Security Council (NSC), the Cabinet Secretariat, different ministries, intelligence agencies and so on. The inputs from the services are channelled through the ministry of defence; neither the service chiefs nor the Chairman Chief's of Staff Committee are members of the CCS, although service chiefs may be called for consultations, like many others.

A National Security Council (NSC) was created in 1999. A National Security Advisor (NSA) was also appointed. We have had three incumbents so far for this appointment—two were retired diplomats and the third is a retired intelligence specialist.

The NSA has a secretariat, which is headed by a Deputy NSA. This appointment too has been held by retired diplomats so far. As far as the secretariat is concerned, officers of various ranks hold senior, middle level and junior staff appointments, but the military is represented only by a handful of junior officers.

An ironical state of affairs, indeed! Within the Ministry of Defence, there is neither integration, nor any methodology for analyzing issues jointly. The Ministry of Defence asks service headquarters individually or jointly to submit their views on issues, whether they are on operational, intelligence or administrative matters or relating to personnel, and thereafter the Ministry deliberates on them, despite having little or no competence to analyze such military matters.

A similar situation prevails within service headquarters, wherein the stance of a particular service on an issue is first finalized in-house, including by obtaining inputs from their respective commands. Thereafter, it is forwarded to the Chief of Staff Committee for consideration. The Committee comprises the three service chiefs, with the seniormost being the Chairman. Such a structure and such formulations cannot hope to deliberate on issues objectively, as service biases are foremost in each member's mind. Since last year, the service headquarters have started calling themselves as Integrated Headquarters. It is a meaningless exercise in semantics, as there is hardly any integration of the three services, let alone with the ministry of defence. Even the establishment of the post of Chief of Defence Staff (CDS) continues to remain unimplemented.

DEVELOPMENT OF INDIAN ARMY

Development of Indian Army is a combination of several changes and improvements that have taken place through the ages. The epic history of Indian Army dates back to more than ten thousand years. The two epics—*Ramayana* and *Mahabharata* constitute the fundamental framework around which the structure of Indian Army has been built. The massive epic war Mahabharata, fought at Kurukshetra in north-central India, has left indelible imprints on the Indian psyche. Though innumerable wars have been fought thenceforth, almost all were in quest of universal peace and Dharma. Recourse to arms was only taken when peace was threatened. With many recent landmark findings refuting the invasion of Asian-European people, or the Aryans, into the Indian sub-continent *en masse*, the military history of India dates back to 6th century BC. The *Arthashastra* is one of the most significant documents of military history ever to be written.

ARMY'S CAPABILITY ACCRETION

The challenges that the army is expected to face in the next decade are not likely to be any less formidable. An appraisal of the emerging threats in fact indicates an increasing complexity of the missions that the army may be expected to execute. The basic character of the Army's responsibilities is unlikely to witness significant changes. Till the boundary disputes with China and Pakistan remain unresolved, Army's most important role of ensuring the nation's territorial integrity will retain primacy. Concurrently, as in the past, the Army will continue to remain embroiled in combating militancy, insurgency and terrorism. With the prevailing instability in the immediate and near neighbourhood, and the growing regional and global role of our country, the Army must also be prepared to undertake missions beyond our borders. It may be added that however much the Army may want to resist, it will continue to be drawn to tackle internal law and order situations and national manmade or natural calamities.

How has the Army fared in the last two decades in the discharge of its responsibilities? At considerable cost to itself it has barely managed to keep the lid on. Given the serious shortage of junior officers, and the indifferent and insufficient weaponry at its disposal, the Army it can be contended, has done exceedingly well. Regrettably the problems of the Army, and the stresses it is subjected to, are understood only by those who are in it. The MOD and the political leadership, or for that matter also the strategic community have a vague awareness, nowhere close to the ground realities. This explains the decades of inertia.

Exploiting the progressive decline of our conventional military capability all through the decade of the eighties, Pakistan launched a well orchestrated offensive through irregulars in Kashmir from about the beginning of 1990. When the momentum of this offensive seemed to be petering out Pakistan did not hesitate to gamble for higher stakes by resorting to Kargil. The Kargil fiasco and the growing domestic instability, however, did not dampen Pakistan's appetite for fomenting trouble for us. The terror attack on our Parliament in 2001 and 26 Nov. 2008-Mumbai is still fresh in our memory.

Over the last few years China too has begun to demonstrate bellicosity, tinged with arrogance, against us. Border intrusions with the purpose of intimidation coupled with force accretions in Tibet and along the LAC, portend problems for us. Its aggressive posturing on other fronts compounds the basket of our concerns.

Viewed from the national security perspective it emerges that our concept of military deterrence has failed or is failing. Clearly then, the Army's conventional war fighting capabilities must be brought to levels that promise if not absolute, sufficient deterrence.

So how do we go about building a credible dissuasive conventional military deterrence? For the past two to three decades the three services have been unsuccessfully trying to drive the process. It would be mindless to persist with the same approach. The responsibility must shift to the PM and his

Cabinet Committee on Security. This is not going to happen without some precipitate action. How this is to be brought about is a matter that the services must address?

The Army could do with a totally fresh appraisal to cover its overall strength, its structure and equipment profile, the quality of its man power, its leadership and its training. Such a review could perhaps be relevant and necessary for the Navy and the Air Force as well. Technological advancements are taking place rapidly. Correspondingly the rate of obsolescence is also increasing. It is therefore imperative that we manage change with much greater sophistication so as to ensure available funds are utilized optimally. It follows that individuals charged with formulating qualitative requirements, induction plans and evaluation of systems must be competent and have the requisite grooming and experience. Even though this issue has been debated before no concrete remedial steps have yet been taken.

INFANTRY

The Infantry is the largest arm of our Army and the only arm which has perhaps never had a respite from combat from the time the Naga insurgency began in the fifties. Matters worsened when we sent the expeditionary force to Sri Lanka for Operation Pawan. Ever since, the Infantry has continued, without break, to climb the stress ladder.

Considering the Infantry's constant engagement, aware that all Army Chiefs from the early nineties have sought to give the Infantry the highest priority in terms of equipping and modernizing it. But if we were to carry out a critical appraisal of the Infantry in 2010 the report card of twenty years effort would be quite dismal. How ironical, especially when costs are lower and the systems involved are relatively not so complex? The story is eloquent testimony to the manner in which the country's higher defence management works. Almost everything that a soldier needs, from the clothes and boots to the weapon he carries, is at present well below par.

Consider the 5.56 family of weapons that the Army is currently equipped. The Army was virtually bulldozed into accepting these weapons. It was told that indigenous R&D must be encouraged. Promises were made that in the production models the user will get a much improved and more reliable version and that a superior Mark 2 will follow. The DRDO also hinted that high volume orders from many foreign customers would be placed soon after the Indian Army accepted the induction and placed orders for delivery. The Army had no choice but to accept though none of the commitments materialized. It has lived with these weapons for more than a decade and paid an incalculable price. A good and reliable personal weapon we know does wonders to a soldier's confidence and morale. But we have failed in giving him such a weapon. Shouldn't there be review and people held accountable?

Conceptually the start point of capability-building and modernization has to be the individual soldier. So we must begin by giving him the best we can. Essentially what the soldier needs is a good and reliable personal weapon, comfortable clothing with stealth and concealment features designed to ergonomically accommodate everything he has to carry, the best protection (body armour) that portable weight permits, stabilized helmet mounted computer screens, sensors and night vision devices for observation and using his weapons, effective communications and position locating/ situational awareness systems. In addition he requires a host of sundry items like eye protection goggles, contemporary light bag pack equipment etc. The approach should be to look at the tactical vest and the helmet (protective gear) as a platform on which the future soldier systems are embedded so that weight reduction and mobility improvements issues are optimally addressed.

The resolve to modernize the infantry soldier has been there for long, but the process has been painfully slow. Ways have to be found to accelerate the process and do it comprehensively. We must therefore begin as of yesterday.

When considering assault rifles we have quite a few options available; each having its unique features. Let us briefly look at the 21st century trends in assault rifles. Essentially they are refinements to the systems developed in the previous decades. Some exciting options that could be considered are:-

- *Heckler & Koch HK 416 firing the 5.56x 45 or the HK 417 firing the 7.62×51 NATO rounds*. Both these weapons have updated features with Picatinny rails, a drop free magazine release, and some other smart features.
- *Israel's IMI Tavor TAR-21*. It has a compact bull pup design and uses the NATO 5.56x 45 cartridges. It can easily be set up for right or left handed shooters and has several modular variants that come with a standard reflex sight.
- *XM 8 from the US*. This has quite a few modular variants with inbuilt electronics such as a laser sight, round counter and integral infra red and visible sights.
- *South Korea's XK11*. This is an interesting new rifle that has a ballistic computer, a laser range finder and a digital scope that provides the soldier with combat data and enables night firing through thermal imaging sights. The product is still at a prototype stage but has considerable promise.
- *The AK Series*. The Kalashnikovs family of assault rifles is much too well known.

An important trend in small arms in the 21st century is that sophisticated electronics is now being built into the design of these weapons. There could be some justification for the approach we have now adopted. A few years ago we had considered integration of night sights in our tender for assault rifles. At that time there weren't many who were offering such embedded systems. To my mind the idea was right though the timing was wrong. But now, with most weapon manufacturers developing weapons with built in electronics.

Given the current employment of the Army and looking at the two vital needs of the infantry soldier i.e. his personal weapon and his body armour, it is difficult to decide which merits greater priority. What is but evident that on both counts the establishment has been found wanting.

Today we have all of the Rashtriya Rifles and a significant proportion of the Army deployed in combating militancy, terrorism and insurgencies. Of these how many of their personnel, are equipped with suitable body armour? And what are the constraints to procuring body armour? On both counts we will get answers that are far from convincing, particularly when today we have a host of companies in India manufacturing body armour and combat helmets. With a dynamic and inclusive approach we can harness the capabilities of these companies to give us quality protection suits and helmets at competitive prices. As a matter of fact with some support in terms of investment in R&D and inducements of assured orders, our companies can well become global leaders in protective solutions.

Assessments suggest that in the development of 'small arms protective inserts' (SAPI), technology today is at only the 40 percent level. Both in the case of X SAPI-silicon carbide and ceramic and E SAPI, and high molecular weight polyethylene (HMW-PE) and aramid fibers, there are possibilities that by improving the quality of resins and making the weave more unidirectional, weight to protection ratios can be substantially improved.

The infantry also needs to acquire better surveillance and target acquisition capabilities as well as more potent fire power at the section level and above. A mission, terrain and adversary based analysis may suggest the induction of special weapons and surveillance systems on a regional basis. It can be assumed that such an exercise would have been undertaken.

INDIAN ARMY 2020

A nation's military is a major but unstated factor in international Realpolitik, howsoever moderated and underplayed, in acknowledgement of international sensitivities. Nevertheless, its existence and capabilities percolate into the public domain, domestic as well as international, and its presence, even unstated, becomes a background presence, which provides a sense of hard-edge backup to the national establishment for undertaking effective front line diplomacy.

It is, therefore, essential in the national interest that the armed forces are upgraded and updated on an ongoing basis, something which governments have been traditionally loath to acknowledge and undertake, the Indian government perhaps more so than others in this respect. Historically, it is to the credit of the Indian Army that it has fulfilled its role as an organ of the state, and undertaken all assigned tasks successfully, except in the Sino-Indian border war of 1962 and reclamation of Indian territory in the Aksai Chin plateau, on the Sino-Indian border in Tibet, for which reasons have to be sought elsewhere. It has functioned effectively in every type of role, in spite of the general lack of a supportive government environment by way of adequate finances, resources, equipment, personnel policies, or higher political direction. The modernization and upgradation of the Indian Army to function in a 21st century environment is, therefore, a priority task for the present as well as successive governments to undertake.

The new millennium opened literally with a thunderclap, as the world witnessed America's new Day of Infamy on live media, with the demolition of the World Trade Centre in New York on September 11, 2001, in an air-assault by Al Qaida fidayeen. In his speech to the Congress on September 20, 2001, President George W Bush proclaimed America's 'War on Terror'. In its aftermath, the tensions of the recently terminated Cold War appeared to revive in a different manifestation, which mutated almost seamlessly into the new conflict that spread rapidly outwards, and impacted Afghanistan and Iraq. In fact, the War on Terror seems to have replaced the earlier geo-political confrontation of the Cold War with another worldwide confrontation, this one an ethno-religious clash of cultures (if not of entire civilizations) between neo-con America and Jihadi Islam.

The doctrines of pre-emptive intervention and regime change by the military superpower and high intensity holy war by non-state terrorists are set to overwhelmingly shape the security environment of the new millennium, and will dominate India's perceptions and security stances in at least the middle term future. Numerous local and regional extensions and variations of the conflict have sprung up all over the world, extending from immigrant communities in Europe, all the way to Indonesia, Thailand, Malaysia and the Philippines in South East Asia, traversing enroute hotspots in Russia and Eastern Europe, Chechnya, Central Asia, Afghanistan, Pakistan, Kashmir, as well as other parts of India, and Bangladesh, with branch lines to Chinese Turkestan along the Silk Route. Some of these new wars have subsumed ongoing confrontations, others are taking the form of proxy wars, sub-ethnic insurgencies, terrorism, narcotics, organized crime, illegal migration, environmental poaching, as also high intensity flare-ups over disputed borders, and perhaps with others yet to come (who knows?) involving exclusive economic zones, oil, seabed and water resources. India's relationships with the Peoples' Republic of China, as well as its strategic surrogate Pakistan, have generally been adversarial, but now repairs to these traditional contentions are being attempted. But any attempts at reconstruction will have to take into account the wider context of the new realities of the War on Terror.

To India, these realities will include, amongst others, the massive and seemingly unstoppable 'peaceful rise' of the Middle Kingdom immediately next door, with its unspoken but implicit connotations of military super-capabilities in the not too distant future, the come-back of Islamic jihad in South and South East Asia, the emergence of 'Maobadi' militias in Nepal on India's doorstep, closely interlinked with their fraternal confederates of the newly consolidated Communist Party of India (Maoist) and other Naxalite affiliates in a nascent Compact Revolutionary Zone, which reaches deep into the Indian heartland. India, shining or not, is nevertheless on its way to be an emerging power whose pluralistic society is under direct attack by the new conflict, which demands the closest attention and can be ignored only at peril; whose ultimate dimensions are as yet unclear. Till that time, there are only wide open questions, difficult, if not impossible to forecast from the present perspective.

Thus, at one extreme, putting a way-out positive spin on the current trends in Indo-Pak and Sino-Indian relations, the possibilities of turning swords into ploughshares appear endless. For instance, with the current upsurge in people-to-people relationships between India and Pakistan and general improvement in the civil environment, could for example a South Asian Federation become a practical reality in 2020, just as the European Union is today, (including, necessarily, resolution of the Kashmir and Siachen problems to the satisfaction of all parties concerned)? Would such a solution emerge as a match winner, or would there still remain some warm embers of national interest, pride and resentments, which would continue to smolder, perhaps requiring to be extinguished later?

Would an international border held only by paramilitary forces replace the Line of Control and Actual Ground Position Line? Ultimately, what impact would all these developments have on the force structure of Army 2020 in terms of mechanized and holding forces for plains and desert warfare; holding forces for the Line of Control and Actual Ground Position Line, and also the ditch-cum-bund and other defense assets and infrastructure painstakingly and painfully developed along the entire front with Pakistan?

Also, if and when outstanding issues with the Peoples' Republic of China are resolved on a permanent basis, what would be the end results for forces holding the Line of Actual Control in Northern, Central and Eastern Commands, right from the Kara Koram Pass in extreme northern Ladakh down to Kibithoo in extreme eastern Arunachal Pradesh? On a similar spin, if the internal security situation also improves to the same extent, will civil administrations manage without continuous recourse to the Army as at present, reducing these unpleasant, thankless, and irksome commitments in aid to civil power, perhaps with substantial savings in manpower in terms of the Rashtriya Rifles? Therefore, at the politically upbeat end of the scale, with conflicts, both domestic and international, being resolved, Army 2020 might well evolve into a minimalist organization, lean perhaps to the point of cadaverousness, based primarily on high technology and special forces, supported by airpower, which many today see as a classical model for the new world.

However, there are also more down market perceptions too, whose darker prognoses cannot be totally set aside. Amongst these are the massive and seemingly unstoppable 'peaceful rise' of the Middle Kingdom immediately next door, with its unarticulated but implicit connotations of military super-capabilities; the come-back of Islamic jihad on India's doorstep in the Islamic Republic of Pakistan, Afghanistan, Bangladesh and Southeast Asia; the emergence of 'Maobadi' militias in Nepal on India's immediate doorstep, with a corresponding Compact Revolutionary Zone of their fraternal confederates, the People's War Group established deep within the Indian heartland; could all suggest a 'Future History' in much deeper tones of sepia.

Taking an in-between perception of the two extremes, it would be realistic to assume that the world would perhaps continue to remain an uncertain and uneasy place, where the only certainty would be uncertainty. Threats would be undefined, unexpected and also omnipresent, in shapes and forms, which cannot be visualised clearly at present. Army 2020 will, therefore, have to be designed to function in an amorphous security environment with capabilities to operate across the entire spectrum of conflict from low intensity warfare to the ultimate unthinkable Kurukshetra of nuclear conflict.

Except in the unlikely event of a major reversal turnabout in India's traditional political worldview within the next decade or so, the role of the defense forces in 2020 will remain unchanged from the traditional one of homeland defense – protection of the territorial integrity of Indian territory by land, sea, or air. This will be consistent with the perceptions that all governments in office, regardless of their political philosophies or domestic policy, have taken all along since Independence, in which international military alignments through power blocs, mutual defense treaties, or major expeditionary commitments overseas (except of course on United Nations missions) have been eschewed.

However, the perception of homeland defense has never passively ruled out pro-active or pre-emptive interventions within or outside the country, wherever considered necessary in the national interest, as have been undertaken on numerous occasions earlier by the Indian Army. This cannot, and indeed must not be wished away or forgotten.

Military intervention in the national interest, to consolidate and nurture the fledgling nation, commenced almost immediately after Independence and through the early years of the Republic, with operations in the (then) princely states of Kashmir, Hyderabad, and Junagadh. The historical process continued with the assimilation of Portuguese colonies in 1961, absorption of the Sikkim Monarchy, assistance and support to the brutalized people of East Pakistan – now Bangladesh – in 1971, attempted peacemaking in Sri Lanka in 1987-1990, the Maldives in 1988, or more recently, the carefully harmonised anti-insurgency operations with Myanmar and Bhutan against separatist elements along contiguous border areas.

Similar contingencies may arise in the future as well, and there is no need to be in any manner apologetic about them, though some ventures can certainly be criticized for incoherent political direction and poor military planning. In addition, the Indian Army has also very successfully displayed its capabilities for operations other than war (OOW) in these regions by way of training missions and assistance in natural calamities, whenever requested by the host countries. Such contingencies could very well arise in future too.

Viewed from the final months of 2004, Indian Army 2020 is only fifteen years ahead on the timeline, within the current 15-Year Defense Perspective, and not really all that distant at all in terms of successive Five Year Defense Plans. The building of the New Army is, therefore, already in progress with the ongoing Tenth, and the future Eleventh, Twelfth and Thirteenth Five Year Defense Plan series. If these proceed even approximately on schedule (which incidentally, has almost never been the case!), Army 2020 should be in place within the Thirteenth Five Year Defense Plan (2017-2022). But defense planning has traditionally been low on the scale of national priorities, with myriad hurdles in the process of planning, decision-making and production.

Political decision-making and effective follow through action by the government have been glacial in terms of results actually achieved. Desperate attempts to expedite the process, even during national emergencies like Kargil 1999, ultimately backfired into low grade, ill informed and crudely partisan political confrontations around the Tehalka sting operation, the CAG Report, and the so-called Coffin-gate scandals, which rocked the political firmament of the time.

Their spill-over effect severely inhibited the official decision-making process, and perhaps damaged it beyond repair. The evolution of Army 2020 will have to live with this and evolve as best as it can. The crux of the issue, as always, will be sustained availability of adequate finances.

Finance ministers controlling the nation's purse strings (including in the current dispensation) generally do not look benignly on resources diverted from the national kitty towards defense, and dole them out grudgingly at the best of times. Plans for Indian Army 2020, integrated into the overall perspective of the Defense Services, are therefore, critically interlinked with the national effort in terms of resources likely to be allotted, as also to timely political and financial decision making.

This is likely to be a fluctuating process, very much influenced by the course of geo-political and economic developments, as well as political philosophies and attitudes of future governments regarding adequate and sustained financial support for defense planning. All these imponderables would impact heavily on the Defense Plan series, and therefore, on the profile of Army 2020, but in what manner and to what effect, remain questions only the future can answer.

Meanwhile, an almost continuous flow of revolutions in military affairs has been underway for over two decades now, which should certainly be incorporated into the profile of Army 2020.

The Indian Army has traditionally been manpower intensive, which many modern intellects disparage as a hangover from the Second or even the First World War era. But it must be understood that these apparent anachronisms linger on even at present, due to certain economic as well as operational compulsions. At one level, the inability of the Indian Army to shed manpower is due to lack of resources to replace it with high-end technologies, primarily because of the generally low priority accorded to defense planning, and inadequate resource allotment. In the absence of equipment, manpower intensive alternatives, somehow have to persist almost by default. The unsatisfactory hybridization, which created the current Reorganized Army Plains Infantry Division – RAPID – is a good example of this. In this case, the divisional structure was reduced by a brigade, on the assumption that manpower thus reduced would be replaced by force multipliers and surveillance.

Needless to say, the Army waited for these in vain, because the financial resources for the technological makeover were simply never allotted. It is to be seen whether these difficulties will persist in future as well. By present indications, it seems that they would still be around for quite some time. At another level, mountain and jungle terrain in the northern and eastern regions combined with extensive deployments on counter insurgency, established operational imperatives for organizations with adequate manpower.

Here, sheer technology, though helpful, was not the dominating factor, and there was no substitute for numbers of well-trained 'boots on the ground', as American forces in Iraq are painfully learning the hard way.

So, in New Age organizations, manpower versus technology will have to be implemented carefully and judiciously.

At present, there is an intense debate within the military and the rest of the strategic community on the shape of warfare in the future, and the type of army required to meet future threats. Will a traditional conventional army, even if technologically upgraded, be adequate to handle these when they occur?

Now that the process of re-construction is already under way, what kind of an Army 2020 should emerge at the end of it? How and to what extent will it or can it reflect the operational compulsions of that future time?

The answer to these and other similar questions must be clearly understood, which is that Indian Army 2020 must retain the basic configuration of a conventional army, and not be mutated by radical doctrinal surgery into some kind of heavy constabulary.

The New Army must possess integral multi-role operational capabilities across the entire spectrum of conflict, whether nuclear, conventional, or low intensity. Any undue emphasis or insistence on a tailor-made orientation focusing primarily on any particular level of warfare would be dangerously misplaced.

To effectively undertake its task of land warfare for homeland defense, India requires a large army, with an armory ranging from land-launched strategic weapons at the high intensity end of the spectrum, to special operations forces at the low intensity end. The middle levels will continue to be bulked out by conventional forces, with adequate manpower – armor, artillery, infantry, as well as integral army aviation, backed up by the requisite support and logistics elements. The basic organizations of the Army require extensive technological upgradation, but are otherwise stable and time-tested under a wide variety of environments. They are flexible enough for structured regrouping for various contingencies. Changes to the existing pattern should be introduced only after careful deliberation.

Amongst other emerging factors are strategic weapons systems, which are still a comparatively recent acquisition and whose command and control methodologies are yet to be fully stabilized. The Strategic Forces Command has been recently established as the designated inter-services agency for overall management of these high-end assets.

The new organization is logical and was originally scheduled to function directly under the much awaited Chief of Defense Staff, but since this appointment is yet to be implemented, it has now been placed de facto under the Chiefs of Staff Committee, through the Integrated Defense Staff. It still remains to be seen how the final shape of the new Command emerges, i.e. whether in the classical sense of a separate command with direct control of operational, logistics, and personnel, or as a functional command for operational employment of dedicated strategic components held with each individual Service.

In the Indian context, perhaps the latter would be more practicable. However, whatever the command structure model ultimately adopted, it must also be optimally calibrated to fulfill the important aspect of 'command satisfaction' within its hierarchy, an aspect not often considered, or, if so, ignored or disregarded. Each Service operates in its own physical environment, and land-based strategic systems are within the Army's domain. Army 2020 must incorporate an integral component of strategic forces, which can be operationally emplaced under the Strategic Forces Command.

A word about Army Aviation, which must be another vital area of focus for Army 2020. Airpower dominates the battlefield, and must be employed to achieve maximum synergy. However, in the inter-services context, this eminently profound article of faith has been allowed to acquire an extended meaning of single service ownership of all air assets.

To the Army, airpower is essentially firepower, surveillance and target acquisition from the sky in close or distant support of ground operations extending up to the operational depth of the tactical battle area. Given the advances in technology, these tasks can now be undertaken by manned as well as unmanned flight platforms, covering a range of unmanned air vehicles / remotely piloted vehicles (UAV / RPV), ground launched precision-guided missiles, and rotary wing ground combat aviation (attack and assault helicopters).

These aerial platforms operate primarily in the environment of the land battle, either independently or in a supplementary role to the air battle, often without diverting high-end airpower from its primary tasks. Army 2020 will have to build up integral air resources for itself, particularly in rotary winged combat aircraft (attack and assault helicopters, airborne early warning, communications and medevac) integral to Army Aviation, which must become the primary agency of rotary wing airpower.

But for all this to be effective within the given timeframe raises the vital issue of the attitudinal and cultural reorientation of the defense forces into a synergized joint-service environment. While acknowledging the supreme importance of individual Service identities and aspirations, by 2020, the Indian Army individually, as well as the Defense Forces collectively, must no longer be allowed to function as independent disconnected entities, without the required inter-service synergy for fullest exploitation of their respective capabilities.

Army 2020 will, therefore, have to be organized, equipped, trained and culturally energized to take its place within an operational triad in conjunction with maritime and aerospace power, functionally interlinked through an integrated politico-military Higher Defense Organization, and a common framework of joint-service doctrines and joint command structures. It takes three to tango, but nevertheless unless the joint services environment is simultaneously developed and implemented, Army 2020 (as indeed Navy 2020 or Air Force 2020) cannot be employed to its fullest capability and effect.

In some senses, provision of an enabling environment of jointmanship (a clumsy term!) and stamping them on the individual ethos and culture of each Service may well be the most challenging task, which should be accorded an overall priority higher than many other issues. In this context, the major area of reconstruction of Indian Army 2020 (and the other Services) might well be in reform of traditional mindsets and approach to battle.

3

Indian Defence Reforms: The Vajpayee Years

Atal Behari Vajpayee's coalition government was at the helm of affairs from 1998 to 2004 and significantly shaped India's defence policies. Some of this was by design, such as the nuclear tests in 1998 which allowed India to come out of the secrecy closet and led to its subsequent accommodation within the existing nuclear order, signified by the 2005

US-India Nuclear deal. Even before the tests, the government also appointed the K.C. Pant Committee to recommend a national security management system for India. These steps eventually led to the creation of the National Security Council (NSC), Strategic Policy Group (SPG) and the National Security Advisory Board (NSAB). In all these activities (from nuclear testing to creating national security structures), Brajesh Mishra, the principal secretary to the Prime Minister, played a key role.1 However the most significant development was the 1999 Kargil War, which was forced on India and revealed many weaknesses. The public outcry at that time led the government to create the Kargil Review Committee (KRC) and the subsequent Group of Ministers (GoM) Committee. These led to one of the most significant attempts at restructuring the Indian military.

With the benefit of hindsight, this chapter re-examines the defence reforms that were initiated during the Vajpayee regime.

In doing so it focuses on the big ideas, their implementation, sources of resistance and the debates therein. To be clear, this chapter does not simply list out what measures were implemented – as this has been done elsewhere – but re-examines the reform committees based on what we know now. It begins by describing the composition, functioning, recommendations and salient debates of the two reform committees. Then, it analyses the reform measures that were accepted and the ones which weren't. The next section gives an overall assessment of defence reforms during this period. It concludes with some observations about the contemporary relevance of the debates surrounding defence reforms.

VAJPAYEE'S THIRD SHOT AT PEACE

Mr. Vajpayee now has the unprecedented combination of international and regional circumstances to push for a final solution to the vexatious dispute with Pakistan over Kashmir.

The Prime Minister, Atal Behari Vajpayee, will soon have a third shot at promoting peace with Pakistan. Although the current military confrontation between India and Pakistan remains to be defused, the speech by Pervez Musharraf, President of Pakistan, on Saturday last and the Indian response suggest that the two sides have turned an important corner. Now it is a matter of time before India and Pakistan will sit down again to find answers to the difficult challenge that confronts them.

After the unsuccessful attempts at Lahore in February 1999 and Agra in July 2001, Mr. Vajpayee appears to have an infinitely better chance at getting it right this time. The announced fundamental change of direction in Pakistan and the intense involvement of the international community in preventing a war between the two nuclear rivals provide a totally different template for Mr. Vajpayee's third attempt at reconciliation with Pakistan. Mr. Vajpayee, who believes he can make a fundamental difference to India-Pakistan relations, now has the chance to move cautiously but decisively to bury the bitter legacy of the Partition in the subcontinent. As he reflects on his past attempts at normalising relations with Pakistan, hindsight should offer Mr. Vajpayee a better perspective and help him avoid the mistakes of the past and take full advantage of the new international situation in going beyond Lahore and Agra.

In retrospect, Mr. Vajpayee's hurriedly undertaken journey to Lahore was an expression of his personal commitment to improve relations with Pakistan. But the hopes generated at Lahore soon crashed against the steep mountains of Kargil. Nevertheless, Mr. Vajpayee did identify a new set of markers for India-Pakistan relations. He sought to overcome the impression in Pakistan that India remains unreconciled to the Partition of the subcontinent, by visiting Minar-e-Pakistan in Lahore. He inscribed there that a stable and prosperous Pakistan was in India's interest. The Lahore visit also marked the Indian recognition of the new nuclear reality between the two nations that called for more responsible approaches to managing the security problems of the subcontinent.

The Kargil aggression that was discovered barely weeks after Lahore showed that Pakistan either did not understand the new realities or was not willing to abide by the new norms demanded by the nuclearisation of the subcontinent. But the approach to the relationship identified by Mr. Vajpayee at Lahore remains important. What we have seen since Lahore is the demonstration of the terrible consequences of departing from the norms of behaviour that must guide nuclear neighbours. If Mr. Vajpayee's good words at Lahore were dismissed as sentimentalism in Pakistan, his actions in the present crisis showed India's resolve to get Pakistan to see the importance of those words.

At Lahore, the amateur poet in Mr.Vajpayee came up with the composition"ab jang na hone denge"(we will not allow a war to happen). But this time, Mr. Vajpayee was reading the riot act to Pakistan. By ordering full-scale preparations for a war against Pakistan after December 13 and calling Islamabad's nuclear bluff, he has tried to force the meaning of the poem he recited in Lahore on the military leadership next door. What the good words at Lahore could not get Pakistan to do _ stop sponsoring terrorism across the border _ India's threat of war and American diplomatic pressure have begun to achieve.

Overcoming the deep personal bitterness over the betrayal at Lahore, Mr. Vajpayee had a second shot at transforming the relationship with Pakistan by inviting Gen. Musharraf to visit India. But the unexpected and intensive exercise at Agra last July to work out a mutually agreeable framework of negotiations collapsed amidst Gen. Musharraf's greediness to gain unilateral advantage. Mistakenly viewing Mr. Vajpayee's sentiment for peace as a national weakness, and wrongly assessing that India was reeling under the bloody effects of cross-border terrorism, the General overplayed his hand at Agra. In refusing to give up the lever of cross-border terrorism and insisting that there could no be normalisation of relations until the Kashmir issue was sorted out, he destroyed the prospects for initiating reconciliation at Agra.

The dramatic international and regional developments since Agra have radically altered the context of any potential peace process between India and Pakistan. The terrorist attacks in New York and Washington on September 11 and the American war against terrorism ended the acquiescence tothe international community of the instrumentality of cross-border terrorism that Pakistan developed against India. The December 13 attack against Parliament House in New Delhi breached India's decade-long tolerance of cross-border terrorism and got the Government to prepare for a military showdown.

But the very fear of a war between India and Pakistan that could result in a nuclear exchange brought the full diplomatic power of the United States into play. Relentless pressure from the Bush administration since December 13 forced Gen. Musharraf to proclaim a basic change of political course for Pakistan as well as agree to discard the instrument of cross-border terrorism. What Agra failed to achieve _ to get a commitment from Gen. Musharraf on ending cross-border terrorism _ has been imposed upon Pakistan by September 11 and December 13. That should make it easier now to initiate a productive peace process between India and Pakistan. The negotiating exercise at Agra covered considerable ground, and if cross-border terrorism is removed from the equations we saw at Agra, a political level dialogue on key issues of India-Pakistan relations can begin fairly quickly.

It is with good reason that Mr. Vajpayee is being advised caution in proceeding towards this third attempt for peace with Pakistan. After all, what we have heard from Gen. Musharraf are mere words on ending cross-border terrorism. India will be right in seeking to ensure that the General's words are put into action, before a de-escalation can begin and talks resume. For, New Delhi cannot afford to negotiate under the continuing threat of cross-border terrorism.

While India makes it certain that cross-border violence sponsored by Pakistan ends soon, it would be wrong in signalling that it might want to delay the initiation of the peace process for other reasons _ including the presumed threats to the political future of Gen. Musharraf who has boldly taken on the jehadis at home. India's objective, instead, must be to step up the diplomatic pressure on Gen. Musharraf to deliver quickly on the ground the promises he has made on cross-border terrorism and at the same time renew India's commitment to begin a serious and substantive negotiation on the Kashmir dispute.

There is a deep sense of anxiety in Pakistan that having been forced to give up the instrument of cross-border terrorism, it will find a New Delhi that is no longer enthusiastic about negotiating about Kashmir.

It should not be difficult for India to dispell those fears. After all, Mr. Vajpayee has repeatedly proclaimed his desire for an engagement with Pakistan on the Kashmir dispute.

In his musings published earlier this month as well as last new year, Mr. Vajpayee had declared the readiness to "get off the beaten track" in finding a solution to the Kashmir dispute. Mr.Vajpayee now has the unprecedented combination of international and regional circumstances to push for a final solution to the vexatious dispute with Pakistan over Kashmir. He might be third time lucky!

The key to the realisation of Mr. Vajpayee's political objectives in Kashmir lies with the U.S., which is in a position to get Gen. Musharraf to deliver on cross-border terrorism and encourage Pakistan to accept a fair and reasonable solution to the dispute that has hobbled the subcontinent since Partition. The visit to the region this week by the U.S. Secretary of State, Colin Powell, provides an important opportunity for India to lay out its terms for the diplomatic and military de-escalation and reiterate its commitment to seek an early solution to the Kashmir dispute as part of a rapid normalisation of India-Pakistan relations.

NUCLEAR PROLIFERATION VS. STRATEGIC ENGAGEMENT

The signing of the nuclear deal in July 2005 was followed by a range of negative reactions in the United States. The main focus of most of these reactions was the impact that this deal would have on other states considering pursuing nuclear weapons. It was argued that the nuclear deal signaled to such states that acquiring nuclear weapons represented a means to recognition as a major global player without any penalty for such actions. Specifically, the issue of Pakistan was raised in so far as Pakistan might also demand the status given to India and a refusal might mean growing anti-U.S. feelings in a state crucial for the success of the global war on terrorism.

India was also criticized for its refusal to curtail the development of its nuclear weapons and delivery systems and for not permitting the full scope of safeguards for its military and civilian facilities. While most in the United States did see India as a major global actor in the coming years, there were concerns whether India could be trusted on such critical issues as U.S.-China relations or Iran's nuclear weapons programme.

Initial reactions from some members of the U.S. Congress were also negative. They argued that the United States could not afford to play favourites and break the rules of the nonproliferation regime to favour one nation at the risk of undermining critical international treaties on nuclear weapons. It was clear at the outset that garnering support from the U.S. Congress for the nuclear pact was going to be an uphill task for the Bush administration.

While many U.S. lawmakers realized India's growing strategic importance and its impeccable track record in nuclear nonproliferation, both domestic U.S. laws and India's status as a nonsignator of the Treaty on the Non- Proliferation of Nuclear Weapons (NPT) meant that Congress would find it difficult to lend their support to the Bush administration's decision to provide India with civilian nuclear reactors. The difficulty was that making an exception in India's case would establish a precedent and open the United States to charges that it lacked commitment to the nonproliferation regime. While most Republican members of the Congress were circumspect, many Democratic members made it abundantly clear that the agreement was highly controversial, and even members of the India caucus were restrained in their views. Moreover, the euphoria over the nuclear deal was soon overtaken by the realities of international politics. India was asked to prove its loyalty by lining up behind the United States on the question of Iran's nuclear programme or risk its own nuclear bargain with Washington. Some members of the U.S. Congress became upset over the visit of the Indian foreign minister to Iran and flayed India during a hearing on the Indo-U.S. nuclear pact. U.S. congressman Tom Lantos (D-CA) went so far as to say that India "will pay a heavy price for a total disregard of U.S. concerns vis-à-vis Iran." It is not clear what part U.S. pressure played in India's decision to vote in support of the European Union- and U.S.-led resolution censuring Tehran in the September 2005 meeting of the IAEA board of governors, but the Bush administration made it clear that if India voted against the U.S. motion, the U.S. Congress would likely not approve the U.S.-India nuclear agreement. Lantos later hailed the Indian vote in the IAEA, arguing that it would promote a positive consideration in Congress of the new U.S.-India nuclear agreement. India, on its part, has continued to claim that its vote had nothing to do with its nuclear agreement with the United States.

The hearings in the U.S. Congress on the Indo-U.S. nuclear pact also brought to light the difficulties involved in its ratification. Most members of the U.S. Congress struggled with the question of whether the net impact of this agreement on U.S. nonproliferation policy would be positive or negative. The majority of the experts testifying before the House Committee on International Relations argued that the deal weakened the international nonproliferation regime.

Only a few, such as Ashley Tellis of the Carnegie Endowment of International Peace, dared to suggest that bringing India into the global nonproliferation fold through a lasting bilateral agreement that defines clearly enforceable benefits and obligations, not merely strengthens American efforts to stem further proliferation but also enhances U.S. national security. The hearings in the U.S. Senate Foreign Relations Committee also highlighted the expectations that the Bush administration had of India regarding the nuclear pact. Not only were India's attitudes vis-à-vis Iran mentioned by senior Bush administration officials as crucial, but it was also made clear that Washington expected India to perform in conformity with U.S. interests.

India's help in building democratic institutions worldwide was deemed essential for the Indo-U.S. partnership. India's support for the multinational Proliferation Security Initiative was also referred to as highly desirable. It was made clear to the Senate that the initiation of legislation by the Bush administration in the U.S. Congress operationalizing the nuclear pact would be based on evidence that the Indian government had begun acting on the most important commitment of separating its civilian and military nuclear facilities in a credible and transparent manner.

Senator Richard Lugar (R-IN), then chairing the U.S. Senate Foreign Relations Committee, made it a point to mention in his 2005 opening statement that India's nuclear record with the international community had been unsatisfying and that India had "in 1974 violated bilateral pledges it made to Washington not to use U.S.-supplied nuclear materials for weapons purposes."

He forcefully reminded everyone that an implementation of the Indo-U.S. nuclear accord requires congressional consent and that it would be his committee and the U.S. Congress that would determine "what effect the Joint Statement will have on U.S. efforts to halt the proliferation of weapons of mass destruction." Senator Lugar laid down very clearly the four benchmarks that would determine the U.S. Congress's consent to the pact: "First, how does civil nuclear cooperation strengthen the U.S.-Indian strategic relationship and why is it so important? Second, how does the Joint Statement address U.S. concerns about India's nuclear programme and policies? Third, what effects will the Joint Statement have on other proliferation challenges such as Iran and North Korea and the export policies of Russia and China? Fourth, what impact will the Joint Statement have on the efficacy and future of the NPT and the international non-proliferation regime?"

Even as this debate was moving apace in the United States, the Bush administration took some significant steps to further strengthen Indo-U.S. civil nuclear ties. It strongly supported India's participation in the International Thermonuclear Experimental Reactor (ITER) consortium, an international enterprise aimed at building a reactor that can use nuclear fusion as a source of energy, and removed India's safeguard reactors from the U.S. Department of Commerce Entities List.

It also made a strong pitch supporting India at the meeting of the Nuclear Suppliers Group (NSG) to enable full peaceful civil nuclear cooperation and trade with India. In a strong signal that the Bush administration was serious about the nuclear deal with India, the U.S. State Department told the Senate Foreign Relations Committee that it could not determine whether India's forty-megawatt nuclear reactor called Cirus had violated a 1956 U.S.-India contract that said that U.S. heavy water could only be used for peaceful purposes. The

Bush administration argued that it is not possible to have a conclusive answer on whether plutonium produced by the Cirus reactor was produced by the U.S. heavy water.

At the same time, hectic lobbying also started in the United States. The U.S.-India Business Council, a group of major U.S. corporations doing business in India, hired one of the most expensive lobbying firms in Washington, Patton Boggs LLP, to help ensure the enactment of legislation permitting the United States to pursue full-scale civilian nuclear cooperation with India. The government of India also worked with its own lobbying firms; Barbour, Griffith and Rogers LLC, which is headed by the former U.S. ambassador to India, Robert Blackwill, and the Venable Law firm.

THE DEBATE IN INDIA: CONVERGENCE OF THE RIGHT AND THE LEFT

A range of opinions was also expressed on the Indo-U.S. nuclear deal in India. The opposition Hindu nationalist Bhartiya Janata Party (BJP) was quick to criticize the pact. Ironically, it was the BJP that had laid the foundations of the emerging Indo-U.S. strategic partnership. The architect of this partnership, former Indian prime minister Atal Bihari Vajpayee, argued that the Indian government had surrendered its right to determine what kind of nuclear deterrent it should have in the future based on its own threat perception.

Vajpayee argued that the new agreement would not only put restrictions on the nuclear research programme, but India would also incur huge costs in separating military and civilian nuclear installations. The Left parties, which are also part of the ruling coalition in India, criticized the government for not consulting them before striking the nuclear deal with the United States.

They also lambasted the government for giving up on India's long-held policy of nuclear disarmament. Other critics of the deal claimed that America's recognition of India as a "responsible state with advanced nuclear technology" that should "acquire the same benefits as other such states" falls short of admitting it into the nuclear club. It was argued that India had committed itself to segregating, in a phased manner, the nation's civilian nuclear facilities; voluntarily placing its civilian nuclear facilities under IAEA safeguards; signing and adhering to an additional protocol with respect to civilian nuclear facilities; continuing the unilateral moratorium on nuclear testing; working with the United States to help conclude a Fissile Material Cut-off Treaty; continuing with stringent nonproliferation export controls; and harmonizing with and adhering to the guidelines of the Missile Technology Control Regime and the NSG. While most of these conditions had long been a part of the Indo-U.S. strategic discourse, for some Indian critics, India had agreed to these conditions without much reciprocity from the United States. Others expressed fears that independent research activities oriented to peaceful purposes, including India's fast breeder programme, might be obstructed or slowed down.

The scientific community in India delivered a mixed verdict. Some, accepting the need for nuclear energy in the coming years, favored the pact, because it would augment India's energy resources. The deal with the United States was also viewed by many as leading the way for other states in the NSG, such as Canada, France, the United Kingdom, and Russia, to supply India with civil nuclear technology. Others were less than enthusiastic and argued that the separation of civilian and military facilities is an onerous task and might entail serious repercussions for research and development in weapons development and for production facilities needed for the nuclear deterrent.

Incidentally, even the Americans conceded that separating its civilian and military nuclear facilities represented an enormously difficult task for India. Some critics have charged that the very premise of the Indo-U.S. nuclear deal is flawed, because meeting energy needs by importing nuclear reactors will only lead to energy insecurity and exorbitant costs. There were also complaints that the scientific community had been kept completely out of the loop during such an important decision. For a long time it seemed as if the Department of Atomic Energy (DAE) in India was not reconciled to the deal, because it continued to be reluctant in coming up with a credible plan for separating India's civilian and military nuclear facilities.

Several rounds of talks between India and the United States failed primarily because of DAE's strong resistance to the deal, especially its opposition to putting its fast breeder programme on the civilian list. Even as this debate was going on in India, India's decision to vote in favour of the U.S.-sponsored motion in the IAEA that was critical of Iran angered the Left parties in India. They came out strongly against the Indian government for not supporting a fellow member of the Nonaligned Movement against what they viewed as America's hegemonistic ambitions and bullying tactics.

In 2006, much to India's chagrin, Iran's nuclear problem once again emerged as a complicating factor in Indian efforts to finalize the nuclear deal with the United States. Iran decided to remove the seals applied by the IAEA for the purpose of verifying the suspension of Iran's P-1 centrifuge uranium enrichment programme in January 2006 just as the Indian government was engaged in some hard bargaining with the United States on the nuclear pact. Iran plans to pursue all activities to build, research, develop, and test the P-1 centrifuge. The uranium enrichment activity is part of a process that could be used both to generate electricity and to make nuclear weapons. In response to this, the EU3 (Britain, France, and Germany), along with the United States, called for an emergency meeting of the IAEA in February 2006 to discuss whether to refer Iran to the UN Security Council.

Once again, India came under pressure as the nature of its decision at the meeting of the IAEA Board of Governors could have repercussions for its own nuclear negotiations with the United States. U.S. ambassador to India David Mulford went public with his warning that if India did not vote to send Iran to the UN Security Council, the effect on the deal would be "devastating," because the U.S. Congress would "simply stop considering the matter" and the "initiative will die." In the end,

India did vote in support of the U.S.- and EU-sponsored resolution and reasoned that it was done keeping in mind India's own security interests, because a nuclear Iran in a highly unstable Middle East country was not in India's interest.

Despite the opposition that the Indo-U.S. deal faced from the right and the left of the political spectrum in India, there were few who were advocating India's withdrawal from the agreement. For most of the Indian strategic community and the media, the Indo-U.S. nuclear deal affirmed the depth and maturity of the India-U.S. partnership. The deal generated a certain sense of euphoria, because it marked an end to India's nuclear isolation and was seen as a tribute to India's growing profile in the global order.

The Indian scientific establishment also started interacting with its U.S. counterpart, giving concrete shape to Indo-U.S. cooperation on areas such as high-energy nuclear physics, nuclear plant design, construction, operation, safety, life extension, and regulatory oversight. Moreover, it was clear to seasoned observers of India's nuclear programme that there was a danger of India's nuclear programme grinding to a halt in a couple of decades if India did not go for international cooperation. India's uranium ore was adequate only for 10,000MW, and India's nuclear weapons programme would have to be accommodated within that. The Indo-U.S. deal, therefore, was seen by most as India's best hope for integrating itself in the global nuclear framework and drawing on its advantages.

INDIA ATTACKS PAKISTANI POSITIONS

The terrain of Kashmir is mountainous and at high altitudes; even the best roads, such as National Highway 1D from Leh to Srinagar, are only two lanes. The rough terrain and narrow roads slowed traffic, and the high altitude, which affected the ability of aircraft to carry loads, made control of NH 1D (the actual stretch of the highway which was under Pakistani fire) a priority for India. From their observation posts, the Pakistani forces had a clear line-of-sight to lay down indirect artillery fire on NH 1D, inflicting heavy casualties on the Indians. This was a serious problem for the Indian Army as the highway was its main logistical and supply route. The Pakistani shelling of the arterial road posed the threat of Leh being cut off, though an alternative (and longer) road to Leh existed via Himachal Pradesh.

The infiltrators, apart from being equipped with small arms and grenade launchers, were also armed with mortars, artillery and anti-aircraft guns. Many posts were also heavilymined, with India later stating to having recovered more than 8,000 anti-personnel mines according to an ICBL report. Pakistan's reconnaissance was done throughunmanned aerial vehicles and AN/TPQ-36 Firefinder radars supplied by the US. The initial Indian attacks were aimed at controlling the hills overlooking NH 1D, with high priority being given to the stretches of the highway near the town of Kargil. The majority of posts along the Line of Control were adjacent to the highway, and therefore the recapture of nearly every infiltrated post increased both the territorial gains and the security of the highway. The protection of this route and the recapture of the forward posts were thus *ongoing objectives* throughout the war.

The Indian Army's first priority was to recapture peaks that were in the immediate vicinity of NH 1D. This resulted in Indian troops first targeting the Tiger Hill and Tololing complex in Dras, which dominated the Srinagar-Leh route. This was soon followed by the Batalik-Turtok sub-sector which provided access to Siachen Glacier. Some of the peaks that were of vital strategic importance to the Pakistani defensive troops were Point 4590 and Point 5353. While 4590 was the nearest point that had a view of NH 1D, point 5353 was the highest feature in the Dras sector, allowing the Pakistani troops to observe NH 1D. The recapture of Point 4590 by Indian troops on June 14 was significant, notwithstanding the fact that it resulted in the Indian Army suffering the most casualties in a single battle during the conflict. Though most of the posts in the vicinity of the highway were cleared by mid-June, some parts of the highway near Drass witnessed sporadic shelling until the end of the war.

Once India regained control of the hills overlooking NH 1D, the Indian Army turned to driving the invading force back across the Line of Control. The Battle of Tololing, among other assaults, slowly tilted the combat in India's favor. The Pakistani troops at Tololing were aided by Pakistani fighters from Kashmir. Some of the posts put up a stiff resistance, including Tiger Hill (Point 5140) that fell only later in the war.

Indian troops found well-entrenched Pakistani soldiers at Tiger Hill, and both sides suffered heavy casualties. After a final assault on the peak in which 10 Pakistani soldiers and 5 Indian soldiers were killed, Tiger Hill finally fell. A few of the assaults occurred atop hitherto unheard of peaks – most of them unnamed with only Point numbers to differentiate them – which witnessed fierce hand to hand combat.

As the operation was fully underway, about 250 artillery guns were brought in to clear the infiltrators in the posts that were in the line-of-sight. The Bofors FH-77B field howitzer played a vital role, with Indian gunners making maximum use of the terrain that assisted such an attack. However, its success was limited elsewhere due to the lack of space and depth to deploy the Bofors gun.

It was in this type of terrain that aerial attacks were used with limited effectiveness. French made Mirage 2000H of the IAF were tasked to drop laser-guided bombs to destroy well-entrenched positions of the Pakistani forces. However, The IAF lost a MiG-27 strike aircraftwhich it attributed to an engine failure as well as a MiG-21 fighter which was shot down by Pakistan; initially Pakistan said it shot down both jets after they crossed into its territory. One Mi-8 helicopter was also lost, due to Stinger SAMs. On May 27, 1999, Flt. Lt. Nachiketa developed engine trouble in the Batalik sector and bailed out of his craft. Sqn Ldr Ajay Ahuja went out of his way to locate his comrade but was shot down by a shoulder-fired Stinger missile. According to reports, he had bailed out of his stricken plane safely but was apparently killed by his captors as his body was returned riddled with bullet wounds.

In many vital points, neither artillery nor air power could dislodge the outposts manned by the Pakistani soldiers, who were out of visible range. The Indian Army mounted some direct frontal ground assaults which were slow and took a heavy toll given the steep ascent that had to be made on peaks as high as 18,000 feet (5,500 m). Since any daylight attack would be suicidal, all the advances had to be made under the cover of darkness, escalating the risk of freezing. Accounting for the wind chill factor, the temperatures were often as low as "15 °C to "11 °C (12 °F to 5 °F) near the mountain tops. Based on military tactics, much of the costly frontal assaults by the Indians could have been avoided if the Indian Military had chosen to blockade the supply route of the opposing force, virtually creating a siege. Such a move would have involved the Indian troops crossing the LoC as well as initiating aerial attacks on Pakistan soil, a manoeuvre India was not willing to exercise fearing an expansion of the theatre of war and reducing international support for its cause. Two months into the conflict, Indian troops had slowly retaken most of the ridges that were encroached by the infiltrators; according to official count, an estimated 75%–80% of the intruded area and nearly all high ground was back under Indian control.

Withdrawal and final battles

Following the outbreak of armed fighting, Pakistan sought American help in de-escalating the conflict. Bruce Riedel, who was then an aide to President Bill Clinton, reported that U.S. intelligence had imaged Pakistani movements of nuclear weapons to forward deployments for fear of the Kargil hostilities escalating into a wider conflict. However, President Clinton refused to intervene until Pakistan had removed all forces from the Indian side of the Line of Control. Following the Washington accord of July 4, 1999, when Sharif agreed to withdraw Pakistani troops, most of the fighting came to a gradual halt, but some Pakistani forces remained in positions on the Indian side of the

LOC. In addition, theUnited Jihad Council (an umbrella for extremist groups) rejected Pakistan's plan for a climb-down, instead deciding to fight on.

The Indian army launched its final attacks in the last week of July; as soon as the Drass subsector had been cleared of Pakistani forces, the fighting ceased on July 26. The day has since been marked as *Kargil Vijay Diwas* (Kargil Victory Day) in India. By the end of the war, Pakistan had to withdraw under international pressure and due to pressure from continued fighting at battle front and left India in control of all territory south and east of the Line of Control, as was established in July 1972 as per the Simla Agreement. Pakistan, however, retained control over some strategic peaks inside the Indian territory.

World opinion

Pakistan was criticised by other countries for instigating the war, as its paramilitary forces and insurgents crossed the Line of Control. Pakistan's primary diplomatic response, one of plausible deniability linking the incursion to what it officially termed as "Kashmiri freedom fighters", was in the end not successful. Veteran analysts argued that the battle was fought at heights where only seasoned troops could survive, so poorly equipped "freedom fighters" would neither have the ability nor the wherewithal to seize land and defend it.

Moreover, while the army had initially denied the involvement of its troops in the intrusion, two soldiers were awarded the Nishan-E-Haider (Pakistan's highest military honour). Another 90 soldiers were also given gallantry awards, most of them posthumously, confirming Pakistan's role in the episode. India also released taped phone conversations between the Army Chief and a senior Pakistani general where the latter is recorded saying: "the scruff of [the militants] necks is in our hands", although Pakistan dismissed it as a "total fabrication". Concurrently, Pakistan made several contradicting statements, confirming its role in Kargil, when it defended the incursions saying that the LOC itself was disputed. Pakistan also attempted to internationalize the Kashmir issue, by linking the crisis in

Kargil to the larger Kashmir conflict but, such a diplomatic stance found few backers on the world stage.

As the Indian counter-attacks picked up momentum, Pakistani prime minister Nawaz Sharif flew to meet U.S. President Bill Clinton on July 4 to obtain support from the United States. Clinton rebuked Sharif, however, and asked him to use his contacts to rein in the militants and withdraw Pakistani soldiers from Indian territory. Clinton would later reveal in his autobiography that "Sharif's moves were perplexing" since the Indian Prime Minister had travelled to Lahore to promote bilateral talks aimed at resolving the Kashmir problem and "by crossing the Line of Control, Pakistan had wrecked the [bilateral] talks". On the other hand, he applauded Indian restraint for not crossing the LoC and escalating the conflict into an all-out war.

G8 nations supported India and condemned the Pakistani violation of the LOC at the Cologne summit. The European Union also opposed Pakistan's violation of the LOC. China, a long-time ally of Pakistan, insisted on a pullout of forces to the pre-conflict positions along the LoC and settling border issues peacefully.

Other organizations like theASEAN Regional Forum too supported India's stand on the inviolability of the LOC.

Faced with growing international pressure, Sharif managed to pull back the remaining soldiers from Indian territory.

The joint statement issued by Clinton and Sharif conveyed the need to respect the Line of Control and resume bilateral talks as the best forum to resolve all disputes.

THE 1999 KARGIL WAR: NOT A GENERALS' VICTORY

Much has been written about the event, including by the Chief of Army Staff at that time, Gen V P Malik, as also by the then Home Minister L K Advani. There was an official inquiry by India's renowned strategic affairs analyst, K Subrahmanyam, but he has pointed out to this writer that he did not go into operational details and accordingly, could not comment on certain weaknesses some top Indian commanders displayed. The mid-level and younger officers and men though fought well, and even though many of them perished, the victory actually belonged to them.

The Pakistani military leadership as well as its Inter Services Intelligence (ISI) have always been indulging in nasty manoeuvers against India. But that they dared to infiltrate troops into India and tried to capture a part of Kashmir yet again was possible because we were negligent, partly because we generally are so by temperament and partly because the government of the day, led by Mr A B Vajpayee, had ordered the forces to be "soft" on Pakistan because of the "positive" talks between him and his Pakistani counterpart, Nawaz Sharif towards maintaining peace and building friendship.

While opportunities for peace must be seized by politicians, there was no reason for the armed forces – the Army in particular – to be lax. In fact, the Pakistani move as it happened had been debated in the Indian Army for years and had been taken up as a strong possibility in periodic exercises. Yet, when it was happening, we were blind to it.

In the foreword to Brig Gurmeet Kanwal's book, Indian Army Vision 2020, Gen Malik says: "The Fact is that even after 60 years of independence, knowledge and experience of defence and military issues is lacking in most of our political leaders and civilian bureaucrats."

But the General has not shared the lapses and neglect of responsibilities of the Army leadership, particularly of the sector commanders, and to an extent, his own. Some of these are by now, well known, including the mindset of the 15 Corps Commander, Lt Gen Krishan Pal, who insisted that there were only a handful of infiltrators – 60 to 80 – and that none of them was a Pakistani soldier. He committed troops without allowing them adequate weapons and strength, and if facts given by Lt Gen Y M Bammi in a book are taken into account, he punished an officer, Brig Devinder Singh, who wanted better preparations insisting that there were a large number of Pakistani soldiers inside the Indian territory. The officer had eight battalions under his charge, and by all accounts, he fought very well, leading the troops from the front. Gen Malik himself has been seen and heard praising this officer at various fora. Yet, Brig Devinder Singh's career was cut short to save those who were wrong.

To recall, the biggest players of the Kargil War were:

a. The Government at the highest echelon of the Political Leadership;
b. The top rung of the military leadership – The Army Chief, GOC-in-C Northern Command, 15 Corps Cdr , and the 3 Div Cdr;
c. The intelligence agencies, primarily the Intelligence Bureau (IB) and Research and Analysis Wing (RAW);
d. The Indian Air Force (IAF) and its exercise of Air Power.
e. The dedicated and committed soldiers and the middle and junior level officers.

The Role Of The Political Leadership

The NDA government was at its pinnacle in May 1998, having successfully conducted the nuclear test that month and having put India in the list of Nuclear Weapon States (NWS). The aim now was to resolve the Kashmir issue by seeking wellmeaning diplomatic and economic relations with Pakistan.

Mrs Indira Gandhi had also attempted that, after the 1971 Bangladesh Liberation War, by trying to tell the then Pakistani leader Z A Bhutto that only peace between the two neighbours would ensure their long-term economic prosperity and growth. In fact, she went out of the way to ensure a comfortable stay for Bhutto, personally choosing even the tapestry of the room he was to stay in Simla during the 1972 summit between them, and by telling Indian officers that the Pakistani leader must be given the respect due to a visiting head of government or state, and not that of a country which had lost war. She agreed to Bhutto's request to release nearly 96,000 Pakistani POWs, and Bhutto promised to work for peace with India.

Needless to say that he backed out. Mrs Gandhi did what was right in those circumstances. But the lesson for the Indian leadership was to understand that Pakistan is never to be trusted. Islamabad built a network of nuclear capability and missiles by smuggling and deceit, lying even to Washington which gave it liberal aid as a friend and mentor.

Prime Minister Vajpayee and his deputy, Advani, tried to establish a political dialogue with Pakistan. Coupled with the nuclear tests, a success with Islamabad would give them respect in the history books forever.

Intelligence organizations were told to be easy, and the armed forces stopped looking for periodic information from them. There was the February 1999 Bus Yatra (journey) by Vajpayee to Lahore to meet with his counterpart, Nawaz Sharif. It was a goodwill mission, seemingly wellresponded by Sharif.

But the fact that the then Pakistani Chief of Army Staff, Gen Parvez Musharraf, did not pay due respects to the visiting Indian leader during the visit, should have been an indication of the Pakistani army's intentions; that it had no intention to accommodate the rapprochement that the political leadership in Islamabad perhaps then wanted.

It may be noted that as a Brigadier on assignment with a think tank in London, Musharraf had written in a thesis that Pakistan must capture Kashmir to secure water from the Himalayan rivers for itself. As a Chief of Staff, he would certainly try to realize his thoughts.

It is a well known fact that the Srinagar-Leh axis runs closest to the Line of Control (LOC) in the Dras–Kargil Sector. Also, the terrain on the Indian side is hostile to defend, whereas the terrain on the Pakistan side is favorable to launch an offensive. Strategically, Pakistan has always intended to block, disrupt or permanently dislocate it.

My first posting after being commissioned into the IAF in 1963 was to Jammu in Squadron 43, flying Dakotas. The main task was to operate to Kargil and Thoise to provide logistic support to the troops deployed in forward areas. I was fortunate to be deputed as the Base Commander of Air Force clement at Kargil from Feb to May 1964, working along with 121 (Ind) Infantry Brigade.

It was an education. Brig Chopra, an Armoured Corps officer who was the Brigade Commander, always used to say that the Dras-Kargil Sector was the most sensitive because of its close proximity to the LOC as well as the terrain factors.

Much later, during a course in 1980-81 at the Army's prestigious College of Combat at MHOW, now renamed Army War College, this lesson was repeated by none other than the Commandant, Lt Gen K Sunderji.

He became the Chief of Army Staff later, and had a sand-model exercise conducted, visualizing exactly what the Pakistanis did to occupy Kargil. A counteroffensive plan was discussed at the 15 Corps Headquarters. I was privy to that along with Lt Gen B C Nanda, Army Commander Northern Command, Air Marshal M M Singh, AOC-in-C Western Command and some other officers.

That in 1998 and 1999, the top brass in the same sector was oblivious to the risk from the Pakistani Army, is absolutely un-understanable.

Raw's Aviation Research Centre (ARC)

Till mid-1997, a user could approach ARC only through the RAW HQ for its operational tasks. This used to delay the process by a week. The legendary Billy Bedi, who headed ARC for several years, initiated userfriendly steps, and a required mission could be launched within hours. Analytical reports were delivered ASAP, within hours if required.

Top 3-star officers from the services were invited and informed of the ARC's capabilities in airborne electronic intelligence, and the then Chief of Air Staff, Air Chief Marshal A Y Tipnis, commended the ARC.

The Kargil Surprise

In May 1999, once reports of Pakistani infiltration had come in, Army's Directorate General of Military Intelligence

(DGMI) sought Air Reconnaissance Mission in the Dras-Kargil sector. I personally flew missions beginning May 13 and soon, on May 18, we had pictures of six Pakistani Army MI-17 helicopters parked in the Mushok Valley area on the Indian side. These photographs were shown to the then Defence Minister George Fernandes, who was aghast and observed that this could have happened only after months of planning and preparation.

Gen Malik also praised ARC for the inputs but strangely, till some three weeks after this input, Lt Gen Krishan Pal still seemed to believe that there were only a few infiltrators on the Indian side. He himself said in a TV statement that he revised his opinion only after India lost many lives in the Battle of Tololing (June 13).

Did the Army HQ fail to convey him the confirmation of the Pakistani helicopters, and presence, inside India? Or he just insisted on ignoring reality?

Perhaps, the Army should come out with the truth after an honest introspection. For record, Gen Malik had told ARC that he had no hesitation in admitting that its inputs enabled the Army to correlate its operational plans and that otherwise the causality figures could have been much higher. The gap between this statement and Lt Gen Krishanpal's observation is glaring, and led to a tragic loss of lives.

The Indian Air Force

IAF does not have combat helicopters for high altitude offensive operations, and on May 25, it was decided to commit aircraft to neutralize the Pakistan-occupied positions on the Indian side. Initially, IAF lost two aircraft and one Mi 17 helicopter.

An IAF spokesman pointed out that the air operations in Kargil had taken place in an environment that was totally new in the history of world military aviation. The IAF had to unlearn what had been taught before, as it was operating with a new set of paradigms such as the ballistic trajectory of weapons in high altitude operations. A well-respected Air Marshal Vinod

Patney, Air Officer Commanding in-Chief (AOC-in-C) Western Air Command, conducted the air operations after a short course to his officers in precision bombing.

The Subrahmanyam Committee

The Subrahmanyam Committee did not attribute any intelligence failures to RAW or ARC, but highlighted equipment inadequacies like the lack of high resolution, all-weather and sub-meter imaging capability.

Lack of UAVs and better coordination between the security agencies was also mentioned but it acknowledged that the IB Director did convey certain inputs on activities in areas under the Gilgit-based FCNA (Force Commander orthern Areas) of Pakistan to the Prime Minister, the Home Minister, the Cabinet Secretary, the Home Secretary and the Director-General Military Operations (DGMO).

There is apparently a general lack of awareness of the critical importance of, and the need for, assessed intelligence, at all levels. Joint Intelligence Committee (JIC) reports do not receive the attention they deserve at the political and higher bureaucratic levels.

One officer in a listening post mentions that a senior bureaucrat asked him about some entertainment programmes only in a span of one year. It is clear that a Kargil-type situation could have been avoided either by plugging gaps as in Siachin, or by a credible declaratory policy of swiftly punishing wanton and willful violation of the sanctity of the LOC, as the Committee observed.

The Nuclear Tangle

Kargil was a stupid adventure for Pakistan. Threats from Islamabad about using nuclear weapons were considered but dismissed as Pakistan would not have been more stupid to invite destructive retaliation. The Kargil War has also helped strengthen India's doctrine that while India would not first use nuclear weapons, it would retaliate by inflicting massive destruction.

Conclusion

There is much evidence available to suggest that the intelligence agencies, RAW and IB, had in fact provided their political masters and military commanders with ample warning about Pakistani intentions and activities. In any case, lack of strategic intelligence could have been made up by the observation on the ground through scouts and patrolling. One did not have to get basic inputs about the Pakistani infiltration from shepherds, which as a matter fact, happened. After all, the Pakistani infiltration was spread over a large front. India deliberately limited its response to the eviction of Pakistani soldiers. But many of our officers and men died needlessly as we were neither prepared for the war nor ready to absorb the inputs towards efficient and better coordination between the security forces. The victory indeed belonged to those officers and men who fought, died or survived, but won.

INSTITUTIONALIZING NATIONAL SECURITY DECISIONMAKING

Vajpayee demonstrated how to handle the larger responsibilities brought on by India's possession of nuclear weapons. Under his stewardship, in 1998, India surprised the world by testing its nuclear weapons, ending the ambiguity surrounding its nuclear program. Despite fighting the Kargil War in 1999 against Pakistan, Vajpayee never lost sight of the imperative of possessing nuclear weapons responsibly. Within a year of its nuclear tests, the Vajpayee government announced India's draft nuclear doctrine, and subsequently created new institutions for managing security challenges for a nuclear-armed India, such as the National Security Advisory Board. The current Indian government's lack of enthusiasm for further institutionalizing and strengthening national security decisionmaking stands in stark contrast to Vajpayee's approach.

Pursuing Dialogue with Pakistan

Second, Vajpayee believed that a state can choose its friends, but not its neighbors. Thus, the only option for India and

Pakistan to resolve outstanding problems was through dialogue. Therefore, in spite of facing challenges to bilateral ties like the 1999 Kargil War and the 2001 terrorist attack on the Indian parliament, Vajpayee persisted in making peace with Pakistan. He also initiated dialoguewith Kashmiri separatist leadership in an effort to find a lasting solution to the Kashmir issue. Despite the Kargil conflict in 1999, Vajpayee visited Pakistan twice—Lahore in 1999 and Islamabad in 2004—and invited General Pervez Musharraf to Agra for talks in 2001. Vajpayee's visit to Pakistan for the South Asian Association for Regional Cooperation summit in 2004 paved the way for a more positive phase of India-Pakistan ties marked by progress on regional cooperation and backchannel talks.

India's current leadership could take a leaf out of Vajpayee's playbook for dealing with Pakistan and Kashmir...Dialogue between India and Pakistan and Kashmiri leadership remains the only way to resolve the Kashmir issue.

The significance of Vajpayee's efforts is underlined by the fact that his successor, Prime Minister Manmohan Singh, continued with these initiatives and built on them. In the current phase of instability in Kashmir and strained India-Pakistan relations, each of these initiatives now holds even more significance. Indeed, India's current leadership could take a leaf out of Vajpayee's playbook for dealing with Pakistan and Kashmir. Notwithstanding the current government's tense relationship with Islamabad and the restive state of the Kashmir valley since 2016, dialogue between India and Pakistan and Kashmiri leadership remains the only way to resolve the Kashmir issue. In any effort to replicate the legacy of Vajpayee's relations with Pakistan, Prime Minister Modi could initiate talks with Pakistan's new leadership to improve relations—something that Pakistan's new Prime Minister Imran Khan has also called for.

Resolving Disputes with China

Third, Vajpayee recognized the importance of a rising China in southern Asia, and therefore made efforts to resolve India-

China boundary disputes and strengthen overall relations. During Vajpayee's landmark visit to China in 2003, India and China signed a "Declaration on Principles for Relations and Comprehensive Cooperation" and decided to appoint Special Representatives (SR) to resolve the two countries' boundary disputes. These SR talks have continued, with twenty rounds of talks held so far. Vajpayee's visit to China and his signing of these agreements paved way for India and China to agree on another major agreement in 2005 outlining guiding principles for resolving their boundary disputes.

While new developments...indicate that India-China ties are on the upswing, the Modi government's on-again, off-again stance towards Beijing does not bode well for the long-term resolution of disputes between India and China.

Vajpayee's move to settle India's border disputes with China was a hallmark of his China policy. In this context, the present state of India's China policy could be reassessed. Under the Modi government, India's China policy since 2014 has alternated between overt displays of friendship and muscular positioning. Last year's Doklam crisis marked the lowest point in India-China relations in the recent past. While recent developments, such as the visit of China's defense minister to India this week, indicate that India-China ties are on the upswing, the Modi government's on-again, off-again stance towards Beijing does not bode well for the long-term resolution of disputes between India and China.

Rebuilding the India-U.S. Relationship

Fourth, and most importantly, Vajpayee understood the importance of rebuilding the India-U.S. relationship, and was instrumental in resetting India's approach towards the United States after the 1998 nuclear tests strained ties between the two countries. He characterized the United States as India's "natural ally," and launched the Next Steps in Strategic Partnership in 2004. Increased cooperation in the commerce, defense, and technology spheres during Vajpayee's tenure laid foundations for further unlocking the potential of bilateral cooperation between India and the United States. The 2005 India-U.S. civilian nuclear deal was an outcome of this process of resetting ties. If Vajpayee could advance India-U.S. relations despite initial differences with the United States over the nuclear tests, India's current leadership could surely find a way to resolve the United States' discomfort with India's close ties to Russia and Iran.

Today, as a more ambitious and powerful India seeks to reshape its regional strategic environment, it should revisit these four lessons from the Vajpayee years.

4

Defence Planning and Policy

INTRODUCTION

As regards the planning process, the Government has taken a number of measures to improve the structure, process and procedure relating to defence planning based on the recommendations of Group of Ministers on 'Reforming the National Security System'. The preparation of Long Term Plans, Five Year Defence Plans and Annual Budgetary proposals have been brought under the newly established Integrated Defence Staff (IDS) to bring about greater inter-service coordination in planning. The IDS also interacts closely with Defence (Finance) in the formulation of Plans and Budgets.

The Government has set up a Defence Acquisition Council headed by the Raksha Mantri and consisting of Raksha Rajya Mantri (s), the three Service Chiefs and Defence Secretary, Secretary (Defence Finance), and Secretary (Defence Production) to assist the Raksha Mantri in taking decisions in the totality of the new planning process, including capital acquisitions and major modernisation projects. The Government has also set up a dedicated institutional structure for defence procurement, the Defence procurement Board, headed by the Defence Secretary for acquisitions on the capital account. Planning processes have been further tightened under budgetary pressures and the need to establish greater synergy and jointness amongst the Armed Forces. This has also necessitated greater coordination in planning and procurement among the three services.

The Ministry in its written note submitted on the current status of the implementation of the 10th Plan has inter alia stated that: "The projections of the Ministry of Defence for the Tenth Defence Plan were reviewed thrice between March 2003 and July 2004 bearing in mind the needs of defence modernization and the likely constraints to the availability of funds for defence in the Tenth Plan. The Ministry of Finance have now agreed in principle to the latest projection made by the Ministry of Defence of Rs. 4,18,101 crore. However, a firm indication of annual outlays for the remaining year of the 10th Plan has not yet been given by the Ministry of Finance.

Meanwhile, in the absence of a formal approval of the allocation for defence in the Tenth Plan, defence planning has been harmonised with the allotments for defence in the annual budgets of the Government. Actual expenditures in 2002-2003 and 2003-2004 were Rs. 55,620 crores and Rs. 60,300 crores respectively. An allocation of Rs. 77,200 crores has been made in the Budget Estimate for 2004-2005 against a projection of Rs. 90,928 crores. About, Rs. 11,000 crores additional funds have been allocated beyond the Budget Estimate for the capital head.

The projected expenditure in 2005-2006 and 2006-2007 are Rs. 1,00,960 crores and Rs. 1,10,251 crores respectively. However, an amount of Rs. 83,000 crores only has been allocated in the Budget Estimate (B.E.) for the current financial year 2005-2006.

While some compromises are inevitable in the absence of a formally approved Plan, every effort has been made to ensure that the annual budgets have been utilized in accordance with the Plan projections of the Ministry of Defence and that any negative impact on ongoing modernization, infrastructure development and procurements of equipment is minimized. Ongoing projects and commitments have been reviewed and prioritized so that the main objective of the Tenth Defence Plan to carry forward the process of modernization of the Armed

Forces is not adversely affected. A modest outlay of over Rs. 950 crores has been made for new schemes for the Army. (No increase is being sought)".

In response to a query regarding the existence of a core plan the Ministry though a written reply has inter alia stated that : "There is no formal draft core plan to make up for the delay in the finalization of the Tenth Defence Plan. Meanwhile, in the absence of a formal approval of the allocation for defence in the Tenth Plan, defence planning has been harmonised with the allotments for defence in the annual budgets of the Government. While, indigenous production/Research and Development is being made in accordance with the decisions flowing from the Defence Acquisition Council, defence procurement is being made in accordance with annual acquisition plans for the three services as approved by the Defence Procurement Board. Adequate measures have been taken to minimise any adverse effect on ongoing modernisation schemes. On-going projects and contractual commitments have been reviewed and prioritised to minimise the effect of any shortfall in actual allocation vis-à-vis projections, both in respect of modernisation plans and in essential procurement. Keeping in view, the rising competing demands on limited resources, the budgetary framework has been fine-turned in such a manner to ensure most effective utilisation of Government resources".

While presenting a detailed picture on the entire planning exercise that has been undertaken in the recent past, the representative of Ministry has stated as under:

"In the year 2001-02, projections for the 10th Plan were examined in the Ministry of Defence. These projections were made by the different Services and the Departments. They added up to Rs. 4.97 lakh crore. In January, 2002 the Ministry of Finance indicated the likely availability of Rs. 4.21 lakh crore. So, there was a gap of about Rs. 75,000 crore. Therefore, the Chief of Integrated Defence Staff and Chief of Staff were requested for giving their views. They recommended slightly reduced allocation of Rs. 4.61 lakh crore. In February 2003, in consonance with the recommendations, it was done. The matter was again taken up with the Finance Ministry in March 2003. But we did not have received any response from them thereafter.

We had to carry out a review of our projections. This was because if some scheme was supposed to be sanctioned in the first year of the Plan, it will involve expenditure in the first, second, third years and leading up to the fifth year. If, for the first two years, projected allocations are not utilized, there is no way the original amount, which was projected for the entire five years could be spent in the last three years. It is because in defence acquisition, we are not really buying things off the shelf and paying out for the whole thing. So, if you take a case of some scheme or project costing Rs. 5,000 crore in five years with simplistic allocation of expenditure of Rs. 1,000 crore each year, and if in the first two years, it is not sanctioned and in the third year it is sanctioned, we are not going to have anything in the first two years, but the expenditure will be Rs.3,000 crore in the remaining three years and not Rs. 5,000 crore. When we received the projects, we reviewed what would be and what would not be sanctioned. Then the revised figures came to something like Rs. 4,18,000 crore as indicated. But they did not give us any annual allocations, not capacity utilization, etc".

On the lessons learnt and the measures that are being implemented to overcome the nagging delays of Defence Planning, the Defence Secretary deposed that : "Presentation of the fourth year Budget is made to the Parliament. As has already been mentioned, there is the Ministry of Defence and there is the Ministry of Finance which are the players in this exercise. The exercise for preparing the plan is undertaken by us well in time, much before the start of the year in which the next Five Year Plan is going to start. For example, for the 11th Plan, to answer your question, we have already started the exercise. For doing that planning as to what would be needed, considering the gaps that is there in the Tenth Plan – if any exercise of this nature is to be undertaken – we might have a wish list; it might represent a large figure. But we still have to have some kind of an indicative figure from the Ministry of Finance saying that we have asked for this much amount, which may not be available, but we can have so much amount at the outer limit, beyond which we cannot go. This kind of an indication is no forthcoming. This is what happened in this current year. If you contrast it with the situation of the Ninth Plan, as the Chairman was enquiring, the Ninth Plan was approved on 1st January, 1998.

Therefore, it was approved in the first year. It was a very major achievement and they indicated a total allocation of Rs. 2,20,000 crore. The Annual Budget, as it took place during those five years if you total up those they came to Rs. 2,43,000 crore. That means the annual allocation was more than the indicative figure of the Plan. That was a situation which was quite in contrast to what is prevalent just now where, firstly, the figure itself was not known to us till December – finally what we wanted and how much they can give. This went till December of 2004. If we were to juxtapose the Tenth Plan indicative figure of Rs. 4,18,000 crore divided by four years, which are known, it is nowhere. There was no relation. Therefore, this figure becomes an academic figure. That is the point that we have been discussing, that is the outlays have to be finalized at the beginning of the plan and secondly Annual Allocation should be conforming to the overall outlay".

Adding further on the issue, the Defence Secretary has also stated that : "As has been mentioned earlier, how initial projections of Rs. 4,97,000 crore was done at the beginning of the Tenth Plan (2001-02).This was also communicated to the Finance Ministry with the break up. They needed it in a particular format. It was given in that format. Subsequently, they had indicated Rs. 4,97,000 crore is too much and we may plan within Rs. 4,21,000 crore. There was a gap of about Rs. 75,724 between the projection and what they had indicated. By that time certain time had elapsed. We were involved in an internal exercise of readjusting. In December 2004 they indicated Rs. 4,18,000 crore, which was what we had projected earlier".

Explaining the details of the ongoing measures to formulate the Eleventh Defence Plan and how these initiatives have a bearing on the implementation of annual plan programmes, the Defence Secretary has briefed the Committee : "As I just said, we have started our exercise of preparing the Eleventh Plan which means that the Integrated Defence Staff which gets inputs from all the three Headquarters puts together the long-term perspective plan requirements of each service and makes them into one composite plan called the Defence Plan. It sees whether there is any overlapping of capabilities or whether there is any repetition or commonalties. So, it does such modifications and vetting and then it is projecting that requirement to the Ministry where we see whether it is all right or whether it needs any change or not.. Accordingly, we pass it on to the Ministry of Finance for approval. Of course, we have discussions with the Ministry of Finance because they might also like to understand the details. So, that dialogue is there. Our request is, if the Ministry of Finance were to give its indications well before the start of the first year of the Eleventh Plan, then that would help everybody to know what is going to be the situation during the five years of the Eleventh Plan. Secondly, we do need some kind of a figure to show that this is the total figure and whatever amount it might be would be divided in the five years in this fashion in the Annual Budget so that the Annual programmes can then be fine tuned to adjust to the availability. Otherwise, there is likely to be a mismatch between what we might project and the money availability".

When asked whether the Ministry of Finance had intimated the details of the 10th Plan allocations in time, the Defence Secretary has stated that : "It was towards the end of the third year. This was one part of the problem. The second part, as I said, is annual allocations are nowhere matching even this figure. Therefore, how do we do the Planning? We do not know what will be the figure for the fifth plan. Budget has been submitted for the fourth year. It totals up to Rs. 2 lakh something".

The Ministry of Defence in its written Action Taken Reply on the recommendation of the Committee on long term planning of three Services contained in the First Report on Demands for

Grants of the Ministry of Defence for the year 2004-05, has stated as under : "A draft Long-Term Integrated Perspective Plan (LTIPP) covering the 15-year period from the Tenth to the Twelfth Plan (2002-2017) was formulated in June 2004 in consultation with the three Services. Since more than two years of the current Tenth Plan period have already elapsed, a new approach paper has been made formulating a Long Term Integrated Perspective Plan (LTIPP) covering the period from 2007-2022. This Plan is expected to be finalised by the Integrated Defence Staff by the last quarter of 2005."

The Committee are unhappy to note that the Ministry of Finance has failed to finalise the 10th Defence plan even after three years of the plan have passed. Non-finalisation of the 10th Defence Plan at its beginning by the Ministry of Finance has created a great deal of uncertainty about the availability of adequate finance for the acquisition of the vital equipment, modernization, etc. The Ministry of Defence had projected a demand of Rs. 4,97,000 crore in 2001 for the Tenth Plan. However, the Ministry of Finance has given indicative figure of Rs.4, 18,000 crore in December 2004,without any firm commitment. The total allocations in the first four years of Tenth Defence Plan just come to about Rs.2, 76,300 crore which is nowhere near their requirements. This gap between the demand and allocations, has adversely affected the defence planning and our preparedness. The Committee take a serious note of this and want the Government to finalise the Tenth Plan immediately and take steps to utilise the committed amount in full. The Committee would like to be apprised of the fmalisation of the Plan as well as the follow-up steps being taken to utilise the total allocation of the Tenth Plan.

The Committee also observe that due to non-finalisation of the Tenth Plan in time, the long term perspective plan of the Forces has got affected and is presently at the fmalisation stage with a revised plan schedule spanning from 2007-2022. The Committee, while expressing their displeasure over the present situation, recommend that the Ministry of Defence should reorient the plans and strive to adhere to the schedules envisaged. As regard the 11th Plan, the Committee desire that it should be finalised at least an year before the plan period starts.

It is high time that the Government prepared a road map for self-reliance. The Committee strongly feels that India should not be taken as a weapons/arms market by the global suppliers and action in this direction should be visible by the end of Tenth Defence Plan and 11th Plan should entirely be devoted to self-reliance.

The Committee has also observed that the surveillance capabilities of our forces are in adequate. This is primarily due to non-availability of low-level radar systems with the three services. The Committee feel that all round effort should be undertaken by the Government to ensure that the entire country is covered. The Committee feel that the Ministry should explore all possibilities of acquiring the required radar systems in adequate numbers without any delay.

CHIEF OF DEFENCE STAFF (CDS)

The Ministerial Committee on National Security had recommended in February 2001 for the creation of the post of Chief of Defence Staff (CDS). When enquired about the present status in this regard, the Ministry of Defence has stated that the Government had constituted a group of Ministers (GoM) on 17 April 2000 to thoroughly review the national security system in its entirety and in particular, to consider the recommendations of the Kargil Review Committee. The GoM had after careful consideration of various issues formulated a comprehensive Report titled 'Reforming the National Security System'. The GoM had inter-alia recommended establishment of the Chief of Defence Staff (CDS).

The recommendations of the GoM were approved by the Government. The Government have not yet come to decision on the post of CDS. Meanwhile, a number of steps have been taken to promote 'synergy' among the Armed Forces, improve inter service coordination on the one hand the Services and the

Ministry of Defence on the other, this would bring about optimal utilisation of resources and strengthen the higher defence management.

Pending a decision on the creation of the post of Chief of Defence Staff (CDS), an Integrated Defence Staff has been set up under a Chief of Integrated Defence staff to the Chiefs of Staff Committee (CISC) to support the Chiefs of Staff Committee and its Chairman in the optimum performance of its roles and functions and bringing together and coordinating several functions common to the Services or involving more than one Service. Tri-Service bodies promoting 'jointness' and 'synergy' among the Armed Forces have also been set up like the Defence Intelligence Agency (DIA), the Strategic Forces Command (SFC) and India's first `theatre' command, the Andaman & Nicobar Command. Individual Service Headquarters have been re-designated as part of the `Integrated Headquarters of the Ministry of Defence'. Administrative and Financial powers have also been delegated from the Ministry of Defence to the Integrated Headquarters to promote expeditious decision-making. These steps are expected to enhance the capabilities of the Armed Forces significantly.

Countries with posts of Chief of Defence Staff or similar or comparable systems include the institutions of the Joint Chief of Staff of the USA, the Chief of Defence Staff of the UK, Chief of Defence Forces of Australia, and the Chief of General Staff of China, amongst others. The Committee on Defence, keeping in view excellent work performed by the armed forces in handling of the rescue and relief operation, in their Action Taken Report on Demands for Grants (2004-05) have recommended that the post of Chief of Defence Staff is very much essential for better management of security.

The Defence Expert also, who appeared before the Committee, while tendering oral evidence has supported the rationale for creating the post of Chief of Defence Staff. During the course of deposition he inter-alia stated as under : "All these benefits are lost because we have not appointed. We have taken time to appoint Chairman of the Chief of Staff Committee.

Therefore, that should be done early. We are losing time as well as the benefits of having the integrated staff and planning because we have not appointed Chiefs of Staff Committee Chairman." The Committee are constrained to note that despite their repeated recommendations in the past for establishment of the Chief of Defence Staff (CDS), Government has not yet come to any decision on the creation of the post even after more than three years has elapsed. The Committee further note that in the existing structure for higher defence management viz. the Chief of Staff Committee had not been able to optimally perform their role and functions in bringing together and promoting coordination amongst the Services.

The Committee feel that keeping in view the security scenario of the country and in order to provide single military advice to the Government and to give administer strategic forces and to enhance the efficiency and effectiveness of the planning process, there is an imperative need to create the post of CDS to provide a focal point for better coordination among the three services in the long term perspective plan in conventional and strategic capabilities, prioritise R & D activities and provide effective coordination leading to the path of self-reliance. The Committee desire that Government should give serious consideration to the recommendations of the Committee.

DEFENCE PROCUREMENT UPDATE

Since the 1960s, the Indian Armed Forces have been the main source of sustenance fuel to the erstwhile USSR and later Russian weapons industry. Over 80 percent of our military hardware is of Soviet origin. In the first 15 years of independent India, no new weapons were procured. The governments then were focusing on the indigenization of the weapon systems. That is why the Indian Army had to fight the 1962 Indo-China war with Second World War era weapons, while the Chinese soldiers were equipped with latest automatic weapons.

After the war, New Delhi learnt the tough lesson and turned towards, USSR for the modernization of its forces. Soon all the three services started getting weapons of USSR make. Initially it was a win-win situation for both the countries, as most of the western countries were not willing to sell their modern weapons to India as they considered it close to the Eastern Bloc. Moreover, western weapon systems were too expensive for the very modest Indian economy. India therefore had to turn towards the USSR which did not ask for hard cash and was willing to sell weapons in lieu of grain, wool, etc. India also got a reliable friend to strategically distract its enemy, China. USSR seized the opportunity of getting a permanent customer for its weapons industry. It helped to ensure a smooth flow of money to the USSR for the development of the next generation weapons. USSR also got a reliable friend in South East Asia to counter the growing influence of the USA.

But the situation has changed now. The IAF has made a great strategic move by turning towards the West for most of the main weapon platforms.

The main reasons for this shift are:

- Consequent to the 1992 financial reforms, India has evolved as the biggest arms market for companies all over the world. So most of the western countries have been doing serious business with India. This has helped in creating a relationship of trust between India and the western countries.
- India is now a strong economy with an average growth rate of almost 9 percent. Increased Defence budgets allow Indian Armed Forces to go for more advanced, reliable and technologically sophisticated western weapon systems.
- In next 10-15 years, India will procure weapon systems worth $40 billion. All the big daddies in the weapon business want to grab the biggest piece of the cake.
- In the past, India had put all its eggs in the same basket. More than one vendor will remove dependency and competition will force all the competitors to field the best weapons and offer the best possible deal.

- Quality standards of western weapons are far superior than that of Russian make. French Mirage aircraft and Israeli weapon systems have scored their impression on the Indian Armed Forces.
- Indian Armed Forces, especially the IAF, have suffered great losses due to lack of spare parts.
- Russia has given India a difficult time in fulfilling its promises like the transfer of technology of T 90 tanks.
- On most occasions, Russia has been failing to meet the promised deadline of delivery, like Project 11356 Krivak IV class guided missile frigates (built in 2004), Aircraft Carrier Gorshkov and IL 76 aircraft for AWACS. Russia miscalculated the time taken to modernize the IL 76 (for AWACS program) by integrating new engine and avionics that caused the whole program to be delayed by 1.5 years.
- $964 millions Aircraft Carrier Admiral Gorshkov deal was signed in 2004 after long negotiations of six years. About two years ago, Moscow informed that it had miscalculated the length of wiring to be done inside the ship. Moscow demanded more money and raised the total cost of the project to $2.2 billion and then to $2.9 billion. Finally, India agreed to pay $2.2 billion, but Moscow insisted on $2.9 billions. This proved to be the last nail in the coffin.

Due to all these factors, Indian forces are now considering and selecting western weapon systems. The contract for of French Scorpene Submarines and contract of developing Barak-NG Missiles are few examples. New Delhi is so annoyed that on the induction ceremony of the AWACS, Defence Minister AK Antony gave a dressing down to Russian and Israeli ambassadors and asked them to ensure that the defence equipments are delivered on scheduled time. There are couple of follow-on orders that Russia was sure of gettin, but the IAF has favored western platforms. These two orders are aircraft for AWACS system and mid-air refueller aircraft. India is set to place a follow-on order for three more AWACS systems and is seriously considering American Gulfstream, Brazilian Embraer jets and European Airbus. An official said, "We will replace the IL-76 by a modern aircraft like the Gulfstream or Embraer. Both have an endurance of nine hours-that is close to what the Russian aircraft has". But selecting any of these two aircraft will have the problem of having too many platforms in the inventory, as the IAF will have to maintain separate maintenance line for each type of aircraft. The IAF is already considering Airbus A330 multi-role tanker transport (MRTT) for an order of six more mid-air refuellers as the IAF found MRTT far better than IL-78 in the crucial flight evaluation. In case the IAF selects Airbus MRTT for both the orders then this the issue of having too many platforms in the inventory will be resolved.

Currently the IAF is using IL-76 and IL-78 and their maintenance line is already in place. Selecting Airbus MRTT will require one more maintenance line but this will remove dependency on Russia and send a signal to Moscow that arm-twisting will not be tolerated any more.

The IAF is also considering Boeing C-17 Globemaster III as its new heavylift aircraft. C-17 is one of the latest and most modern cargo aircraft that has a capability of taking-off and landing on short runways with 70 tons, whereas IL-76 has a capacity of 45 tons only. Moreover, IL-76 is a thirty year old platform and can be upgraded with more powerful engines, better equipments and avionics, but the old platform has its own limitations. Sources said, "The IAF has selected C-17 as the new heavylift aircraft and is all set to place an initial order of 10 aircraft through the US government's Foreign Military Sales (FMS) route, and may later go in for a follow-on order. The defence ministry is considering the proposal and the first aircraft will be delivered in three years after signing of the contract."

In August this year, India will start the flight evaluation trials for the 197 Light Utility Helicopters LUH. Five competitors for the $3 billion contract are Russian Kazan and Mil, American Sikorsky, Italian Finnmeccanica and European helicopter manufacturers Eurocopter. Last year, Request For Proposal (RFP) was sent to six companies.

Five out of the six companies responded. Bell Helicopters of America backed out of the race due to 50 percent offset clause associated with this contract. Previously, Eurocopter was selected by the armed forces but the contract was cancelled by the Defence Ministry in December, 1997 because Eurocopter had sent the civilian version of the helicopter for field trials. This time, Eurocopter will be sending the military version of the helicopter and is expected to win the contract. Out of the 197 helicopters, 133 will be given to the Army and the rest will be given to the Air Force to replace their aging fleet of Cheetah and Chetak helicopters that are being used in high altitude conditions in air maintenance roles and for surveillance, as well as search and rescue missions.

All these developments are giving the desired results to New Delhi. Moscow is now on the back-foot and has understood that it will face competition in the market it has been ruling. Russia has indicated that it is ready to look at a downward revision of the price for the Aircraft carrier, Admiral Gorshkov.

Moscow has also resolved the issue of Transfer of Technology of T-90 tanks and has released $64 million for the development of multi-role transport aircraft (MTA). Russia and India signed an agreement in 2007 to develop a 20 ton cargo capacity plane to fulfil futuristic needs of both the countries. Ilyushin design bureau, Irkut Corporation and Hindustan Aearonautics Ltd will develop the aircraft.

Production of the aircraft is expected to begin in about eight years and both the countries will equally share the cost of the $600 million project. India will procure about 45 aircraft and Russia is expected to get 100 aircraft to replace An-12, An-26 and An-32 aircraft. Thus the IAF will have three different maintenance lines for three types of aircraft of different cargo capacity (Boeing c-17, Airbus A330 MRTT and Russian MTA) and will not be dependent on of any particular vendor. IAF will also have the option to switch to any vendor at any time.

DOMESTIC INDUSTRY IN DEFENCE PLANNING

Private entities are answerable to their shareholders and are in the business to make profits, whether in defence or any other sector. Attractive return on investment, more than what can be expected in non-defence sectors, is the only mantra that can make them divert their finite resources to the defence sector. Gestation period is also quite high in defence sector as establishing a defence venture can take more time than other commercial ventures. Therefore, advance information of the acquisition plans of the government can give potential domestic investors the lead time and the opportunity to study the prospects of raising funds and also seek foreign collaborations. This is a necessary precondition for creating the right atmosphere for developing an indigenous defence industry.

At present, private players do not have prior knowledge of the defence plans of the country. Though we have 15-year long-term integrated perspective plan (LTIPP) that flows into the 5-year Services Capital Acquisition Plan (SCAP), which in turn flows into the 2-year roll-on plan for Capital Acquisitions, the acquisition proposals are most often than not guarded as secrets. The Indian domestic industry is not privy to these plans. As a consequence, information is sent to them only when requests for proposals (RFPs) are issued. Potential Indian investors, therefore, lose the lead time that is required to plan and prepare for such large investments.

The solution may lie in sharing with a select group of Indian industries the LTIPP and the SCAPs to the extent they relate to items proposed for acquisition. The argument that revealing in advance what the nation seeks to acquire will be detrimental to national security also does not hold much water. Private companies have been involved in the development of closely guarded defence projects in India. Even those relating to some of the most sensitive projects, find their way into leading arms publications sooner than later. Again, there is no reason to believe that private sector can be less trusted in keeping state secrets than the public sector. In any case, we lose some of our eminent public sector personnel to private sector. Like in the US, we should involve the private sector at the planning stage itself. To ensure secrecy of information, suitable regulations may be put in place, like in the US. If necessary, in very sensitive projects, the information need not be shared.

Defence Items

As argued above, private entities will not embark on any manufacturing venture, defence or otherwise, unless they are confident of reaping dividends from it. Therefore, prudence lies in opening up this sector. Let the market forces regulate the industry.

Defence contractors are most often not large. Even large entities source components and subcomponents that make up complex systems from countless small enterprises. In India too, there are thousands of small and medium producers. Several of them do not have licenses as many of the items used in defence equipment also have civilian application. Therefore, the requirement of licenses for the manufacture of defence-related items not only complicates the existing situation but also destroys individual and entrepreneurial initiatives.

Introduce Offset Credit Trading

The 2008 procedure has introduced offset banking. According to the guidelines, offset banking is permissible for a maximum of two-and-a-half years. Given the lead time available from the time RFPs are issued, this time-frame may be around 5 years or even 10 depending on the completion schedule of the project. This is a very positive step and has been very widely welcomed. But the bankable years should not end with the end of the project as "rather than linked to the life of a specific offset project, the technology strategy needs to embrace productive opportunities across the broader economy. Offset policy thus needs to be framed accordingly." It has been estimated that credit transfers account for around 7.5 per cent of all offset transactions and that the banking of offsets has resulted in a trend to permit offset commitments over longer periods of time covering several projects rather than limited to specific projects. This will undoubtedly give confidence to foreign firms hoping to bag Indian contracts get a return for their investment. But this alone is not enough. The most encouraging step will be to introduce offset trading.

Offset trading is the sale of credits accumulated by firms over a defined period. The introduction of this provision will make it possible to sell offset credits to any firm that bags a contract in India and has certain offset obligations to fulfil. It will yield several benefits. First, every prospective firm that is hopeful of bagging any defence contract in India will be assured return on their investment even if they are unsuccessful in securing the contract they may have targeted. It may at least ensure that they may have no losses and also obtain profit in many cases.

This may motivate firms to shed their fears of investing in the military sector in India. Second, India has attractive factors of production. The prospect of offset trading will only increase the willingness of foreign firms to capitalise on these advantages and invest in the defence sector in India. While allowing offset trading, government can also consider prescribing diminishing value to credits over a period of time unless there is value addition to the product. This will encourage firms to sustain their investments in India over a longer time horizon. Third, a firm that is already discharging its offset obligations can continue producing defence equipment over a longer period of time, hoping to accumulate credits for future contracts. Even if it does not bag the contract it may have hoped to, it will be able to trade the offsets. This policy can lead to a win-win situation for both foreign firms and India. The key to success is the prosperity of all the key stakeholders and hope of future profits for investors. Nothing else will succeed. Success will come from giving foreign firms the incentive to sustain their interests in India by encouraging innovativeness and hope of profits through it.

Directing Offsets

The 2008 procedure (Annexure-VI) lists the defence products that qualify for the discharge of offset obligations. This list is generic in nature and ranges from small arms to directed energy weapon systems. In effect, there is no precise direction in which offsets are channelised. Any vendor will be well within his right to produce any item related to the aforementioned list to fulfil its offset obligations. But this will not yield optimum results.

For instance, it has been concluded that the Netherlands and Switzerland have been able to displace jobs in the US through offset arrangements by transferring production facilities to themselves. To achieve this, the two nations exercised careful control to ensure the "precise direction in which offset-resources are steered. Almost never are they aimed at increasing indigenous military production capacity." In the study by Brauer, he has cited Molas-Gallart to argue that Spain had to abandon its dream of an "integrated, comprehensive, indigenous industry to be generated via arms trade offsets." It was also argued that when offsets are bureaucratically mandated and applied to some vaguely specified national interests, net benefits may not exist. Therefore, prescribing a generic list from which offset obligations are to be chosen for implementation may not be the best strategy to serve India's defence needs. This issue deserves further examination.

India is a nation that has a reasonable defence industrial capability. It is more advanced in some areas than in others. For instance, in the field of naval shipbuilding, India has been able to achieve a fair degree of indigenisation and in some cases around 76 per cent. India today is designing stealth frigates and constructing them in Indian yards. But almost all the weapon systems are imported though India has developed and is using many indigenous sensors. Therefore, for instance, the navy should be able to identify areas of high priority such as the weapon systems that it will prefer to produce indigenously and incorporate them in the list. Through this process, the benefits of offset can be channelised into identified areas. For instance, given the plan of the navy for a 160-plus ship force by 2022 from the 145 that it has at present, a prospective vendor will be inclined to invest in identified areas included in the list to: 1) fulfil its offset obligations; 2) accumulate offset credits knowing that orders for the weapons or other naval items will be assured for a known period, given the navy's maritime plan; and 3) be reasonably assured of future orders.

Assured of continuing orders, firms will also be inclined to provide value addition over time. To give further impetus to foreign vendors to endeavour towards this goal, a system of procurement through repeat orders, say for 10 years or so, from the same source that had produced indigenously such critical items should be seriously considered. Provision of value addition, etc., can also be made mandatory for such repeat orders. Similarly, critical items for the three services can be compiled and included in the list eligible for discharging offset obligations.

INDIA'S DEFENCE POLICY

India inherited some defence industries from Great Britain. They included Hindustan Aeronautics Limited (HAL), which is today India's largest defence public sector undertaking (DPSU), Mazagon Docks Limited (MDL), the largest shipyard in the nation, and more than half a dozen ordnance factories. The growth of the domestic defence industry has, however, been sporadic since Independence. It did not follow any definite plan though emphasis was placed on enhancing indigenous defence production capability.

Some analysts have also traced certain vigorousness in the Indian effort at developing an indigenous defence capability to the early 1960s spawned by the 1962 India-China war. The war is seen as having underscored the urgency of building a domestic defence industry through foreign assistance. It was also in consonance with Nehru's policy of building a strong industrial base patterned on the Soviet model. But while the war with China has been identified as the catalyst in the effort at developing a domestic defence base, there was no concerted, systematic and well-orchestrated effort towards the achievement of this goal. There were many factors that stood in the way of India building a strong military-industrial base. India's comparatively easy access to various types of defence equipment from the former Soviet Union (FSU) and their purchase against deferred rupee payments and on "friendship" price were some of them. Sophisticated defence equipment was transferred to India under the favourable rupee-rouble arrangements from FSU. Some license production facilities were also established in India, for instance for the Mig-21 aircraft. The Cold War also ensured that India continued to have a favourable and preferred source of defence systems and equipment from FSU. It did not find the superpower wanting in any critical manner in fulfilling India's defence requirements. However, this had the unintended consequences of dampening any sense of urgency in India to develop an indigenous defence industry. Coupled with this was the reluctance of the US to help in India's effort to develop a domestic defence production base. Nevertheless, trudging along, India was able to develop the largest defence industry among developing nations.

However, with the collapse of the FSU, India lost easy access to sophisticated defence equipment at cheap prices. The problem was compounded by the absence of an alternate source of modern defence equipment. The situation became worse with the almost complete disruption in the supply of services and spare parts necessary to maintain the predominantly Soviet-equipped Indian armed forces. The navy was particularly affected, as it was dependent on Soviet designs and equipment for some of the ships that were under construction in India. This led to huge cost and time overruns in the indigenous construction programme of naval vessels.

Ironically, the need to service and maintain various kinds of equipment imported from FSU compelled India to seek ways and means to develop some level of indigenous capability. Towards this goal, certain technologies and know-how were obtained, both for the repairs and for the local production of some critical spare parts. These efforts were, however, largely case-specific and were not components of any systematic strategy for the comprehensive development of an indigenous defence industry. They were also service-driven in the absence of any coherent strategy to achieve self-reliance. However, the liberalisation of the Indian economy that almost coincided with the collapse of FSU and promised to unlock India's productive capabilities gave impetus to the goal of developing a domestic military-industrial complex.

It was, however, not until 2005 that India formulated a defence offset policy to contribute to the nation's goal of developing its domestic defence industry. This policy was incorporated in the Defence Procurement Procedure (DPP) 2005. The policy introduced a 30 per cent offset in contracts valued above Rs 3 billion under "buy" and 'buy and make" categories.

Under the policy, foreign vendors had the liberty to discharge their obligations either through the execution of defence exports of Indian items and services or through investments in India's defence infrastructure.

They also had the option of selecting Indian firms in consultation with an industry associate of their choice to implement their offset obligations. The hallmark of this policy was its non-obligatory nature, or in other words, these offsets were non-mandatory.

It was left to the Services Capital Acquisition Plan Categorisation Committee (SCAPCC) to recommend the incorporation of offset obligation in acquisition proposals. The offset policy was, however, in the nascent stage and it lacked clarity in many areas. It also suffered from the absence of any designated agency in the Ministry of Defence (MoD) for guiding, overseeing, executing and monitoring the implementation of the policy. In reality, confusion reigned in equal measure in the corridors of South Block as in the minds of the vendors on how to implement the offset obligations. Consequently, the offset policy did not yield any dividend.

The absence of any offset benefit to the Indian defence industry led the Government of India (GoI) to make significant changes in DPP 2006 and they included the following:

- offset was made mandatory in defence contracts of the size and nature as prescribed in the 2005 policy;
- foreign firms were allowed the flexibility of forming joint ventures (JVs) with Indian firms, and;
- a new organisation called the Defence Offset Facilitation Agency (DOFA) was established comprising of representatives of all stakeholders; the Services, DPSUs, Defence and Research Organisation (DRDO), etc.

Defence Offsets

Offsets have been variously defined. In essence, offsets in defence, as in civil trade, are compensations that a buyer seeks from the seller for the purchase of goods and/or services. The demand for offsets in defence has exhibited an upward trajectory since the 1950s. It gained further momentum in the 1980s and has been growing ever since. From around 20 nations about two decades ago, this practice has now been now adopted by more than 130 nations.

European nations have been able to generate more offsets than others. During the period 1993-2004, European countries were able to obtain offsets valued at 99.1 per cent of their defence imports while non-European countries achieved 46.6 per cent of their imports.

Significantly, 72.9 per cent of the offsets obtained by European nations were 100 per cent or more of the value of the weapon systems imported by them. The data on arms sales and offsets show that demands for offsets "are increasing over time in all regions."

India was, however, late in adopting an official offset policy though it had obtained some compensatory benefits since Independence through a series of bilateral arrangements. It was only in 2005 that the nation, through its Defence Procurement Procedure (DPP), announced an official policy to secure offsets for its defence imports. The policy was amended to give it greater clarity and direction in 2006 and again in 2008. Consequently, as a late entrant in the field, India's polices are yet to be fully tested against the complex process of managing offsets and it is yet to traverse the path of achieving its declared objective of creating a vibrant military-industrial base.

Objective of Paper

This paper seeks to critically examine the salient features of India's offset policy and answer the following questions.

- Will the policy outlined in DPP 2008 contribute substantially to the development of a military-industrial base in India?
- What are the shortcomings of the policy?
- What modifications are required in the offset policy and connected government procedures to maximise the benefits that can accrue to the nation from capital acquisition of defence equipment?

In order to understand the basic arguments contained in this paper, a few concepts relating to offsets in general and in defence trade in particular are explained.

Offsets Explained

Offset, as the term implies, is an element that counterbalances or compensates an act. It is a set-off from a development, in this case, military acquisition. However defined, the term offset primarily signifies an element of 'compensation' as the predominant import of the term. It occurs "when a supplier places work to an agreed value with firms in the buying country, over and above what it would have brought in the absence of the offset."

As is commonly understood, in trade, offsets have been classified as direct or indirect offsets. Direct offsets are those that are directly connected with the item being sold by the seller and can take the form of co-production, component production, licensed production, etc.

Indirect offsets are those not directly related to the product being imported and here compensations can be secured in any other area with the aim of obtaining for the economy what would otherwise have not been available to the buyer but for the purchase. Though the above two forms characterise the two widely-accepted compensatory strategies, it is necessary to add a new terminology to describe a hybrid form of offsets that is between the direct and indirect offsets that India is seeking to obtain.

This may be termed as quasi-direct offsets. It can be defined as compensation given in the sector under which the purchase falls, but is not directly connected with the product that is being imported. For instance, when tanks are imported, and the offset is obtained in the form of assistance for the co-production of a warship, then it will fall within this definition (quasi-direct) as it enhances the defence capability of the importing nation, though the compensatory arrangement is not directly connected with the item being imported.

Therefore, though analysts have largely described India's policy as seeking direct offsets, it would be more accurate to describe it as quasi-direct offsets.

DEMOCRACY AND DEFENCE POLICY

Democracy influences both the process and the content of defence policy. Thus, in a democratic set-up, defence policy is based on a consultative process. Its goals and objectives, as well as many finer details, are often debated in Parliament, the media, by think-tanks and during election campaigns. This process ensures a more participative, inclusive and transparent defence policy. This indeed is the case in India and other democracies. An important outcome of this process is that democratic governments cannot concentrate on militarisation alone.

They have to balance the needs of other sectors like the economy, health and education, with the requirements of defence. This ensures that there is no emphasis on militarisation and on an aggressive defence policy. It is well known that democracies do not go to war with each other. The reason for this is that ordinary people want peace and prosperity and democratic governments have to reflect this aspiration in their defence policy. On the other hand, dictatorial regimes have compulsions to spend large amounts on military to take care of both domestic instability and regime survival against external intervention. History is replete with such instances in the past and there are many contemporary examples today. This indeed is the case with democratic India's defence policy which has always focused on its own defence and has never contemplated aggression, even against its smallest neighbour. India's defence expenditure in early years of its independence was below two per cent of GDP.

Even now, it is less than 2.5 per cent, despite many real threats it has to face. Compare this to the amounts that some of our neighbours spend on military! Another important outcome of defence policy making through a democratic process is that such a process enables nations to develop comprehensive national strength. The concept of comprehensive national strength includes economic strength, technological strength, infrastructure and other important aspects that help to build up a nation's power. A country cannot be defended by its military power alone. Recent history shows that even great powers with huge militaries can face serious difficulties in achieving their goals and can even disintegrate due to the weight of their own internal contradictions. In India, we have been able to develop comprehensive national strength and, today we are counted amongst the world's most important powers. This is not only on account of our military but also due to our economy, our science and technology, our knowledge power, our sunrise industries and our democracy. Given its vigilant citizens with a stake in the security of the nation, the genuine requirements of defence are taken care of in democracies.

Thus, despite the fact that India has been peace-loving, it has always made an effort to keep pace with the latest defence technologies. In its initial years, India had opposed nuclear weapons tooth and nail and favoured complete disarmament. But, when the powerful nations of the world did not give up nuclear weapons and when our neighbours developed their own nuclear weapons, the Indian democracy showed enough dynamism and flexibility to change its policy and develop nuclear deterrence. However, our nuclear doctrine affirms that India will not resort to first strike and never use nuclear weapons against non-nuclear weapon states. Thus, even India's nuclear doctrine has a purely defensive orientation. India's nuclear policy has evolved over time and is based on its essentially consensual approach in matters of national security. India's defence policy is flexible enough to respond to changes in the international strategic environment.

The primary task of the Indian Armed Forces has been to provide security for our citizens and to defend our vital interests at home and abroad. Democratic India also wishes to play a friendly and responsible role in the international arena. India has always been in the forefront of UN peace-keeping missions. It has been an important actor in international fora, particularly the United Nations. In accordance with its growing profile and role, it deserves a place in the United Nations Security Council. India also seeks to provide an adequate military capability for operations to promote international stability, and humanitarian missions after natural or other disasters, providing assistance to the civil authorities at home, and maintenance of essential national services. India has worked for regional peace and stability and rendered exemplary service to provide relief in times of disaster. A recent example is that of relief operations following the Tsunami disaster. We are also ready to cooperate with the nations of the region to provide maritime security and participate in disaster management and disaster forecasting mechanisms.

In its external dimension, India has always sought a cooperative relationship with all nations. It has also made continuous efforts towards peace at the international level. It was in this background that in the Cold War era, India had refused to side with one bloc or another. India led the Non-Aligned Movement to mitigate tensions at the international level and to play a positive role in resolving conflicts. However, its proximity to the Soviet bloc for defence supplies was misinterpreted. Due to the configuration of the Cold War era, India and some western nations were unable to come together and form a strong partnership. Now that the Cold War has ended and India is rapidly integrating with a globalising world, it has entered into either a strategic partnership or a strategic dialogue with all important powers of the world.

Our growing friendship with United States, Russia, European Union and Japan is a testimony to this positive development. India and China have set aside their boundary dispute to come together in the area of economic cooperation. Earnest efforts are also being made by the two sides to resolve the boundary issue but this does not allow our growing cooperation to be affected. We are trying to develop close and cooperative relationship with all our neighbours, including Pakistan. Our future vision of South Asia is a region which is stable, at peace with each other and cooperating to accelerate economic growth and prosperity of its people. We want our neighbours to take full advantage of our growing market and a rapidly globalising economy.

India has suffered from terrorism for many decades and has been able to cope with the problem effectively. In doing so, it has respected human rights. It is an important player in the war against terrorism which is seen as an assault on our secular, inclusive and democratic polity. Countries which are undemocratic in their orientation are often a heaven for terrorists and even pursue terrorism as a part of state policy. This is an important distinction between the defence and security policies of democracies and autocratic rulers. Because democracies do not favour draconian measures and respect the rule of law, they are some times perceived to be soft or weak. The process of debate and consultation also can be a stretched out process at time. However, democracies are inherently strong and tend to promote defence policies which are conducive to the welfare of their own people and to peace and stability in the world.

DEFENCE PLANNING AND SERVICES

Before independence, the defence services worked on a system of contract budget. Defence expenditure was pegged at Rs 55 crore per year, which was more than half of the Central Government's revenue. There was no serious threat from outside (except during World War II, when a fresh agreement was signed) and this amount was more than adequate to maintain the establishment.

The savings were not allowed to lapse but put away in the Defence Reserve Fund that was utilised to finance measures for re-equipment of the Defence Services, thus freeing the Government from having to provide fund money greater than the contract amount. Expenditure on defence rose steeply soon after independence. However, there was no planned effort and defence programmes consisted mainly of outright purchases from abroad, drawing heavily on available Sterling reserves. In the late 1950s, some efforts were made to initiate domestic weapons production by the Ministry of Defence when Mr. Krishna Menon was the Defence Minister. The Sino-Indian conflict in 1962 aroused a new defence consciousness in the country. After taking care of immediate postwar requirements, systematic defence planning started in 1964. Defence requirements were assessed on a five-year basis and the First Five Year Defence Plan (1964-69) was drawn up. This plan took into account the resources available and assistance which could be expected from friendly foreign countries. The plan was primarily based on an expansion and modernisation programme considered necessary by each Service in the light of the respective threat perception assessed. It also proposed a defence production base that would gradually reduce the country's external dependence, provide for improvements in border roads and communications, and a modest expansion of DRDO. The Government recognised the imperative need to synergise 'defence' and 'development' instead of planning each on a separate and unrelated level. The MoD emphasised the "inevitable need to harness all resources of the country for the country's defence and for the defence effort to derive full sustenance from the country's economic development plans".

Thereafter, the National Development Council authorised the Chairman of the Planning Commission to review the needs of both development and defence. A Planning Cell was established in 1965 in the Ministry of Defence 'to deal with the wider aspects of defence planning'. The new system was intended to facilitate medium and long-term defence planning and to maintain constant liaison with the Planning Commission and other ministries.

It was expected that the MoD would derive maximum advantage from the development effort by being able to place its priorities for consideration along with the overall economic and industrial plans drawn up by the Planning Commission. The experience of the First Five Year Defence Plan showed that the development of weapons and equipment was a long drawn out process. The Government realised that there could be no forward movement in attaining self-sufficiency in weapons and equipment unless these requirements were planned over a reasonably long period, long enough to cover the span of development and production of new weapons systems and other fighting tools.

The inadequacy of foreign exchange reserves was another hindrance in planning and implementation. In order to mitigate some of these drawbacks, the Second Five Year Defence Plan (1969-74) was instituted on a "roll-on" basis. After a year, an additional year was added so that the Defence Services would have before them a revised and updated five-year plan. In this context, the MoD commented: "Opportunity is taken by this annual exercise to take note of and reflect the change in priorities, the shifts in emphasis and the latest concepts and programmes to reorient the plan within the scheme of resources so that the aims and means are most effectively balanced." This system was expected to facilitate the planning of projects that took five years or more and to revise or eliminate projects, depending on the prevailing foreign exchange situation and availability of domestic resources.

For a period of five years, firm assurances were to be given on the availability of resources. This, unfortunately, never happened. In 1971, it was impossible to adhere to the discipline and the pattern of the roll-on plan. Instead of roll-on annual revisions, immediate requirements dominated the Government's attention that pre-empted plan efforts. In its 1971-72 Annual Report, the MoD acknowledged that having a Planning Cell in the ministry was an insufficient and unsatisfactory method of meeting a crisis.

The Planning Cell was not taken seriously in the crucial stages of economic planning and the argument that defence needs would be adjusted in the over-all allocation of resources was proved wrong.

In 1974, an Apex Group headed by the Union Minister for Planning again suggested that steady long-term defence programmes would be more cost effective and economical rather than fluctuating allocations due to periodic economic and security crises. In order to integrate defence planning with the overall economic planning effort, defence and economic development plans were made co-terminus.

Defence Planning Machinery

Most of the defence planning machinery and planning methodology was developed in the decade 1964-74. The Joint Intelligence Committee (JIC) was established in the Cabinet Secretariat to provide external and internal threat assessments.

Inputs for this purpose were to be provided by all Intelligence agencies of the Government. The Service Chiefs were to assess the broad military aims and a strategy, coordinated in the Chiefs of Staff Committee, was to be approved by the Defence Minister.

However, this was seldom done. Each Service ended up planning its own force level, choice of weapons and equipment, and build-up of infrastructure. In 1977, the Government formed a Committee for Defence Planning (CDP) to "undertake regular assessments relevant to defence planning in the light of all factors having a bearing on national security and defence". However, this committee could not function smoothly nor meet the desired goals.

Planning units were also established in the Department of Defence Production and DRDO. A Planning and Coordination Cell was created in the MoD to coordinate and compile various plans into a 'Defence Plan' for Cabinet approval.

As the bureaucrats in the ministry had no professional knowledge or background, this cell could only compile different requirements without any analysis. In Army Headquarters, the Deputy Chief of Army Staff was made responsible for preparing the Army plan.

A Perspective Planning Directorate was established in the late 1970s. Naval and Air plans were prepared in the respective Planning Directorates. Financial considerations, nonexistent at this level earlier, were introduced through Finance Planning Sections attached to these Directorates.

In 1986, the Directorate General of Defence Planning Staff (DGDPS), comprising officers from the three Services, DRDO, and Ministries of Defence and External Affairs, was established under the Chiefs of Staff Committee (COSC) to coordinate and harmonise defence planning. Civilian officers from the Ministries probably did not find the job professionally satisfying and were gradually withdrawn, thus leaving the DGDPS a tri-Service set up.

All these measures enabled each Service headquarters to prepare defence plans in a more rational manner. But due to lack of clear political direction and each Service primarily planning for itself, joint planning, coordination between Services and other departmental plans of the MoD, were largely ignored.

After the Kargil conflict in 1999, the Group of Ministers (GoM) and later the Cabinet Committee on Security (CCS) approved several reforms. An Integrated Defence Headquarters (IDH) was established and the DGDPS was merged with it.

The creation of the post of Chief of Defence Staff (CDS), whose tasks would include ensuring intra and inter-Services prioritisation of defence plans and improvement in joint functioning of the Defence Services, was recommended. The reforms also included establishment of a Defence Intelligence Agency and creation of Defence Equipment Production, Research and Planning councils in the IDH and MoD, respectively. Unfortunately, the CDS, who would be the cornerstone of integrated operational planning for defence, has not been appointed.

Analysis of the Planning System

Despite several years of planning efforts, defence planning in India is characterised by seesaw bouts of frenzied activity followed by long periods of relative inaction. Five-year defence plans have rarely been formally approved before commencement.

The Tenth Defence Plan, now in its third year, is yet to be accorded formal government approval. Adhocism is the order of the day, leading to knee-jerk responses and haphazard planning, making India a reactive rather than proactive nation in matters pertaining to national security.

Whenever India's major adversaries plan a big defence purchase, there is an outcry for similar acquisitions, resulting in piecemeal decisions regardless of long-term impact and overall requirements.

The Defence Forces are forced to follow "a case-by-case" approach to modernisation and procurement of arms, ammunition and equipment to replace obsolescent items, in many cases long after their life cycle is over and they cannot be maintained in a cost effective manner. The Army's Vijayanta tanks, MiG-21s of the IAF, and IL-38 maritime reconnaissance aircraft of the Navy are some examples.

Weapons development, procurement and absorption are complex processes. A lead-time of 15-20 years is required to plan and execute major projects. Despite this, for several years, a large amount of the capital acquisition budget has been surrendered. In the prevailing era of strategic uncertainty, the changing nature of warfare demands a judicious mix of threat and capabilities-based forces that can operate efficiently as combined arms, joint Services teams and components of multinational coalition forces.

CONCEPT OF NATIONAL SECURITY POLICY AND STRATEGY

The concept of national security rests mainly on the proposition that many foreign and domestic political, economic and military issues are interrelated, each with implications on the other. In India's case, this has been highlighted by insurgencies and other political events, particularly in border-states, and other outside pressures, which are brought to bear on the country's economy and technological progress from time to time.

A response to this type of environment calls for a highly focused national security policy and strategy. Effective guidance on national security and defence policy objectives is fundamental to the defence planning process.

National security is a relative matter without a firm criteria but unless firm national security objectives are set and a defence policy evolved, there can be no military doctrine or balancing of defence effort with other national objectives and priorities such as maintaining a viable economy and supporting development of society.

The lack of a cohesive national security strategy and defence policy has many implications. First, it results in the absence of clear political direction regarding politico-military objectives, which is the very basis of sound defence planning. Secondly, there is inadequate coordination of defence plans and economic development. Finally, science and technology policies for defence, general industrialisation and other development programmes are not coordinated properly to achieve security goals and objectives.

Defence Perspective and Integrated Planning

A Defence Plan has to be prepared on the basis of a 15-year long perspective planning system, such that the first five years of the plan are very firm (Definitive Plan), the second five years less firm (Indicative Plan) and the third five-year term tentative (Vision Plan).

There has to be a reasonably firm allocation of financial resources for the first five years and an indicative allocation for the subsequent period. Perspective planning needs to be done in the Integrated Defence Headquarters, where military, technical and R&D experts take an integrated view of future threats and challenges.

This has to be based on future battlefield scenarios, and array of forecasts, evaluation of strategic options and force mixes, and analysis of potential technical and industrial capabilities. Based on this, the respective Service should work on their perspective plans and the R&D and Defence Production/ Supplies experts should spell out their requirements in terms of effort, technology and indigenous production.

As stated earlier, the CDS, who would be the cornerstone of integrated operational planning for defence, has not been appointed. India's defence planning, therefore, continues to be Service based. Often, the threat perception of one Service is at variance with that of another Service. What emerges is essentially a sum of total of Service or department wise programmes. The focus is not on overall goals or priorities but on what is required by a particular Service. In its endeavour to lay the groundwork for an increased share of the budget, each Service tends to exercise its own priorities, favouring its own plans to the detriment of joint plans.

Subjects like surveillance, air defence, electronic warfare, and amphibious operations, which relate to more than one Service, do not get adequate attention. Integrated planning for defence is essential for creating balanced force structures and for the successful execution of all military missions.

In fact, it is the most effective manner of ensuring effective defence. According to Charles Hitch, "the revolution in military technology has not only changed the character of our military programmes, it has also to a significant degree blurred the lines of demarcation among various Services". Most major military missions today require the participation of more than one military service.

Therefore, the principal concern now must be centred on what is required by the defence establishment as a whole to perform a particular mission—not what is required by a particular Service to perform its individual part of that 'mission'. The areas of commonality in modern weapon systems are immense and growing rapidly. Communications, guidance systems, missiles, radars, lasers—even traditional equipment such as guns, fuses, ammunition and vehicles are common. Integrated defence planning is necessary in view of escalating costs of these weapons and equipment.

Self-reliance in Defence Technology

The DRDO has a network of 51 laboratories and establishments. The Scientific Advisor (SA) to the Raksha Mantri (RM) is the Secretary of this Department. The DRDO has a staff of 30,000, including 6,800 scientists and engineers. It receives approximately four to six per cent of the defence budget annually. The DRDO is engaged in the pursuit of self-reliance in critical technologies relevant to defence. It formulates and executes a programme of scientific research, design and development for the induction into the Armed Forces of state-of-the-art weapons and other equipments.

In April 1984, the DRDO envisaged a programme "to transform the Department into a leader of international class with the mission to capture and retain commanding heights in critical technologies". A 'mission mode' organisational structure and approach was approved by the Government with a view to increasing the element of self-reliance from the current 30 per cent to 70 per cent by 2005. This goal, however, is nowhere in sight. The Department has developed more than 1,100 items of weapon systems and equipment with a production value of over Rs 6,000 crore. But it has not been able to make any major contribution to the state-of-art weapons and equipment. Most of its programmes, like Prithvi (sea borne version), Trishul (short-range surface to air missile), Akash (medium-range surface to air missile), Nag (anti-tank missile), Light Combat Aircraft with Kaveri engine, Pinaka (multiple-barrel rocket system), MBT Arjun, Electronic Warfare equipment, new radio sets for the Army, Sonar system for Navy, and many other items, are way behind schedule.

Because of the failure to deliver the required weapons and equipment, defence planning and Force structuring by the Services has suffered continuously. The DRDO's inability to deliver in time has caused a crisis of confidence and constant dissatisfaction in the Services. In order to ensure smooth progress towards self-reliance in defence technology, the Government must undertake a periodic performance audit of DRDO projects to reinforce efforts in areas of success and weed out projects that are unproductive.

5

Military Force to Military Power

2020: DEFENDING INDIAN FORCE

The Flashpoint. NATO's Allied Force saw induction of more than 400 planes into the Balkan skies. Phase-I witnessed cruise missiles, F-117 Nighthawks, B-2 bombers, F-15/16 Eagles, F-16 Falcons and B-52 bombers which rolled in from as the diverse directions and places as Adriatic Sea, Missouri, Italy and England. With that Kosovo moved to a new level of misery. The largest air attacks since WWII commenced on a country which does not threaten the global equilibrium nor its neighbours. And none know the precise exit strategy nor the endgame. However, this much is clear that the resultant giagantic refugee problem will heavily eat into the NATO manpower and resources for a long time to come.

Of late, unfortunately, the American foreign policy has been driven by ultimatums. Whenever, a disagreement occurs, the lone super power needs to deliver on such threats. But the air attacks without ground troops support cannot always win. So Osama bin Laden remains where he was. Saddam continues to visit his mistresses. And now NATO's credibility is up for grabs. The Balkans is likely to be the graveyard of air-attacks-alone theory. For history argues that a determined infantry cannot be evicted by massive air attacks. The Kosovo spillover will not only impact on the health of the EU, but also put a question mark on the American global dominance.

However, Americans are likely to continue with such ill-advised actions on a variety of flashpoints worldwide in a desperate attempt to disallow emerging new power equations. This will further tie down in knots the NATO credibility. Let's try to visualise how India can re-organise internally to meet the new challenges arising out of the deteriorating international scenario.

The Indian Faultline. This faultline can be traced back to the Mauryan empire's unwise decision of renouncing war. Like corporate graphs, the military power graph of a nation either gradually creeps upwards or if not in use, the law of gravity pulls it downwards!

Thus unwittingly, in subsequent centuries the neglect of the military component resulted in unprecedented foreign invasions. Incomprehension of the dynamics of military power by the subsequent rulers and the attempts to absorb, appease and amalgamate the invading armies put the foreign rulers at the seat of power in Delhi with ease. This is akin to allowing an adversary in a soccer match to dominate your half of the field. Obviously goals will be scored.

The other aspect of the Indian Faultline rests on the fact that majority of the Indian rulers employed the military power ruthlessly internally to pacify the outlying provinces (instead of attempting economic development) while refusing to correctly posture it to meet the threats from invasion. This short sighted approach continued on India's attaining independence. Many elders (product of a similar mindset) tend to defend the actions of Indian political leadership of 1947 on singular ground of inexperience. One tends to disagree because all it needed was to review the historical evidence of foreign subjugation and the leadership would automatically have deduced the reasons. And initiated corrective measures. This small exercise really did not require a very high caliber in leadership either.

On one hand, the international stability appears to be in a tail spin. Because the lone super power is determined to rise and shine at every flashpoint despite the time tested principle of never jump into somebody else's civil war. On the other hand, India is finally waking up to the fact that the world does not feed on morals! India needs to re-look and re-fashion its internal factors to meet the prevailing new external lawlessness.

The Have-Nots. Indians over the centuries have done to the Untouchables, what the Americans did to the Blacks. Suppression. The Blacks even today cannot easily rise in the American society because of one simple fear that they will return the favour in ample measures. Fortunately for India, the Untouchables retain their levels of tolerance like the rest of the Indians. Therefore, rapid education and economic development of the backward/rural areas needs to be implemented on a war footing. Time lost in this respect will be directly proportionate to heightened levels of social disharmony which India can ill-afford as an emerging power.

Unity-in-Diversity. The Indian tragedy is that this slogan since 1947 has only harped on the aspect concerning *diversity,* encouraging divisive tendencies from Kashmir to Kanyakumari! For aspirations towards building a modem nation-state, the buzz word has to be integration and not disintegration. Give spin to integration by merging the MoD with Service Headquarters and right down the line to the Theatre Command. More efficiency at a much lesser cost with availability of a larger fire power. A unique functional role model of unity in diversity for India is its military. Be it the Sikhs, Rajputs, Jats or the Madras Regiments, the cultural diversity is adequately maintained at the lower end of the spectrum. Uniformity through training is achieved at the higher end of the spectrum.

The social scientist and the economist must sit together with the military analyst to understand, innovate and devise methods to integrate the society accordingly. The military role model respects and encourages secularism and yet manages to effectively knit the diversity in a rare unity. Overall national uniformity in approach is vital for the national health and cannot be disputed. Nor should it be erroneously mistaken as militerization of the Indian mind. Internal harmony will also reduce consumption of military power within. Such surplus of military component then readily will be available to face the external threats.

To develop national uniformity in approach, the following elementary steps are recommended.

- Post-independence military actions, battles and wars must be taught to students from the ninth standard onwards. This literature is not only secular but can galvanize the young through acts of courage, compassion and bravery exemplified by the Indian soldier, sailor and the airman. It will also be of immense help to create a larger vision of a diverse India in the young mind. Further, to hone the skills of civilian instructors in the teaching of post independence history in military science departments in colleges, officers from the three services should be put on deputation for two years under study leave provisions.
- On scrutiny, the only all India services are the Army, Navy and the Air Force. Indian Administrative Service or Indian Police Service merely adorn an all India nomenclature. For example an IAS officer from Bihar cadre normally ends up spending his professional tenure between Bihar and Delhi. This needs to be modified like the military. Officers of the civil services like IAS, IPS, etc. should be posted through out the country to increase their vision and interaction with diverse regions and communities. This will provide a fillip to integration.
- A major boost to uniformity in approach can be achieved by lateral induction of the military in civil services. Officers of the Armed Forces imbibe in them the best man and material management techniques that the country can offer. If they are laterally inducted into central and state administrative and police structures with their seniority intact, they will perform miracles in providing a responsive and a responsible administration. Similarly jawans can be absorbed in the state and central police forces. Training costs come down,

efficiency goes up, shortages of manpower ends, and the military remains young. Besides, this simple measure bestows honour and recognition of the soldier's contribution to the nation. Above all this will act as a force-multiplier in national integration.

Internal Reforms. Analysing the Indian genius and skills, one factor stands out. It works the best in a free atmosphere. Scores of Indian fast food joints are now ahead of those owned by multinationals.

Infact, for the first time, the latter are forced to cut down their retail prices and cater to the Indian palate. Modern banking facilities at a lesser cost provided by HDFC Ltd. Bank is ahead of the foreign banks. Zee TV revenues score over a foreign channel.

Therefore, accelerated pace of internal reforms to free and unleash the Indian enterprenuial energy in the next five years is a must-must. Simultaneously lowering the over-whelming government structures by 35% in the next five years is mandatory for India to gain momentum. The system is not only clogged but eats up revenue in far excess of what it can collect. And hardly delivers.

However, the social net for the next twenty years needs to remain intact till the have-nots are brought into the main stream through education. Here, I emphasize on the spread of education in the rural areas because this not only creates new skills and competence but helps check the explosion in population. In actualities, India can afford to cxport vast amount of brains and yet have an internal surplus! The government needs to exploit this factor.

Defending India. To defend India, we have everything going for us except a vision and a will to ruthlessly implement it. Indians must remember that despite building up of sufficient alliances in our region and out-of-the-region, we must not become complacent and neglect the growth of military power in future. Education of the masses, encouraging the free enterprise, developing the economy of the outlying provinces through an efficient administrative machinery on a war footing (and thus freeing the military power from enormous internal consumption), disallowing demographic changes in the border areas from outside in particular, and giving thrust to national integration while retaining diversity at the lower end of the spectrum are the areas that need to be conceptually worked upon. Simply, put to defend India, the India First generation must take over from the fading elders of India Last generation.-

MODERNISING THE INDIAN ARMY

For over a decade the Indian Army's efforts to modernise have been thwarted due to political neglect and lack of adequate budgetary support. The defence budget for Financial Year 2008-09 increased 10 per cent in nominal terms, barely adequate to keep up with inflation and the fall in the value of the rupee against the US dollar, but decreased to less than 2.0 per cent of India's projected GDP. A sum of US $12 billion was provided for capital acquisitions (US $9 billion for the army), but of this US $0.6 billion (Rs 3,000 crore) is expected to be surrendered as unspent. Nothing exemplified the army's lack of preparedness for war more than the fact that 155 mm ammunition for the Bofors howitzer had to be imported from South Africa during the Kargil conflict in 1999. Had the conflict not been confined to the 150 km frontage of the Kargil sector, T-72 and 130mm medium gun ammunition too may have run short and it would have been politically embarrassing for the government as well as the army.

Not only that, in the plains the army would have had to fight with obsolete Vijayant tanks and several other vintage equipment that were unsuitable for combat. Even though A.K. Antony, the Defence Minister, has said, 'We need to cut down on the unnecessary procedures, bottlenecks and red tape in our procurement mechanism,' the Ministry of Defence has been unable to give modernisation of the armed forces the priority that it deserves. The Army Chief's modernisation vision is to 'adapt to high-end technology, improve night-fighting capability... (and) information technology, information warfare and network centric warfare.' The indigenously designed Arjun main battle tank (MBT) has been in the pipeline for over two decades. Though the tank has many good features, it has consistently failed to meet the army's GSQR for an MBT and orders have been placed for only 124 tanks to be manufactured. The lack of progress on the Arjun MBT has significantly slowed down the pace of armour modernisation. In the year 2000 India signed a deal with Russia to acquire 310 T-90S tanks. Subsequently, India began to assemble these tanks at Avadi. It has recently been reported that in addition to these, India has decided to acquire another 347 T-90S tanks and assemble them within the country.

The first Indian assembled T-90S (Bhishma) rolled off the production line on 8 January 2004. Meanwhile, a large number of T-72M1 (Ajeya) tanks are still awaiting modernisation. The lack of a suitable fire control system and night fighting capability are major handicaps. In a future conventional war that will be fought under the nuclear shadow, manoeuvre will be extremely limited. This restriction will lead to much greater emphasis being placed on firepower to achieve the laid down military aim. Hence, it is imperative that artillery modernisation is undertaken with alacrity so as to generate firepower asymmetries on the future battlefield. The last major acquisition of towed gun-howitzers was that of about 400 pieces of 39-calibre 155mm FH-77B howitzers from Bofors of Sweden in the mid-1980s. This gun had proved its mettle in the Kargil conflict. Just when a contract for 120 tracked and 180 wheeled self-propelled (SP) 155mm guns was about to be concluded after years of protracted trials, South African arms manufacturer Denel, a leading contender for the contract, was alleged to have been involved in a corruption scam in an earlier deal for anti-material rifles (AMRs).

Since January 2008, the Ministry of Defence (MoD) has issued three global tenders for 155mm guns and howitzers for the mountains, the plains and self-propelled guns for the deserts. Summer and winter trials were expected to be held in 2009-10, but so far the bids received are still being evaluated. The artillery modernisation programme is bound to see further delays.

The probability of the next conventional war breaking out in the mountains is far higher than that of a war in the plains. With this in view, the artillery recently conceptualised a requirement for a lightweight towed howitzer of 155mm calibre for employment in the mountains. Neither the present Bofors howitzer nor its 52-calibre replacement will be capable of effective operations in the mountains. A lightweight 45-calibre 155mm howitzer weighing less than 5,000 kg, with a light but adequately powered prime mover, is ideal for the mountains. In January 2008, the MoD floated a Request for Proposal (RfP) for 140 pieces of ultra-light 39 calibre 155mm towed howitzers for use by the Indian Army's mountain formations. Presumably, these will also be employed by its rapid reaction divisions – as and when they are raised – as the howitzers will be easy to transport by air. India has floated a global tender for the purchase of 400 52-calibre 155mm towed artillery guns for the army, to be followed by indigenous manufacture of another 1,100 howitzers. An RfP has also been issued for 180 wheeled self-propelled guns for around Rs 4,700 crore for employment by mechanised forces in the plains and semi-desert sectors. Approximately 180 pieces of 130mm M46 Russian medium guns have been successfully 'up-gunned' to 155mm calibre with ordnance supplied by Soltam of Israel. The new barrel length of 45 calibres has enhanced the range of the gun to about 40 km with extended range ammunition.

A contract for the acquisition of two regiments of the 12-tube, 300mm Smerch multi-barrel rocket launcher (MBRL) system with 90 km range was signed with Russia's Rosoboron-export in early 2006. This will be a major boost for the long-range firepower capabilities of the army. Extended range (ER) rockets are being introduced for the 122 mm Grad MBRL that has been in service for over three decades. The ER rockets will enhance the weapon system's range from 22 to about 40 km. A Rs 5,000 crore (US $1billion) contract has also been signed for the serial production of the Pinaka MBRL weapon system, another DRDO project plagued by time delays and completed with help from Larsen and Toubro and the Tatas.

Since the Bofors 155mm Howitzer was introduced into service, the indigenously designed and manufactured 105 mm Indian Field Gun (IFG) and its (not so) light version, the Light Field Gun (LFG), have joined the 75/24 Indian Mountain Gun, the 100mm Russian field gun and the 122mm Russian howitzer on the obsolescence list.

Counter-bombardment (US term counter-fire) capability is also being upgraded, but at a slow pace. At least about 40 to 50 weapon locating radars (WLRs) are required for effective counter-bombardment, especially in the plains, and only a dozen have been procured so far. In addition to the 12 AN-TPQ 37 Firefinder WLRs acquired from Raytheon, USA, under a 2002 contract worth US $200 million, Bharat Electronics Limited is reported to be assembling 28 WLRs. These radars will be based on both indigenous and imported components and have been approved for introduction into service after extensive tests. The radar is expected to match the capabilities of the Firefinder system and will have a detection range of about 40 kilometre.

The BrahMos supersonic cruise missile , with a precision strike capability, very high kill energy and range of 290 km, was inducted into the army in July 2007. It is a versatile missile that can be launched from TATRA mobile launchers and silos on land, aircraft and ships and, perhaps in future, also from submarines. 50 BrahMos missiles are expected to be produced every year. Efforts are underway to further increase its strike range. BrahMos Aerospace has orders worth Rs 3,500 crore (US $0.65 billion) from the army and the navy, which has opted for the anti-ship as well as the land attack cruise missile (LACM) versions. These terrain hugging missiles are virtually immune to counter measures due to their high speed and very low radar cross section and are far superior to subsonic cruise missiles like Pakistan's Babur.

Despite its large-scale employment on border management and extensive commitments in IS and CI operations, infantry modernisation had been languishing for several decades when the Ministry of Defence (MoD) finally cleared a visionary plan to modernise the army's infantry battalions by according 'in principle' approval in the form of Modification 4B to the war establishment (WE) of a standard infantry battalion in 1998. However, no funds were specially sanctioned for this purpose till the NDA government approved the expenditure of Rs 3,500 crore (US $0.6 billion) in September 2003. The army has initiated a project for a Future Infantry Soldier as a System (F-INSAS). 'F-INSAS basically aims at "converting an infantryman into a fully-networked all-terrain, all-weather, weapons platform with enhanced lethality, survivability, sustainability, mobility and situational awareness" for the digitised battlefield of the future.'

While 250 Kornet-E anti-tank guided missiles (ATGMs) with thermal imaging sights have substantially increased the anti-tank capability of infantry battalions, most efforts to modernise the equipment held by infantry and Rashtriya Rifles (RR) units are aimed at enhancing their capability for surveillance and target acquisition at night and boosting their firepower for precise retaliation against infiltrating columns and terrorists holed up in built-up areas. 200 hand-held BFSRs with practical ranges up to seven to eight km where clear line of sight is available, 2,000 hand-held thermal imaging devices (HHTIs) with ranges up to 2,000 metres for observation at night and stand-alone infrared, seismic and acoustic sensors with varying capabilities have enabled infantrymen to dominate the Line of Control so completely that infiltration has come down to almost a trickle. The newly acquired weapons, which complement these surveillance and observation devices, include: 1,500x 84 mm rocket launchers, including some disposable ones; 1,000 AMRs (anti-material rifles); 8,000 UBGLs (under-barrel grenade launchers); 4,000 new generation carbines; 300 bullet proof vehicles; and, several hundred accurate sniper rifles.

However, the numbers acquired and the ammunition stocks are still inadequate and need to be made up more rapidly. While the INSAS 5.56 mm assault rifles have now been in service for almost 10 years and proved to be effective, the light machine gun (LNG) version is still facing teething problems and the carbine version for close quarter battle has not found favour with the army. New 5.56 mm assault rifles of bull-pup design with an integrated laser range finder and grenade launcher are under development. Efforts are also being made to provide infantry platoons and sections with integrated GPS-based navigation system, secure lightweight walkie-talkie radio sets and better protective gear with a helmet that incorporates a built-in head-up display.

The mechanised infantry is now equipped with the BMP-2 ICV Sarath of which over 1,000 have been built since 1987. A new variant is the 81 mm Carrier Mortar Tracked Vehicle (CMTV) that is based on the chassis of the Sarath ICV and has been indigenously developed to enhance the integral firepower available to mechanised infantry battalions. Other variants include a command post, an ambulance, armoured dozer and engineer and reconnaissance vehicles. Mechanised reconnaissance and support battalions need better surveillance radars, fire-and-forget ATGMs and effective night fighting capability.

A new DRDO project that is reported to be ongoing aims to equip future soldiers with lightweight force multipliers. Soldiers of the future will have miniaturised communication and GPS systems, small power packs, weapon platforms and smart vests with fibre-optic sensors. For over 350 infantry battalions, plus about 150 Rashtriya Rifles, Assam Rifles and Territorial Army battalions, these major changes will be extremely costly to implement and will spill over at least 10 to 12 years – that is, if the funds can be found. Without modernising this cutting edge of its sword, the army will soon begin to resemble the armies of India's lesser neighbours.

Another DRDO project that is way behind schedule is the Nag anti-tank missile system. The antiquated Jonga-mounted SS-11 B1 anti-tank guided missile (ATGM) system has been replaced in missile battalions by MILAN shoulder-fired ATGMs. However, a vehicle-mounted missile system like the Nag is definitely necessary for reconnaissance and attrition tasks and for anti-tank screens. The experimental Plan AREN tactical communications system for strike formations needs early replacement. The ability to carry broadband data needs to be enhanced in particular. Even the more recent static communications network called ASCON lacks ISDN capability for the real-time transmission of maps and streaming video.

The Defence Minister, A.K. Antony, recently admitted that there are gaps in India's air defence coverage. While the allusion was primarily to the lack of sufficient radar coverage to detect aerial threats to India's air space, the air defence (AD) of field formations continues to be given a much lower priority than it deserves. With the DRDO's indigenous Akash medium-range and Trishul short-range surface-to-air (SAM) missile projects not making major headway, it is time to start looking at substitutes from abroad. The air defence of mechanised forces is another area that is crying for attention. The SAM-6 and SAM-7 Kvadrat-Strela medium range missile system, the backbone of AD for strike formations since the early 1970s, is now ageing and needs urgent replacement. The Tungushka and the OSA-AK (SA-8) missile systems are on the obsolescence list and the 23mm, multi-barrelled Schilka tracked air defence gun system is already obsolete. In fact, the assets of the Army Air Defence corps are grossly inadequate to provide high quality low-level air defence to the field formations. Hence, forward combat echelons will lack effective protection against enemy aircraft during a future war. The young Army Air Defence corps requires substantial capital infusion to really come into its own.

For the future, the Defence Research and Development Organisation (DRDO) is planning to develop an integrated air defence system with exo-atmosphere (above 40 km altitude) and endo-atmosphere (below 30 km) capabilities by 2009-10. The system may also have built-in features to double up as a tactical missile, apart from functioning as an extended air defence system to engage target aircraft beyond 100 km. This was stated by V.K. Saraswat, Chief Controller, DRDO R&D

(Missiles and Strategic Systems), after the successful test launch of a high-altitude interceptor missile from the Wheeler Island in December 2007. This programme will also lead to the development of an indigenous ballistic missile defence (BMD) capability.

An automated command and control and decision support system for use by the General Staff is still far from becoming a reality, as also supporting systems like the battlefield surveillance system and air space management system. The urgent requirement of real-time satellite reconnaissance systems has still not been operationalised despite the nuclear overhang under which the armed forces now operate. Even though the cameras on India's remote sensing and cartographic satellites now have sharply enhanced resolutions, less than one metre, military-grade photographs of still better resolution are needed to be purchased from the open market. These sources may dry up quickly during war.

A 'system of systems' approach must be followed so that scarce RSTA and communications resources can be synergistically configured and optimally exploited, based on the concept of 'network-centric warfare' in which surveillance sensors, targeting systems and 'shooters' are fused together in a seamless 'system of systems' that reduces response time between the acquisition of a target and its destruction to 15-20 minutes.

Though some modern frequency hopping radio sets with integral encryption devices have been introduced into service in recent years, networked communications, which form the backbone of an effective C4I2SR system, need substantial upgradation. The tactical-level Tac C3I system for field formations is in urgent need of an upgrade. The Plan AREN system has been in service for almost three decades and is based on outdated and bulky technologies. The ASCON communication system for voice and data links between static HQ and those in peacetime locations, still has some years of service left as it is of modular design and can be upgraded to a limited extent. However, its capability to provide data links is rather limited as data requirements have grown by leaps and bounds over the last decade or so. A tri-service Defence Communication Network (DCN) is in an advanced stage of planning.

While some Stentor long-range BFSRs have been in service for over a decade, medium-range radars are still to be acquired. Israeli Searcher-I and Heron unmanned aerial vehicles (UAVs) have been introduced into service but these are few in number and it will be a long time before they really make a difference by providing a real-time surveillance capability so that ground forces can initiate action even as a fresh input is received. Only a small number of Searcher-II UAVs, with an upper ceiling that makes them suitable for the mountains, have been acquired.

PGMs are increasingly gaining currency as weapons of choice in conflict on land, however, the Indian artillery does not have PGMs in quantities large enough to matter. Only limited quantities of the Russian Krasnopol PGM have been imported for the Bofors 155mm howitzer. Among others, the Bofors Bonus PGM is a suitable candidate, subject to successful trials in the deserts and mountains. Despite a Long-term Integrated Perspective Plan (LTIPP) and five-year Defence Plans, approval has to be sought on file for each new weapon system or piece of equipment on a 'case-by-case' basis. It is by now well-known how each such case chronicles the saga of an uphill struggle to get approval first from the MoD, then MoD (Finance), the Ministry of Finance (MoF) and, finally, the Cabinet Committee on Security. All this is only possible after the DRDO has first certified that the weapon system or equipment in question cannot be developed and manufactured indigenously and such a certificate is hard to come by. Gradually these archaic procurement and acquisition procedures are being reviewed and improved. The Defence Procurement Procedure (DPP) 2008 was promulgated recently.

The approach to army modernisation must be more focused; the priorities need to be clearly established and then adhered to. The government must give a firm commitment in terms of funds and the MoD should streamline its procedures and processes for speedy procurement of high priority weapons and equipment. It is time to institute a rolling, non-lapsable defence modernisation fund of Rs 25,000 crore (US $5 billion) as a viable method of ensuring that defence procurement is not subjected to the vagaries of annual budgets. The present situation is disturbing and, if allowed to go on indefinitely, will seriously compromise the army's preparedness to fight the next border war that inimical neighbours like Pakistan can be expected to thrust on India. The MoD 'has assured the army of full support for its around 600 modernisation schemes, worth about Rs 70,000 crore in the 11th Plan (2007-2012) period,' but it remains to be seen whether this will actually materialise.

MILITARY MANPOWER AND STRATEGIC ENVIRONMENT

India's regional security environment is marked by Afghanistan's endless civil war despite US-led North Atlantic Treaty Organization (NATO) intervention and the overthrow of the despotic Taliban regime and its tense relations with Iran and the Central Asian Republics (CARs). Pakistan's half-hearted struggle against the remnants of the al Qaeda and the Taliban, the fissiparous tendencies in Balochistan and the Pushtun heartland, the continuing rise of the cancer of radical extremism and creeping Talibanisation, the unstable civilian government, the floundering economy and, consequently, the nation's gradual slide towards becoming a 'failed state', pose a major security threat to India.

The collusive nuclear weapon-cummissile development programme of China, North Korea and Pakistan and Iran's quest for nuclear weapons are issues of concern. Sri Lanka's inability to find a lasting solution to its ethnic problems despite the comprehensive defeat of the LTTE (Liberation Tigers of Tamil Eelam) has serious repercussions for India. Bangladesh's emergence as the new hub of Islamist fundamentalist terrorism even as it struggles for economic upliftment to subsistence levels, could trigger a new wave of terrorism in India. The Maoist ascendancy in Nepal and its adverse impact on Nepal's fledgling democracy, as also Nepal's newfound inclination to seek neutrality between India and China, are a blow to what has historically been a stable relationship. Simmering discontentment in Tibet and Xingjian against China's repressive regime is gathering momentum and could result in an open revolt.

The peoples' nascent movement for democracy in Myanmar and several long festering insurgencies may destabilise the military Junta. The spill over of religious extremism and terrorism from Afghanistan and political instability in the CARs (Central Asian Republics) are undermining development and governance. Other vitiating factors impacting regional stability in India's neighbourhood is unchecked proliferation of small arms which has been nurtured and encouraged by large-scale narcotics trafficking.

India's unresolved territorial and boundary dispute with China and an un-demarcated Line of Actual Control (LAC) on the India-Tibet border do not augur well for long-term peace and stability between these two Asian giants. Though the border is relatively stable, a future border war with China, though improbable, cannot be ruled out.

China's carefully orchestrated plan aimed at the strategic encirclement of India is evident from its unjustifiable opposition to India's nuclear weapons programme; its strong military support to the ruling regime in Myanmar; its diabolical assistance to the LTTE in Sri Lanka; its increasing proclivity to build and acquire ports in the Bay of Bengal and the Arabian Sea – the so-called "string of pearls" strategy; its attempts to isolate India in the ASEAN Regional Forum (ARF) and to prevent India's entry to the Shanghai Cooperation Organisation (SCO); and, its relentless efforts to increase its influence in Nepal, Bhutan and Bangladesh.

Clearly, China's growing power and influence in Asia poses a long-term strategic challenge to India as a competing regional power. The 60-year old dispute over Jammu and Kashmir (J&K) continues to bedevil India-Pakistan relations. The Line of Control (LoC) in J&K and the Actual Ground Position Line (AGPL) at Siachen Glacier were perpetual flashpoints and witnessed active military hostilities for most of these 60 years.

Violations of the LoC, such as the intrusions engineered by Pakistan in the Kargil district of J&K in the summer months of 1999, are fraught with danger and have the potential to lead to full-scale conventional conflict. Also, India accuses Pakistan of sponsoring a "proxy war" through terrorist outfits nurtured by the Inter-Services Intelligence (ISI) Directorate in J&K.

With the military continuing to drive from the backseat in Pakistan, the recurrence of such misadventures remains likely, particularly if the domestic political and security situations continue to deteriorate. Pakistan's 450,000 combatant personnel remain India's foremost military threat. Progress on the India-Pakistan Composite Dialogue process has been stalled due to Pakistan's disinclination to bring to justice the perpetrators of the Mumbai terror attacks. The only positive factor is that a mutually respected cease-fire has been in place on the LoC since November 25, 2003.

Though it is an ancient civilisation, India is a young nation state that is still engaged in the process of nation building. This process has been marked by ethnic tensions, fissiparous tendencies and socio-economic challenges. India has been saddled with a long-drawn low level insurgency in J&K due to its inability to fully integrate all parts of the state with the national mainstream.

Failure to find an amicable solution and end the alienation of the people of the Kashmir Valley, in particular, could have widespread repercussions in other parts of the country and in the region. Similarly, several of India's north-eastern states have been in turmoil for many decades due to political and economic neglect, poor governance and, consequently, inadequate socio-economic development. Left Wing Extremism or Maoist terrorism is the latest manifestation of India's internal instability. These internal security challenges are likely to continue to prevail over the next two decades.

The end of the Cold War led to what could be characterised as an era of strategic uncertainty. Defence planning has become more difficult in several ways. The sources and types of conflicts for which planning must be carried out have become more diverse and less predictable even as the number of potential adversaries continues to grow. The range of missions that armed forces need to undertake is expanding to include those likely to be assigned in sub-conventional conflict, including low-intensity border wars and insurgency fuelled by foreign powers. And, the global security agenda has expanded in functional terms.

Yesterday's peripheral challenges such as the security of energy sources and the threat from mass migrations now compete with conventional threats for a share in the defence pie. Systemic changes in the structure of the global economy, communications and military technologies are likely to alter the strategic stakes.

These changes in the security paradigm are changing the strategic terms in which policymakers, military leaders and defence analysts must address long-term defence planning so as to evolve defence capabilities that will be relevant to the emerging threats.

The asymmetric character of contemporary conflict challenges conventional thinking and demands fresh responses. General Rupert Smith has identified six key trends that define modern warfare:1 the growing role of non-state actors as well as multinational forces as combatants; looking for creative new uses for old weapons; emphasis on force protection rather than using force at any cost; the prolonged nature of modern wars; a new focus on winning the hearts and minds of people; and, a shift from absolute objectives to more flexible ones.

He writes that in the Clausewitzian trinity (army, state and people), the balance between the three has changed. "There was a time when armies dominated — as they still do in the country of warlords; later, states were able to command the complete obedience of their people. Now it is the people who are in charge and the strategic objective is their hearts and minds." The aim of this book is to examine the salient issues affecting the recruitment, training and retention of suitable personnel in the Indian armed forces, understanding the linkage between manpower and technology and recommending measures to reduce the cost of manpower in the light of India's strategic environment. The chapter also takes stock of similar re-structuring issues across major Western armies.

MILITARY TECHNOLOGY

The military funding of science has had a powerful transformative effect on the practice and products of scientific research since the early 20th century. Particularly since World War I, advanced science-based technologies have been viewed as essential elements of a successful military. World War I is often called "the chemists' war", both for the extensive use of poison gas and the importance of nitrates and advanced high explosives. Poison gas, beginning in 1915 with chlorine from the powerful German dye industry, was used extensively by the Germans and the British ; over the course of the war, scientists on both sides raced to develop more and more potent chemicals and devise countermeasures against the newest enemy gases. Physicists also contributed to the war effort, developing wireless communication technologies and sound-based methods of detecting U-boats, resulting in the first tenuous long-term connections between academic science and the military.

World War II marked a massive increase in the military funding of science, particularly physics. In addition to the Manhattan Project and the resulting atomic bomb, British and American work on radar was widespread and ultimately highly influential in the course of the war; radar enabled detection of enemy ships and aircraft, as well as the radar-based proximity fuze.

Mathematical cryptography, meteorology, and rocket science were also central to the war effort, with military-funded wartime advances having a significant long-term effect on each discipline. The technologies employed at the end—jet aircraft, radar and proximity fuzes, and the atomic bomb—were radically different from pre-war technology; military leaders came to view continued advances in technology as the critical element for success in future wars. The advent of the Cold War solidified the links between military institutions and academic science, particularly in the United States and the Soviet Union, so that even during a period of nominal peace military funding continued to expand. Funding spread to the social sciences as well as the natural sciences, and whole new fields, such as digital computing, were born of military patronage. Following the end of the Cold War and the dissolution of the Soviet Union, military funding of science has decreased substantially, but much of the American military-scientific complex remains in place. The sheer scale of military funding for science since World War II has instigated a large body of historical literature analyzing the effects of that funding, especially for American science.

Since Paul Forman's 1987 article "Behind quantum electronics: National security as a basis for physical research in the United State, 1940-1960," there has been an ongoing historical debate over precisely how and to what extent military funding affected the course of scientific research and discovery. Forman and others have argued that military funding fundamentally redirected science—particularly physics—toward applied research, and that military technologies predominantly formed the basis for subsequent research even in areas of basic science; ultimately the very culture and ideals of science were colored by extensive collaboration between scientists and military planners. An alternate view has been presented by Daniel Kevles, that while military funding provided many new opportunities for scientists and dramatically expanded the scope of physical research, scientists by-and-large retained their intellectual autonomy.

Science and Military Technology before the Modern Era

While there were numerous instances of military support for scientific work before the 20th century, these were typically isolated instances; knowledge gained from technology was generally far more important for the development of science than scientific knowledge was to technological innovation. Thermodynamics, for example, is a science partly born from military technology: one of the many sources of the first law of thermodynamics was Count Rumford's observation of the heat produced by boring cannon barrels.

Mathematics was important in the development of the Greek catapult and other weapons, but analysis of ballistics was also important for the development of mathematics, while Galileo tried to promote the telescope as a military instrument to the military-minded Republic of Venice before turning it to the skies while seeking the patronage of the Medici court in Florence.

In general, craft-based innovation, disconnected from the formal systems of science, was the key to military technology well into the 19th century.

Even craft-based military technologies were not generally produced by military funding. Instead, craftsmen and inventors developed weapons and military tools independently and actively sought the interest of military patrons afterward. Following the rise of engineering as a profession in the 18th century, governments and military leaders did try to harness the methods of both science and engineering for more specific ends, but frequently without success.

In the decades leading up to the French Revolution, French artillery officers were often trained as engineers, and military leaders from this mathematical tradition attempted to transform the process of weapons manufacture from a craft-based enterprise to an organized and standardized system based on engineering principles and interchangeable parts (pre-dating the work of Eli Whitney in the U.S.).

During the Revolution, even natural scientists participated directly, attempting to create "weapons more powerful than any we possess" to aid the cause of the new French Republic, though there were no means for the revolutionary army to fund such work. Each of these efforts, however, was ultimately unsuccessful in producing militarily useful results. A slightly different outcome came from the longitude prize of the 18th century, offered by the British government for an accurate method of determining a ship's longitude at sea (essential for the safe navigation of the powerful British navy): intended to promote—and financially reward—a scientific solution, it was instead won by a scientific outsider, the clockmaker John Harrison.

However, the naval utility of astronomy did help increase the number of capable astronomers and focus research on developing more powerful and versatile instruments.

Through the 19th century, science and technology grew closer together, particularly through electrical and acoustic inventions and the corresponding mathematical theories. The late 19th and early 20th centuries witnessed a trend toward military mechanization, with the advent of repeating rifles with smokeless powder, long-range artillery, high explosives, machine guns, and mechanized transport along with telegraphic and later wireless battlefield communication.

Still, independent inventors, scientists and engineers were largely responsible for these drastic changes in military technology (with the exception of the development of battleships, which could only have been created through organized large-scale effort).

CHANGING GEARS A SOFT POWER APPROACH?

India's neighbours occupy much of its attention in its overall foreign policy dilemmas. Except Bhutan and Maldives, India is facing security challenges from all its neighbours. Most of these challenges are traditional in nature; however non-traditional challenges such as environmental issue are also prominently emerging in their security discourse. The foreign policy strategy of India is fundamentally aimed to protect its core national interests; safeguarding territorial integrity and sovereignty, and economic prosperity. Ensuring these interests has been the principal foreign policy agenda for successive governments post-independence. Though the tools and approach used to achieve the desired foreign policy objectives have varied.

For instance, Nehru attempted to demonstrate India's leadership at regional as well global level by projecting Gandhian ideals of non-violence and socialistic values of peaceful co-existence despite India's feeble position in the community of nations. This could also be seen as India's soft-power projection in the region. Unfortunately, this neither changed India's image in its neighbourhood nor did it help to secure a permanent membership in the UNSC.

Realizing the fact that ethics and values serve little in foreign policy in a rapidly changing global security environment, Indira Gandhi brazenly adopted a pragmatic approach towards the neighbours. The liberation of Bangladesh in 1970 through direct Indian military intervention and subsequent creation of a nation in South Asia demonstrated India's ability to exercise hard-power in its foreign policy options. Since then, military power has been an indispensible component of India's foreign policy even though it incurs huge drain on its overall GDP. Alas, India's national security challenges such as cross-border terrorism and illegal migration have not been culminated despite piling up of weapons and building arsenal, thus making hard power options futile in persuading its neighbours to act cooperatively.

The end of cold war, which heralded the rise of multipolar world order, dramatically altered India's foreign policy priorities followed by rapid liberalization. Inspired by Joseph Nye's idea of 'Soft-Power', India began to embrace its neighbours with soft-power skills which involved striking a common cord with neighbours on religion, culture, ethnicity and linguistic basis. This realisation was reflected in the famous Gujral Doctrine, the first official Neighbourhood Policy, which sets out five principles to guide India's foreign policy towards its immediate neighbours.

The most convincing reason for this shift from hard-power to soft-power approach was the growing Chinese influence in its neighbourhood. Yet, the lack of a comprehensive neighbourhood policy strategy and dearth of broad understanding of security challenges blurred India's prospect to become an effective regional power. The big question now is how soft power works in India's neighbourhood policy? Sri Lanka can be a best case to examine this question due to two specific reasons: India's hard power approach towards Sri Lanka in the past had been unsuccessful and counter-productive and the new approach is focused on soft power resources.

INDIA AND THE BALANCE OF POWER

After disappointing itself for decades, India is now on the verge of becoming a great power. The world started to take notice of India's rise when New Delhi signed a nuclear pact with President George W. Bush in July 2005, but that breakthrough is only one dimension of the dramatic transformation of Indian foreign policy that has taken place since the end of the Cold War. After more than a half century of false starts and unrealized potential, India is now emerging as the swing state in the global balance of power. In the coming years, it will have an opportunity to shape outcomes on the most critical issues of the twenty-first century: the construction of Asian stability, the political modernization of the greater Middle East, and the management of globalization.

Although India's economic growth, its new foreign policy has been less noted. Unlike their U.S. counterparts, Indian leaders do not announce new foreign policy doctrines. Nonetheless, in recent years, they have worked relentlessly to elevate India's regional and international standing and to increase its power.

New Delhi has made concerted efforts to reshape its immediate neighborhood, find a modus vivendi with China and Pakistan (its two regional rivals), and reclaim its standing in the "near abroad": parts of Africa, the Persian Gulf, Central and Southeast Asia, and the Indian Ocean region. At the same time, it has expanded relations with the existing great powers — especially the United States.

India is arriving on the world stage as the first large, economically powerful, culturally vibrant, multiethnic, multireligious democracy outside of the geographic West. As it rises, India has the potential to become a leading member of the "political West" and to play a key role in the great political struggles of the next decades. Whether it will, and how soon, depends above all on the readiness of the Western powers to engage India on its own terms.

MILITARY POWER PROJECTION

To some, the phrase "power projection" suggests imposing regime change on a state far away from home for strategic gain. In this view, a prototypical example might be Operation Iraqi Freedom, the 2003 U.S.-led invasion of Iraq. While such a conceptualization captures some key elements of power projection, it is far too narrow. The U.S. Department of Defense (DoD) defines power projection much more broadly as being "[t]he ability of a nation to apply all or some of its elements of national power—political, economic, informational, or military—to rapidly and effectively deploy and sustain forces in and from multiple dispersed locations to respond to crises, to contribute to deterrence, and to enhance regional stability."

Focusing specifically on the final element of national power in the DoD's definition—the use of military tools—it is possible to disaggregate military power projection into nine different aspects based on the political goals being sought and the level of force employed. Four of these relate to the employment of "soft" military power (securing sea lanes of communication, non-combatant evacuation operations, humanitarian relief, and peacekeeping), and five are primarily concerned with "hard" military power (showing the flag, compellence/deterrence, punishment, armed intervention, and conquest).

Soft Military Power Projection

Securing Sea Lanes of Communication. The protection of shipping lanes from attack by hostile states or irregular threats. As the Indian Navy's maritime doctrine notes, trade is increasingly critical to the Indian economy, which makes the protection of the sea lanes transiting the Indian Ocean a significant priority. Following the attacks of September 11, 2001, the Indian Navy played a high-profile role in escorting U.S. shipping through the Straits of Malacca.

More recently, Indian naval vessels have been deployed to the Gulf of Aden, where they have thwarted several attempted hijackings by pirates.

Non-combatant Evacuation Operations. The evacuation of Indian or friendly third country civilians from a foreign country when they are endangered by war or civil unrest. For example, during Operation Sukoon (Urdu: Relief) the navy evacuated 2,280 Indian, Sri Lankan, and Nepalese civilians from Lebanon ahead of the 2006 Israeli-Hizbollah War. Several orders of magnitude larger was the airlift of over 100,000 Indians from Iraq and Kuwait ahead of the 1991 Gulf War.

Humanitarian Relief. The use of military forces abroad to assist in the aftermath of a natural disaster.

Following the 2004 Asian tsunami, the Indian Navy mobilized 32 ships and over 20,000 naval personnel to evacuate casualties, as well as provide emergency sources of power and water to the peoples of Sri Lanka, the Maldives, Indonesia, Thailand, and Malaysia.

Peacekeeping. Military operations designed to support diplomatic efforts to reach a long-term political settlement to an ongoing dispute. India has been one of the most significant contributors to U.N. peacekeeping missions. As of 2009, the Indian Army had roughly 8,000 personnel deployed in the Democratic Republic of Congo, Lebanon, East Timor, the Ivory Coast, and the Golan Heights.

Hard Military Power Projection

Showing the Flag. The symbolic deployment of military forces to a region to demonstrate political interest, resolve, or willingness to take more forceful military action. For example, in June 1987 the Indian Air Force violated Sri Lankan airspace when it undertook Operation Poomalai (Tamil: Garland), the forced airdrop of relief supplies to ethnic Tamils during the siege of Jaffna. This action sent a clear message to the government in Colombo about New Delhi's desire to see a negotiated end to the conflict and helped lead to the signing of the Indo-Sri Lankan accord. More recently, the Indian Navy has undertaken several high-profile deployments to the South China Sea and the Persian Gulf, which have been interpreted as important signals of Indian interest in these regions.

Compellence and Deterrence. The use or the threat of military force against another state to induce it into or dissuade it from pursuing a given policy. In this form, power projection acts as a diplomatic tool, attempting to influence the decision-making process and calculus of foreign actors. For example, the governor of East Pakistan's decision to surrender to India in 1971 has been attributed to the compellence effect of well-timed air strikes on his residence in Dhaka at the very moment he was conducting a crisis response meeting. In the same conflict, the destruction of East Pakistani airfields after the air force in the territory had been attritted was an exercise in deterrence by denial that sought to preclude intervention by an outside power.

Punishment. The punitive use of force against another state in response to its pursuit of a given policy. Aside from limited punitive strikes on Pakistani posts across the Line of Control in Kashmir in response to militant activity (not an expeditionary use of force), punishment has not been widely employed by the Indian military.

Armed Intervention. The forcible movement of military units into another nation's territory to influence the internal affairs of the target country, short of outright conquest. Historical examples in India's immediate neighborhood range in size from the 1988 deployment of a parachute battalion to the Maldives (Operation Cactus) to put down a coup to the 1971 intervention in East Pakistan by three corps of the Indian Army to assist guerillas fighting for independence.

Conquest. The offensive use of military assets to forcibly occupy non-contiguous territory controlled or claimed by another state. This has not been an aspect of power projection pursued by independent India, although at the time some observers believed that the use of military forces in Hyderabad (Operation Polo), Goa (Operation Vijay), and elsewhere as part of the post-Independence consolidation of the Indian Union was "an act of military aggression and conquest."

Given this disaggregation, it is clear that power projection is a much broader concept than mere invasion seeking regime change. Military assets, depending on how they are employed, can advance a state's foreign policy goals by facilitating the projection of either hard or soft forms of military power. Moreover, since Independence, India has employed at least seven, and perhaps eight, of the nine aspects of military power projection.

6

Defence Budget

DEFENCE BUDGETING OF INDIA

The Union Budget 2010-11 has raised the defence outlays to Rs. 1,47,344 crore (US $31.9 billion). This represents a growth rate of a mere 3.98 per cent, in nominal terms (or 0.3 per cent in real terms) over the previous years' allocation of Rs. 1,41,703 crore, and far below the 34 per cent nominal increase witnessed in the budget for 2009-10.

The sudden dip in the defence budget's growth rate follows two related steps taken by the government. While the first one is related to the government's resolve about fiscal consolidation, the second is on account of the acceptance by the government of the recommendation of the Thirteenth Finance Commission (TFC). This commentary analyses the latest defence budget as well as the likely impact of TFC's recommendation on India's future defence spending.

INDIA'S DEFENCE BUDGET 2017-18: AN ANALYSIS

While presenting the Union Budget 2017-18 on February 01, 2017, the Finance Minister (FM), Arun Jaitley, allocated Rs. 3,59,854 crore (US$ 53.5 billion) to the Ministry of Defence (MoD). As in his previous budget, the FM also made certain changes in the format of the defence Demand for Grants (under which defence money is distributed among the armed forces and other defence agencies), bringing further complexity to the task of estimating the various heads that make up India's official defence budget.

The complexity apart, the bigger question that faces the defence community is whether the latest allocation is adequate to meet the security needs of the country. This *Issue Brief* examines the latest defence allocation in the light of its possible impact on modernisation and operational preparedness of the defence forces. It however, begins with a macro survey of Indian economy and the context of the Union Budget, both of which have a direct bearing on defence.

Macroeconomic Scenario and the Context of the Union Budget 2017-18

Despite a gloomy global economic environment, the Indian economy continues to a bright spot, with the initial estimates of the Gross Domestic Product (GDP) showing a growth of over seven per cent per annum for three consecutive years between 2014-15 and 2016-17.

The growth momentum is likely to be sustained at around 6.75-7.5 per cent in 2017-18, as projected by the latest Economic Survey. Besides the GDP growth, the economy has also witnessed other robust macro-economic indices pertaining to inflation, fiscal consolidation, current account deficit, rupee-dollar exchange rate, foreign exchange reserves and foreign investment inflows.

The impressive macro fundamentals notwithstanding, the Indian economy is widely perceived to be growing at much slower than its growth potential of 8-10 per cent. There is a growing concern that the sluggish recovery of world economy and recent anti-globalisation tendencies seen in the West could affect India's effort to push for an export-led economic development.

Back home, the subdued corporate investment and depressing private final consumption expenditure are major markers of concern which, if left unaddressed, would likely halt the growth momentum. It is in this context that the Union

Budget has focussed on a government-led investment approach to spur the domestic economy.

Investment on infrastructure, rural economy and the like have been the primary focus of the Union Budget 2017-18. The emphasis on these sectors is such that the government has deviated from its promised fiscal consolidation path to provide extra resources on these fronts.

More significantly, the deviation has come even after a hefty 17 per cent growth in the estimated gross tax receipts. From the MoD's point of view, however, the Union Budget 2017-18 is a missed opportunity as neither the fiscal expansion nor the revenue buoyancy has resulted in a significant hike of resources.

Defence Budget: Reconciling the Figures

While presenting the Union Budget to the Parliament, the FM stated that "[f]or Defence expenditure excluding pensions, I have provided a sum of Rs. 2,74,114 crores including Rs. 86,488 crores for Defence capital." The FM's overall stated figure of Rs. 2,74,114 is, however, not what the defence ministry considers as India's official defence budget.

An attempt is made in Table below to reconcile the defence-related allocations provided in the Union Budget with the traditional format used by thc MoD and compare it with the previous years' allocation and expenditure. Using the MoD format, the defence budget for 2017-18 amounts to Rs. 2,62,390 crore.

The difference in amount (between FM's and MoD's figures) of Rs.11,724 crore is allocated under what is considered Defence (Civil Estimates) which, inclusive of defence pension of Rs. 85,740 crore, does not form part of the official defence budget.

A noticeable aspect of the Table below is the underutilisation of capital allocations provided in the 2016-17 budget, resulting in a surrender of Rs. 6,970 crore (8.1 per cent). The surrendered amount has largely been absorbed in the revenue expenditure which has increased from its original estimates by Rs. 5,876 crore.

Table : Official Defence Budget, 2016-17 and 2017-18

	Revenue Expenditure (Rs. in Crore)	Capital Expenditure (Rs. in Crore)	Total (Rs. in Crore)
2015-16	145937	79958	225895
2016-17 (BE)	162759	86340	249099
2016-17 (RE)	168635	79370	248005
2017-18 (BE)	175861	86529	262390

Note: BE: Budget Estimate; RE: Revised Estimate. Figures for 2015-16 are actual expenditure. Rs. 1.0 crore = Rs. 10 million = US$ 148772 (alternatively, $1 million = Rs. 6.7 crore) as per the average exchange rate for the first 10 months of 2016-17.

Defence Budget: The Highlights and the Major Trends

Table below provides comparative statistics of defence budget and related figures for 2016-17 and 2017-18.

The noticeable feature of the table is the further decline in the defence budget's share in both central government expenditure and the GDP. With a share of 1.56 per cent of the estimated GDP of 2017-18, the defence budget is the lowest since 1956-57.

Table : Comparative Statistics of Defence Budget: 2016-17 & 2017-18

	2016-17	2017-18
Defence Budget (Rs. in Crore)	249099.0	262389.8
Growth of Defence Budget (%)	0.96	5.34
Revenue Expenditure (Rs. in Crore)	162759.0	175861
Growth of Revenue Expenditure (%)	6.98	8.05
Share of Revenue Expenditure in Defence Budget (%)	**65.3**	**67.0**
Capital Expenditure (Rs. in Crore)	86340.0	86528.7
Growth of Capital Expenditure (%)	-8.7	0.22
Share of Capital Expenditure in Defence Budget (%)	34.7	33.0
Capital Acquisition (Rs. in Crore)	70000	69783*

Growth of Capital Acquisition (%)	-9.4	-0.3
Share of Defence Budget in GDP (%)	1.65	1.56
Share of Defence Budget in Central Government Expenditure (%)	12.6	12.2
Defence Pension	82332.66	85740.00
MoD's Budget (Rs. in Crore)	340921.98	359854.12
Growth in MoD's Budget (%)	9.95	5.55
Share of MoD Budget in GDP (%)	2.26	2.14
Share of MoD Budget in Central Government Expenditure (%)	17.24	16.76

Note: *: approximate figure.

Another major feature of Table above is the further increase in the share of the revenue expenditure in the total defence budget. The increase is primarily due to the hike in the manpower cost of the armed forces, which accounts for over 83 per cent (or Rs. 11,071 crore) of the overall growth of Rs. 13,291 crore in the defence budget. It is significant to note that the manpower driven defence budget is not unique to 2017-18. In the last several years, it has been a recurring feature with a debilitating effect on two vital elements of the defence budget: revenue stores and capital modernization which together play a vital role in the operational preparedness of the armed forces. The combined share of these two elements has declined from 55 per cent in 2007-08 to 40 per cent in 2016-17. This does not augur well, especially when there exists a huge void in India' defence preparedness, and the armed forces have grave shortages in many areas ranging from ammunition, assault rifles, bullet-proof jackets, night fighting-devices to howitzers, missiles, helicopters, fighters and warships. Needless to say, for adequate defence preparedness, the present ratio needs to change for the better, for which allocation under revenue stores and capital modernisation needs to be augmented substantially.

INDIA'S DEFENCE BUDGET 2008-09

Union Budget 2008-09 has allocated Rs. 105,600 crores for India's Defence. Crossing the one lakh barrier for the first time, and accounting for nearly 14.1 per cent of total central government expenditure, the Defence Budget looks quite impressive. But when seen in the context of India's expanding interests, this allocation remains as moderate as ever. Moreover, an in-depth analysis reveals problems in defence and budgetary management, none of which show signs of abating.

For fiscal year 2008-09, India's defence allocation has increased by 10 per cent over the previous year's allocation of Rs. 96, 000 crores, and by little over 14 per cent compared to last year's revised allocation of Rs. 92,500 cores. In the last five years, the defence budget has increased by nearly 37 per cent from Rs. 77,000 crores in 2004-05, which represents over 8 per cent growth per annum. Notwithstanding the current allocation and growth of the defence budget over the years, the question remains whether India's defence spending is compatible with its economic and security interests.

A brief survey of the Indian economy reveals its great potential and global reach. The economy registered an average growth of nearly 8 per cent a year during the 10th Plan, and seems set to continue the growth momentum in the 11th Plan period. What is more important is that much of this growth is driven by the external sector, mainly growing trade with the rest of world. India' total trade (exports plus imports) has increased by more than five times in the last decade and now accounts for over 35 per cent of its gross domestic product (GDP). This testifies to the fact that the economy is much more globalized than, say, 10 years ago when trade accounted for less than 20 per cent of GDP. The growth of the Indian economy and its global character has also infused confidence among international investors who see India as an attractive place for investment. The growing inflow of foreign direct investment is testimony to this fact. This process of greater integration with, and concomitant acquisition of greater stakes in, the international economic system is likely to continue in the coming decades. Military capability is necessary, for instance, to protect the country's sea lines of communication – 90 per cent India's trade by volume and 70 per cent in value moves by sea.

A survey of the regional military balance shows India's unfavourable position vis-à-vis its neighbours. China's relentless military modernisation, backed by double-digit growth in military expenditure for more than a decade, is a case in point. Its military modernisation, exemplified by the recent demonstration of IT-and space-based capability, has expanded its military reach from the traditional battlefield into the 'space and cyber-space domains'. This is besides the other 'anti-access/ area denial capabilities' developed through a range of modern weapons systems that, according to a 2008 Pentagon Report, have left even the United States worried. Given the long-standing India-China border dispute, China's war preparations for winning "local wars under conditions of informationalization" together with its massive infrastructure development along the border, have certainly given it a definite military advantage.

At the same time, the sharpening of Pakistan's armoury, especially with the help of US military aid, is no less worrying. Since 9/11, Pakistan has received more than US $10 billion worth of military assistance from the United States. Such assistance, which includes F-16 fighter aircraft, air-to-air missiles, cluster bombs, air defence radars and surveillance technologies, has direct security implications for India, since it narrows the advantage in conventional warfare that has been in India's favour.

The moderate nature of India's defence spending, the question arises as to how much India should spend on defence. Though an answer lies in a complex set of issues ranging from the nature of threats, the fiscal health of the government and the kind of diplomacy it chooses to pursue, yet some statistical references can be drawn from other countries that are devoted to building or have attained world-class military capability.

While the United States, with a military budget (for Fiscal Year 2009) of more than $700 billion and a share of nearly 50 per cent of global military expenditure, remains the largest military spender in modern times, India's defence budget estimated roughly at $26.5 billion for 2008-09 constitutes a mere two per cent of the global total.

In terms of proportion of economic resources devoted to defence, India's latest defence budget, which accounts for 1.99 per cent of expected GDP in the coming Fiscal Year, is less than the global average of around 2.5 per cent, and lags behind America's 4.1 per cent and Pakistan's 3.5 per cent. In absolute terms, India's defence spending, ranked 10th in the list of major spenders in the world, constitutes a fraction of the American military budget and less than half of China's 'under-reported' but official defence budget of $57.22 billion for 2008.

Given the higher proportion of economic resources being devoted to defence in these countries, should India raise its defence allocation, say, to 3 per cent of GDP? The answer lies in the adequacy of the present budget to meet the country's security requirements. As the evidence shows, the proportion of financial allocations made available to the defence establishment vis-à-vis its demand has increased to nearly 95 per cent in recent years, even though its share in GDP has decreased significantly in the same period.

This indicates that there is hardly any shortage of funds to meet the defence establishment's financial requirements irrespective of its share in GDP. In any case, the fixing of defence allocation to a certain portion of GDP is not theoretically a sound proposition, given the volatilities in economic growth rates and threat perceptions in the long run. What is more important is that the security requirements, which ultimately get translated into the annual defence budget, need to be adequately financed.

A close look at the formulation of the Indian defence budget, however, reveals little evidence of the country's security concerns being properly addressed or financed. The annual defence budget, which follows from the Defence Capability Plan, 15-year Long Term Integrated Perspective Plan, 5-year Services Capital Acquisition Plan and Annual Acquisition Plan, is handicapped in terms of catering to the true security needs of the country because of the poor formulation and execution of, and inordinate delays in, planning. In other words, the security needs of the country are poorly reflected in the budget, and the capability requirements of the Armed Forces either get delayed or come to possess a short shelf-life. As a result, the Armed Forces are under-prepared to meet any worsening in the security scenario as well as technological upgrades by adversaries.

Another major problem in defence management, as reflected time and again in successive budgets, is the inability of the defence establishment to fully utilise the allocated funds, especially those meant for the modernisation of the country's security infrastructure.

Though the modernisation expenditure, credited under the 'capital expenditure' of the budget, has increased considerably from nearly 25 per cent in 2000-01 to over 45 per cent in 2008-09, the problem of timely utilisation of allotted resources continues to haunt the defence Services.

As the latest budget reveals, out of Rs. 41,922 crores earmarked for 'capital expenditure' for 2007-08, Rs. 4412 crores, or over 10 per cent, remained unutilised. These unutilised funds, which mean opportunities lost or delayed in acquiring needed capability, have become a regular feature despite reforms in the acquisition structures/procedures.

An examination of the capital acquisition structure/procedure reveals several weaknesses in the system: poor planning; deficiency in formulation of qualitative requirements; lack of motivation for indigenisation efforts; single-vendor approach towards selection of weapon systems; poor human resource and information management; 'large number of submission and approval points'; and 'multiple agencies with dispersed centres of accountability'.

The cumulative effect of all this is a gap in the capabilities sought by the Armed Forces; under-optimisation of the huge resources spent over the years; and a poor self-reliance index.

The Indian acquisition system defies the best international practices prevalent in counties such as France, the UK and Australia. In contrast to the Indian system, the acquisition process in these countries is undertaken by an integrated body encompassing all the stakeholders – Armed Forces, Industry,

R&D organisation, quality assurance organisation, civilian bureaucrats and other skilled workforce.

This integrated body is responsible for all acquisition functions, right from the planning level to the disposal of equipment, and thus owns the responsibility of the whole life-cycle process of any equipment or system. The advantage of this integrated body lies in its single-point accountability to provide timely solutions to the Armed Forces' requirements and, in the process, it provides the best value for money and also a thrust towards self-reliance. Keeping the above merits of the integrated acquisition organisation in mind, India could possibly adopt a similar institutional arrangement for expediting its acquisition process.

As regards self-reliance in critical military technology and production of advanced weapons systems, India, despite decades of effort, has remained import-dependent. The poor self-reliance index of 30 to 35 per cent against the target of 70 per cent by the end of 10th Plan testifies to this fact. Inadequate budgetary provision for defence research and development (R&D) is the major reason behind India's poor defence industrial production and heavy outflow of financial resources to foreign suppliers. Overdependence on foreign suppliers not only has its costs and industrial disadvantages but also provides opportunities for corruption and delays in procurement.

The present allocation of Rs. 6,486.35 crores for defence R&D constitutes a mere 6.1 per cent of the defence budget. In contrast, major military powers spend a much higher proportion of their budgets on military R&D. For instance, the United States spends around 16 per cent of its defence budget on R&D. American dominance in military technology and production of sophisticated weapons systems is the result of higher allocation, concerted efforts in the right direction and involvement of industries in research activities.

In India, almost the entire defence R&D activity is undertaken by the DRDO (Defence Research and Development Organisation), with little budgetary or technological support from the defence industry, which largely comprises of state-owned Ordnance Factories and Defence Public Sector Undertakings (DPSUs). The private sector, which is a key contributor to civilian technology and a key driver of economic growth since liberalisation began in the early nineties, is still kept out from contributing to military technological advancement.

The absence of R&D efforts by the defence industry has forced the DRDO to concentrate on every aspect of military technology, many of which could be undertaken by the industry itself. As a result, a very small proportion – 8 to 10 per cent of R&D budget – is percolated down for fundamental research. If India wants to be self-reliant in critical military technology and defence production, it needs to enhance its R&D spending. At the same time, increased allocations need to be channelled in the proper direction, and industry, including in the private sector, needs to be engaged in R&D activities so as to make DRDO focus on key and critical technologies.

Considering its economic and security imperatives, India's defence spending is not only moderate but also fails to capture the true security needs of the nation. The defence budget, because of the problems in the acquisition system, is constrained to translate budgetary resources into required military capability in the given time and at optimal cost. To augment defence spending, what India needs is an efficient defence planning mechanism, backed by an integrated acquisition organisation. Also, given its poor self-reliance index, India needs to enhance R&D spending. Enhanced budgetary allocations should be channelled in the right direction, with the industry (including private sector) taking a lead in technology development.

BUDGETING PROCESS AND SOME ISSUES

This budget as usual was prepared under limited space available to Finance Minister and his team the current political equation with Left-parties sharing the policy platform with congress. In some way it has kept check on runaway liberalization euphoria, which has till date proved to be anti-poor, if we go by various indices of socioeconomic welfare and growth. The same old beaten practice of cut and paste technique and lowering taxes on a few things and then increase on some other things has been adopted. Nowhere concept of zero-base budgeting, setting growth targets and addressing distortion in economic and social administration systems is evident. This way you can always favour 2-3 industries by turn every year and collect moneybags for party funds and favours to politicians and their cronies.

Taking past budget as a base and then trying to mobilize more taxes is an idiotic approach. It is not 'budgeting' as a policy instrument. It is merely routine accounting of {Munims}. There is hardly anything radically different in 2006 budget. I don't understand what government wants to achieve by varying taxes on umbrella and lipsticks? Is this the job of Union government? How it affects economy and productivity of country? Does it really matter if excise duty is 4% or8% on lipsticks or writing chalks? What government should do is have simple three slabs 4 % 8% and 10% in all kinds of indirect taxes and duties and straight two slabs of 10% and 20% in Income tax with dividing income line of Rs 1 million per annum. All incentives and rebates should be withdrawn except for Provident funds and pension plans for social security and interest paid on housing purchase. We are not addressing viability of a product industry by building its fundamental strengths and removing structural weaknesses, but merely through tax regulation of government by giving tax relief and grants. This is old and outdated model of economics management and has no relevance left. Politicians are still functioning in 1956 mode. In fact all tax manuals should be 4-5 page booklets with simple procedures and automated formats so that corrupt tax officials are taken out from scene and put on monitoring and recovery process in cases of tax evaders. They should be given tough targets and thrown out if not successful.

Middle class is again under attack this time through different route. Service taxes have been hiked which is bad decision.12% is too high a rate. You can't tax everything. Tomorrow you will tax housemaids and tutorial services and public toilets. It is absurd and stupid. It will result in now more tax evasion. It is unjustified too.{now 95 services will be under service tax-existing 81+15 new proposed including ATM withdrawal}. The argument to tax ATM use is bizarre and reflects old mindset of bureaucrats to try to regulate systems through taxation route. It is odd that you have to pay for taking out your own cash put in banks at virtual no returns on savings bank. Banks can charge overheads but how government can tax this? An average Indian pays out almost 60% of his expenditure amount on account of various taxes only. So he gets merely 40% component as real value i.e. labour, material, design and benefits of products required in his average life routine. India is one of the most unproductive, mismanaged and highly taxed country. Still the funds collected by government annually in range of just Rs 4 lac-crores {INR 4000 Billions or US $ 82 Billion} is just peanuts.

This works out to only INR 3800/-per year per citizen. What any Government can do by this meager amount and plan for citizens? And imagine almost 50% out of this being siphoned off or spent on government officials and clerks themselves, their salaries, perquisites and pensions etc. All welfare schemes are meant for public servants only and not for people whom they are to serve.

Average Per capita income of a government (public servant in India currently) is 10 times that of per capita income of India. This is ridiculous. Is this country working to feed corrupt, unproductive public servants? 98% of Indian people are feeding a package of luxury to just 2% civil servants at cost of their two time meals. There is need to contain the rot of corruption, slim down government machinery and freeze their salaries and perks which are umpteen numbers. The productivity of public servants is very poor and they are generally corrupt and misbehaved because of job security and lack of accountability. This is anti thesis in model of democracy.

Why government has so small collection? Reason is simple-Mass scale rampant tax evasion and parallel economy running in country. Actually India's GDP is at least double of official figures {may be close to three times}. This has direct impact on inflation, hidden currency circulation, *havala* transactions and pressure on resources. People who consume most services actually pay least as percent of their real income. Widespread theft of basic services and energy is causing havoc in economic and social welfare planning. Only middle class is squeezed out every year more and more.

Politicians are party to this game. Income gap is increasing between rich and poor. Prostitution, illegal affairs and now organized crimes are increasing in bigger cities and also small too, just because cost of living has gone up tremendously and there are virtually no jobs. Police force is totally criminalized and ineffective reduced to brokerage centres. Over last 15 years of so-called reforms and competition being encouraged, the prices of general use household items and even simple OTC medicines have gone up by in at least 3-5 times range excepting for auto and electronic goods, meaning average 20% annual escalation in Consumer prices. And every year government data lie about actual inflation rate.

Against this double-digit inflation rate we have fixed 6% FDR rate and are reducing Provident fund interest thereby impoverishing old citizens who will die of deprivation and penury. There is no social security net in India. Government is virtually forcing people to divert to stock markets whose operations are highly shady at the moment and illogically elevated prices are ruling in stock markets. These prices defy all theories and concepts. Greed and manipulation is behind this. Mutual Funds are dumping common men's money there. Who is going to loose? Warning signals are clear.

The budget is not at all a long term or even mid-term planning document. It is based on very poor intellectual and expertise inputs. Problems like employment generation, increasing of productivity in economy, investment in long overdue judicial reforms and expansion, social security schemes like old age homes, effective logistics for commodities and goods distribution and storage facilities and a good infrastructure have not been addressed. India badly needs large number of decentralized new townships that are self contained with housing, hospitals, utilities, business centres and industries to release pressure on real estate and bring down soaring prices of land. Where black money is dumped too. Housing loans should be provided at low interest rates of 7-8% to encourage people to invest in housing and bring down prices of houses and commercial property. Stamp duties are too high in States forcing people to convert property into black assets. But knowingly politicians continue this.

Higher education is unnecessarily under control of State governments whereas most universities should now be privatized with well-defined UGC aid criteria, tighter quality control by setting up autonomous college councils and fixing of fair fees by an empowered panel in Ministry of HRD for private sector to meet expenses of quality education and seriously enter here. Same way allocation of funds in absolute terms for the schooling sector is peanuts despite charging of education *cess*. The biggest drain is government salaries and perquisites on unproductive, corrupt and unfit employees recruited by bribes, political connections and caste and reservations basis. This is of immense concern. Coupled with corruption in bureaucracy and siphoning off of almost 50% of public expenditures to the coffers of politicians, bureaucrats, engineers and contractors, hardly anything is left for actual public investment and welfare. Some new approach to public administration system coupled with fast automation and slimming down of civil services with moderate salaries to them should be implemented. There is need to tame corruption in civil services and defense services too. Defense outlay should be reduced by India and Pakistan sitting together and resolving issues. Education, healthcare, social security and basic services are lacking seriously in the country. We are moving towards chaos and crisis after about a decade's time. India is going to be largest polluting nation including local colony level pollution. There is going to be acute shortage of housing, land, water and electricity.

Selling cheap cars is not priority of this nation, nor to sell mobile phones and boast about highest growth rate of this sector in world. This is idiotic. These sectors are a liability and expenditure of resources with shortage of petroleum. In a country Where 1.5 crores people are added every year and you go and fight in WTO for Agriculture Market Access for exports of agro-goods, you should be talking about agriculture growth rate and not auto-sector and electronic equipment growth rate. Condition of agriculture in India is pathetic. The growth rate is too low. Farm productivity is poor. Basic commodities are not available to poor citizens and not at all affordable. What you will export?

India has no petroleum. So expansion of auto sector is foolish. Instead we should focus on mass rapid transport and decentralization of self-contained townships in massive drive to reduce land scarcity, which is causing meteoric, rises in property.

Basic and radical reforms are required to make country a healthy society to live where people feel safe, get two times square meals, have opportunities for employment and where honest can work productively Nothing of this sort has been addressed in the mere accounting jugglery of figures called Union budget. This certainly is not budgeting. I fail to understand why so many rebates and clauses are there in all tax manuals. Why can't they have simply a 4-5-page manual with simple procedures and all types of taxes pegged below 10% cap? No one wants to pay taxes in two digit rates? It is psychological barrier and there is no need for high taxes. But then how black money will be generated, how politicians and corrupt bureaucrats will thrive. From 1991 to 2005,economic planning and public administration in India are more or less failure. Current budget is on beaten track and will lead to more misery to people in coming times. It is mediocre exercise without application of brain and not with good intents and future focus.

Conclusions: The budget document should first list budgeting premises, the indicators used and the targets of growth and reforms set for next 5 and 10 years period, shortcomings identified in economy and the methods of budgeting adopted so people can critically evaluate proposals after approving the budgeting premises of government. Economic survey is not adequate document for this purpose and why it is put only one day in advance? It should come out at least 30 days in advance for people and experts to digest and comment and send budgetary proposals. Finance minister and his team should not think that they have got a unilateral license to impose whatever they think good or right just because they have been elected and empowered to do this. They are answerable to people and should consult in major issues before bringing out laws and budgets. This is how democracy should function. Indian politicians and bureaucrats are still living in British colonial era just mentally replacing British and acting like them instead. That is how an IPS or IAS behaves when you visit him or her. Arrogant, superior, elite and unaccountable with little indications of humility and realization that s/he is public servants and paid by visitors to work for their welfare and for general service of humanity. Their only qualification is that they have slogged and passed one UPSC examination with little proven background. It is imperative to reduce Government establishment expenses of union and state governments to less than 10% of their annual budget or 2% of India's GDP. It is much more directly and indirectly. In fact corrupt nexus of Businessmen-politicians and bureaucrats drains off 50% of India's official GDP.

Citizens' satisfaction and feedback survey on an ongoing basis through Internet portals: In the end I would suggest FM to come out next year with Draft budget after economic survey of India and circulate it. Ministry of Finance or Planning Commission should setup a portal where public suggestions and opinion about draft budget should be invited. These information and objections should be compiled and then incorporated in Final Budget document.

Citizen's satisfaction survey should be started in India for all major government services including police and judiciary as is done in several countries like US, Canada, Australia,

Singapore to get broad public feedback about required reforms rather than from only a handful of psuedo-experts and opinion makers in power corridors.

MAKE IN INDIA AND DEFENCE PRODUCTION

Unlike in the previous budget, the Union Budget has not provided any specific incentives to push the Make in India initiative in the defence sector, although some industry-wide proposals have been promised. Among others, the government has promised to reduce income tax from present 30 per cent to 25 per cent for Micro, Small and Medium Enterprises (MSMEs) with an annual turnover of upto Rs. 50 crore. This is likely to benefit some 6000 MSMEs which are presently supplying parts, components and sub-systems to players like DRDO, Defence Public Sector Undertakings, OFs and the large private companies.

The lack of any specific incentive for the defence industry may be a source of disappointment, as industry has repeatedly demanded certain concessions which are currently extended to other sectors. In the Union Budget itself, the FM extended the 'Infrastructure Status' to the 'Affordable Housing', sector, allowing the industry in that sector to avail certain tax-related benefits. Needless to say, Infrastructure Status is one of several demands long demanded by the defence industry.

Within the defence budget, however, there has been a small allocation of Rs. 44.63 crore made for prototype development under the 'Make' procedures which have recently been revised by the MoD and some 23 projects have been identified for execution. Of the total amount, Rs. 30.08 crore is earmarked for Army and the balance Rs. 14.55 crore for the Air Force.

Conclusion

The meagre increase of five per cent in the official defence budget is grossly inadequate especially in view of the vast voids existing in military capability and the diminished and incremental effect on modernisation and operational preparedness. There is a need to augment rcsources substantially, particularly under two critical heads of the defence budget – stores and capital procurement – which have come under severe pressure in the last several years with a huge negative consequence on India's defence preparedness.

From the MoD's perspective, while the demand for higher allocations is a genuine one, it must also be fully geared up to utilise the available resources in a time-bound manner. There is hardly any merit in asking for more resources while the present capacity to utilise the available resources, particularly those under the capital head, is constrained. The defence establishment must, therefore, look inward and find lasting solutions to procurement impediments. At the same time, the MoD also needs to look at the current profile of the defence budget and lose no opportunity for controlling manpower costs so as to allow other items of expenditure to grow in a healthy manner.

FUTURE DEFENCE SPENDING UP TO 2014-15

If the Finance Ministry's emphasis on fiscal prudence and inclusive growth has resulted in a smaller increase in the latest defence budget, the Report of the Thirteenth Finance Commission, tabled in Parliament on February 25, 2010, also does not paint a very optimistic scenario for India's future defence spending.

The Constitutional Commission, which has recommended on specific aspects of Centre-State fiscal relations, has also proposed a roadmap for defence spending for the period 2010/11-2014/15. As per the roadmap, defence spending is to grow by an annual average of 8.33 per cent during this period, with the revenue and capital components slated to increase by an annual average of seven per cent and ten per cent, respectively. As a percentage of GDP, defence spending is to be progressively decreased to 1.76 per cent in 2014-15. The fiscal consolidation part outlined by the Commission. More importantly, the Finance Ministry, which is in charge of implementing the Commission's recommendations, is not only in agreement with the path but also tries to better the fiscal roadmap suggested by the

Commission. This means that MoD's future spending as outlined in the TFC could come under further stress in coming years.

The Road Ahead

While projecting the MoD's budget through 2014-15, the TFC took into account the projections made by both the Finance Ministry and the MoD. The final projection by the TFC however turned out to be the same as made by the Finance Ministry-possibly to the dissatisfaction of the MoD, which argued for "the need to provide adequately for enhanced force multipliers." The TFC however stuck to its guns, saying "the Finance Ministry's projections address these needs [of the MoD]" and further added that:

"we [the Thirteenth Finance Commission] are of the view that there exists considerable scope to improve the quality and efficiency of defence expenditure through increased private sector engagement, import substitution and indigenisation; improvements in procedures and practices and better project management, within the parameters of Government of India's policy. Efforts in this direction will further expand the fiscal space available for defence spending."

The Finance Commission needs careful consideration, given the indication that India's future defence budget may not grow as desired by the MoD. In this regard, the Defence Ministry needs to carve out a plan as to where it can bring efficiency in its spending.

At present, the defence budget is broadly divided into Revenue and Capital expenditures, with the former accounting for nearly 60 per cent of total budget. However, given the cost-intensive nature of capital acquisition, the MoD, as argued rightly before the Finance Commission, needs more resources for 'enhanced force multipliers'.

This makes a case for rationalisation of revenue expenditure, if the overall budget is to grow by a fixed 10 per cent annually. The MoD has therefore to revisit its spending on major revenue components such as Pay and Allowance; Stores and Equipment;

and Transportation, among others. Of particular focus should be Pay and Allowances, which has increased significantly from Rs. 24,690 crore in 2007-08 (budget estimate) to approximately Rs. 46,767 crore in 2010-11.

The way defence Capital budget is spent has been major a source of major concern, expressed by various authorities, particularly the Comptroller and Auditor General of India (C&AG). Besides, the repeated surrender of capital funds and India's heavy import dependency have probably attracted the maximum attention for remedial measures.

Although the MoD has taken a keen interest in alleviating the problems by way of revising the Defence (Capital) Procurement Procedure (DPP), some lacunae still persist. The biggest problem perhaps is the lack of an integrated acquisition structure, as brought out by the Reports of Group of Ministers (2001) and C&AG (2007).

In the absence of accountability at one place, various acquisition functions, carried out by different agencies, lack a mission-oriented approach, often at the cost of optimum time-cost trade offs and indigenisation/self-reliance. This not only raises the acquisition cost but also delays or hampers defence preparedness. It is high time the MoD looks deep into this issue.

INDIA'S UNENDING DEFENCE EXPENDITURE

Despite criticism from various circles that India is not investing more to tackle development issues as millions remain mired in poverty; the Indian government's ambitious modernisation plan for its military is in full swing. In February this year, Indian military procurement units descended on the DefExpo 2010 trade fair in New Delhi. Inaugurating the Indian Defence Exhibition, Defence Minister A.K. Antony said that India's defence expenditure, which is 2.5 percent of its gross domestic product (GDP), is going to increase. He pointed out, "our defence industry is open up to 100 percent for Indian private sector, while foreign direct investment is allowed up to

26 percent." Antony further indicated that our government is committed to rapid modernisation of armed forces. Over the next 12 years, India is set to spend a whopping US$200 billion on defence acquisitions to replace its outdated inventory. In this regard, on February 15, 2010, a report of the Indian strategic defence magazine (India Strategic's DefExpo) revealed that 70 per cent of the inventory of the Indian armed forces is 20-plus years old, and needs to be replaced with the modern technology.

It explained that nearly half of this funding ($100b) will go to the Indian Air Force (IAF), which would need to replace more than half of its combat jet fleet as well as the entire transport aircraft and helicopter fleet. The army needs new guns, tanks, rocket launchers, multi-terrain vehicles, while the navy needs ships, aircraft carriers and new range of nuclear submarines.

In three from 1994 to 1997 India's defence budget was increased from 20 percent to 24.4 percent. For the financial year 2001-2002 defence has been allocated Rs 620,000.00 million. This amount shows an increase of Rs 75,000 million as compared to previous year's revised estimates of Rs 544,610 million. In 2009, India increased its defence budget by a whopping 28.2 percent or Rs 130,000.00 million. Some experts estimate that military spending will increase further, totalling as much as 200 billion dollars over the period to 2022.

India's military has planned a massive upgrade of its mainly 1990s-era weapons systems which is mostly from the former Russia. The plans include the purchase of 126 new combat aircraft to replace an ageing fleet of MiG-21s..The US has emerged as a potential military supplier to India since the two countries signed a deal of civil energy technology in 2008, which lifted sanctions on New Delhi in order to import nuclear technology.

India is likely to become a major customer for the US military-industrial complex over the next few years. During the recent visit of the US Secretary of State Robert Gates to New Delhi, American Defence officials, however, have said that US weapons sales to India would not be a focus of the trip.

Regardless of such denials, the key reason for the Gates' visit can be found in the fact that India is planning to raise its military budget by 50% to almost $40 billion, making military expenditure 3% of the annual GDP. In contrast to India's planned defence expenditures, Pakistan's entire 2009-10 budget amounts to little over $30 billion.

India, the largest arms buyer among emerging nations, accounted for 7.5 per cent of all international arms sales between 2000 and 2007. It has spent billions of dollars in the past few years on purchases of planes, radars and ships from Britain, France, Germany and Russia and Israel.

In recent years, India has bought reconnaissance aircraft from US aerospace major Boeing worth 2.1 billion-dollars, medium range missiles for 1.4 billion dollars from Israeli Aerospace Industries, and signed an upgrade service contract with the Russian Aircraft Corporation to upgrade its MiG 29 squadrons for 965 million dollars. Several deals are planned for the near future including one of the largest arms contracts of recent times—a 11-billion-dollar project to acquire 126 multi-role combat aircraft.

It is mentionable that after 9/11, both India and Israel which had openly jumped on Bush's anti-terrorism enterprise are acting upon a secret diplomacy, targeting Pakistan China, Iran and Syria. In this context, Indo-Israeli secret diplomacy could be assessed from the interview of Israel's ambassador to India, Mark Sofer published in the Indian weekly Outlook on February 18, 2008. Regarding India's defence arrangements with Tel Aviv, Sofer had surprisingly disclosed "We do have a defence relationship with India, which is no secret" and "with all due respect, the secret part will remain a secret." As regards joint exercises, Sofer replied, "Certain issues need to remain under wraps for whatever reason."

Notably, India's 'The Tribune' wrote on September 10, 2003, "India and Israel took giant leaps forward in bolstering the existing strategic ties", and Tel Aviv has "agreed to share its expertise with India in various fields such as anti-fidayeen operations, surveillance satellites, intelligence sharing and space exploration." With the support of Israel, New Delhi has been acquiring an element of strategic depth by setting up logistical bases in the Indian Ocean for its navy. In fact, India wants to become a mini-superpower of the region and hence it uses the pretext of deterrence against Pakistan and China. In this context, New Delhi with the support of US and Israel has presumed peace-loving Pakistan and China as their arch enemies, but it does not admit officially.

In May, 1998, when India detonated five nuclear tests, Islamabad was compelled to follow the suit through its own atomic experiments. But Pakistan which so far relied upon the minimum nuclear deterrence has again been forced by India's unending spending on arms purchases to counterbalance the former. In this regard, Pakistan has signed a number of agreements with China. Nevertheless, currently, more than half of India's budget is allocated for military, paramilitary, various security forces and debt servicing. That leaves less than half for everything else including infrastructure development projects, education, healthcare, poverty alleviation, and various human services. New Delhi' s latest arms buildup will leave even less for what India needs most to lift hundreds of millions of its citizens from abject poverty, hunger illiteracy and disease.

Indian civil society organisations, while complaining of excessive defence spending indicated that the government spends 2.35 per cent of GDP on defence, but only 1.72 per cent on the social sector.

The defence budget for 2009-2010 is 29 billion dollars, up 34 percent over the previous one. Indian defence analyst Ravinder Pal Singh, while calling New Delhi's unending defence spending at the cost of poverty-alleviation—with security requirements competing with socioeconomic concerns for money calls it guns-versus-butter question.

Even some of Indian officials are surprised in relation to Indian defence expenditure which has no bounds.

For example, an official of the country's finance ministry remarked, "There is a dilemma...poverty needs to be eradicated to prevent men from taking to the guns...but more funds for security means less money for poverty alleviation."

Meanwhile, a report of United Nations pointed out that India ranks 134th of 182 countries on the United Nations Development Programme's Human Development Index. It estimated that 50 per cent of the world's undernourished population lives in India. Nearly 31 per cent of the billion-plus Indians earn less than a dollar a day.

Secretary General of the Control Arms Foundation of India Binalakshmi Nepram said, "When people are dying of poverty and bad sanitation, what protection will arms provide them?"

On the one hand, international community has been making strenuous efforts for world peace in wake of global financial crisis and war against terrorism, on the other, India has initiated deadly nuclear arms in South Asia where people are already facing multiple problems of grave nature. Majority of South Asian people are living below the poverty level, lacking basic facilities like fresh food and clean water. While yielding to acute poverty, every day, some persons commit suicide in India, Pakistan, Sri Lanka etc.

7

Indian Defence Industry: A Reform Agenda

POLICY CHANGES IN DEFENCE INDUSTRY

The first set of major policy changes were promulgated by the Government to give a fillip to our stagnating and moribund defence industry. The fundamental underpinnings to the policy changes were two: firstly, bring in the private sector; and secondly, opening the door for foreign companies by permitting up to 26 percent investment, so that technology inflows are facilitated. It was perhaps rightly believed that these were the two principle measures that were required to catalyse our ailing military industrial capabilities.

While most observers welcomed the policy announcements, there was considerable scepticism over the Governments' resolve to implement them. Could a system that was wedded to the philosophy of state led industrialisation for almost fifty years, change course that easily? Unlikely! Then there was the problem of our establishments' recognised and reputed talent for conceptualising great ideas, but seldom demonstrating the capacity to execute them. However, after having out-of-habit taken recourse to castigating the Government, it would be prudent to also try and understand its compulsions and concerns. The first is that given the nature of the UPA Government, no reforms can be implemented without the Left's concurrence.

The Left's dogma is to stonewall any measure that appears to threaten the interests of the PSUs and the Ordnance Factory Board (OFB). Thus the Left would not be inclined to acquiesce to proposals that contemplate the relaxation of state control over most core industrial sectors. Similarly, the defence PSUs and the OFB, would also not be willing to dilute their monopoly of their defence market.

Then there is the problem of the huge investments and the capacities created in all our Government owned defence industrial under-takings. Logically, it cannot be any one's case, that these assets are permitted to decay instead of putting them to optimal use. With the private sectors' case for a level playing field, the fear that over time, the Government owned defence industrial establishments would be progressively edged out of business, is genuine.

The third concern, and not easy to counter, pertains to the argument of national security. Since the private sector is not under Government control, in times of a crisis it may not respond to national requirements in the same manner that a Government owned unit would do. It is a combination of the preceding concerns that explain the Government's hesitation in letting go the control that we have witnessed since the policy changes were promulgated in May 2001. Having acknowledged the issues, it must be conceded that these are not new or unique to us. All nations have had to grapple with the same set of dilemmas, and since we are in the catch-up game, our problems ought to be easier to solve, for we have the experience of other countries to learn and benefit from.

So, while the Government at one level remained wedded to the policy of reforms, in its implementation, it dragged its feet. Consequently, the practice of doing business only with the Government owned industries did continue unchanged for three to four years, much to the frustration of the private sector. This ambivalence of the Government impacted negatively on the private sectors' attempts at collaboration with foreign companies. It should therefore be accepted that foreign partnership was, and is, vital for our industry to take off. Indigenously we do not have the technology, nor the know-how, for state-of-the-art systems that the defence services aspire for. Since foreign defence companies were unclear of the Governments' intent, they were not prepared to enter into collaborative arrangements with the private sector. For quite a while they remained cautious, indulged in fence sitting-hedging their bets.

The air was finally cleared with the Government's announcement of the Defence Procurement Policy of 2006. The most significant features of this policy were its 'offset clauses' and the concept of RURs (Raksha Utpadan Ratnas). Of the two, it is the offset policy that has the potential to yield spectacular results in energising our defence industry.

The billions of dollars of business that this policy will bring to the Indian industry has generated unprecedented excitement among our domestic players. In excitement lies the challenge. They will have to be prepared to absorb complex technologies and engineering skills, and then manufacture components, assemble subsystems, and systems, at a cost that is competitive and sufficiently profitable. Ever since the idea of the offset policy was mooted, all foreign multi-nationals have been lobbying intensely to sabotage it. Arguments-that the policy would push up prices, that the Indian industry is incapable of absorbing high technology 'direct offsets', that monitoring mechanisms cannot be effective etc-have been in the air for a while.

The Government is considering some relaxation in the policy. The areas mentioned were the adjustment of the cost of technology transfer against offsets, banking of offsets and the acceptance of indirect offsets. Though these issues may merit consideration, it would be somewhat premature to accept policy changes even before we have begun. The pressure on foreign vendors to fulfil their offset obligations must remain undiluted. Concurrently, we must concentrate on finding satisfactory solutions to the issues being raised. Having dwelt somewhat cursorily on policy issues, an objective assessment of our present industrial capability and its growth potential would now be in order. The Defence industry cannot be viewed in isolation. It has to be a manifestation of the nation's overall industrial and technological capabilities. Often we tend to ignore this fundamental.

The first place to begin this survey would be to look at the captains of our industry. There is a growing realisation that they have arrived. Globally, they are winning admiration and recognition. In the early nineties, when the first steps of liberalisation were initiated, they nurtured apprehensions about their survival. Having successfully negotiated that phase of transition in our economy, they have at the beginning of the twenty first century emerged with renewed strategic sense that has a global sweep. Witness the takeovers and the expansion plans of quite a few of our companies. Just a decade ago, who could have imagined, that the Jaguar brand car would be owned by an Indian Company? They have in the recent past displayed vision, and matched that vision with the capacity to implement.

The next requirement is of the work force. It is abundantly available in all categories; managerial, technical and in terms of working hands-our biggest asset being the young age profile of our people. Some intervention can be expected from the government in its labour policies. But being a politically sensitive issue, the Industry will have to live with this problem, till a change becomes environmentally possible. In terms of spheres in which we have advanced to global standards our range has remained somewhat limited to the automobile sector, pharmaceuticals and a few other disciplines. We have hardly any capabilities in electronics, communications, optics and in the field of aviation. Our industrial policies should focus on these voids. To become a meaningful player in the defence sector, these technologies are vital.

Our biggest strength is software services. Infosys, Wipro and TCS are globally among the best. In addition, there are a host of second tier companies, clocking rapid growth, while doing both domestic and international business. Unfortunately, this strength has not been effectively harnessed to give the requisite impetus to our defence industry. Particularly, because the new generation of weapon systems and related support systems, are all heavily dependent on extremely sophisticated software, the cost of which may be as high as 30-40 percent of the total value of the platform. Electronics we know takes up another 30-40 percent.

The Left and a few other groups have consistently opposed the opening up of the defence industry to the private sector. They have repeatedly been claiming that the public sector units can produce all that our armed forces need. A brief look at their track record will establish that such confidence in the state owned establishments is quite misplaced.

We have 39 Ordnance Factories, 8 Defence PSUs and 50 Defence Research Laboratories, ie. close to 100 establishments, all well equipped, extravagantly staffed, with some excellent scientists and managers, and yet no creditworthy achievements to show. And what equipment do they produce which is to the satisfaction of our Armed Forces?

It would be difficult to list any, other than the ALH from HAL, which has the potential to be a good product. The DRDO might want to take credit for the Agni (1 and 2) and the Prithvi. These are good systems but lose a fair amount of their sheen since they come twenty to thirty years after similar systems were inducted in China.

Our process of reforms in the management of the Government controlled defence research and production establishments, have regrettably floundered. Many studies have been done, yet-to all intent and purposes-the drift continues. Over the last three to four years the Government has been pushing for public private partnership. The idea being that such association would bring about the desired efficiencies in the public sector. But the problem is that such forced marriages do not really work. Driven by expediency, some private companies, may consider coming to an under-standing with PSUs for the short term, but such arrangements are not likely to be conducive to the real growth of the defence industry.

The policy of opening up of the defence industry to the private sector was successful in attracting quite a few industrial houses-large, medium and small, to enter the fray. Even prior to the formal opening of the defence sector, some had indirectly been in the business by manufacturing components, subsystems and systems-for integration by the defence PSUs.

Besides, our nuclear and space programmes had involved the private industry. Such companies have executed sophisticated design and engineering jobs that include special metals and alloys, and therefore have acquired the confidence to take on the development and manufacture of defence systems. L&T, Tatas, Mahindras, Godrej Boyce, Bharat Forge and more recently Punj Lloyd, are some of the major industrial houses that have staked their claim for defence contracts. Following them, are a large number of second and third tier companies covering a wide range of technologies.

The basic handicap of all these companies at the time the policy change was announced in 2001 was their lack of domain knowledge. They did not know weapon systems, or what force multipliers were, or how the procurement procedures worked. They also did not know how the global arms market operated. They were equally unaware of the equipment profile of our armed forces and their future requirement.

Even though these companies inducted service officers whose advice was available, lack of personal knowledge of the business inhibited executives from pursuing projects that entailed taking investment decisions. Increased involvement in the defence sector; and interaction with the defence services, the procurement arm of the Ministry of Defence, and the big multinational defence companies, over the last five to six years; has impacted positively on the confidence levels of company executives.

The role of defence service officers in galvanising the industry merits special attention. Other than these officers, not many in India, have any idea of modern warfare, military organisations, weapon systems, munitions and the support systems. Such domain knowledge within the industry is imperative. All over the world companies engaged in the business of military hardware extensively employ service officers to develop products and promote business. Not only this, even governments in order to support domestic industries, lend serving officers and men to participate in trials or make presentations. We may recall some of the service-industry seminars held in Delhi in the recent past which had serving officers endorsing products.

Unfortunately, the environment that we have nurtured in India discourages our retired/retiring officers from being employed. If employed they cannot be optimally used because of the establishments' attitude towards them. Who benefits? Only the foreign companies and maybe our adversaries! This must change. By encouraging the absorption of service officers by the defence industry, the nation will reap multiple benefits. Firstly, the users would have access to informed inputs on developments, which would contribute to better decisions on choice of systems and the formulation of specifications. Rather the industry would gain from the expertise of these officers in an area which they have much to learn about. Secondly, to some extent, the problem of rehabilitation of officers who retire at relatively younger ages would get addressed. It is important that the Government revisits this issue.

The central issue facing the defence industry is access to contemporary technology, its absorption and assimilation, and then the use of domestic research and development to graduate to next generation systems. South Africa, Israel, China, South Korea, Brazil, and even Singapore, have learnt to successfully navigate this cycle. There is no reason why we cannot emulate their example. In our case, so far, technology transfers have taken place only to the OFB and the defence PSUs. Their experience should not become the only basis for drawing conclusions on this subject. The appetite for growth of the private sector, and its new found confidence, would undoubtedly yield different results.

A survey of the global defence market will reveal that we are currently the biggest importers of defence systems. The US and China do spend more but they mostly buy domestic. The figures of our projected purchases are being regularly quoted in thousands of crores. They do give us sufficient strength to extract terms that could be used to considerable advantage. Look at the pending procurements: some 200 helicopters, 126 advanced fighters, approximately 800-1000 artillery guns, and half a dozen submarines. Each of these would run into billions of dollars. The conclusion is obvious-buy sensibly. With these purchases in the pipeline, if we did not get all the technologies we need, we will have only ourselves to blame. Procurement terms must state our purchase imperatives unambiguously. As a matter of fact we could consider modifying our procedures when acquiring big ticket items. Take the case of advanced fighters. All contenders have proven comparable systems. The differences essentially stem from design philosophies and the source of subsystems and systems that have been selected for integration.

The gaps in features are so narrow that quite often the choice can be a matter of individual predilection. The same arguments can be applied to the helicopters we want or the submarines. Selection could therefore be based on the totality of the package a vendor offers and not just the L-1 criteria after qualifying. To what extent and in what manner is technology being offered? What are the long term buy back agreements? What kind of investments is the vendor making in India? For such high value transactions we must extract much more than what we have done hither to. We need to therefore delve deeper into the manner in which we pursue major acquisitions. There could also be a case for some coordination with say the Civil Aviation Ministry taking into account the carriers that Air India would be planning to induct. An important caveat at this point would be in order: under no circumstances should the views of the concerned service headquarter not be the ultimate deciding factor.

While charting the strategy for the development of our domestic defence industry we must identify technologies that require special attention; technologies where our capabilities merit quantum upgradation. It can be assumed that the DRDO, the services headquarters, and also the CII, would have undertaken studies on this subject. Our acquisition plans must look at integrating the road map that we should have drawn for technology inflows and digestion. Electronics, optics, communications and avionics, are generally the areas that we should be focusing on. We have for a few decades depended exclusively on Bharat Electronics for all our communication requirements as also all our electro-optical products.

Today Bharat Electronics may be a profit making company but has little to offer in terms of future technologies or next generation products. The same story applies to HAL, notwithstanding the successful development of the ALH, which should have been offered at least ten years earlier. There is therefore a strong case to encourage private sector companies to enter these fields. The logic that since the Government has made investments in creating capabilities, all orders must be confined to these companies has proven over time to be counterproductive.

A change in approach is long overdue. India urgently needs an HAL/BE in the private sector. The Government must encourage and support their emergence. The subject of exports has also been grossly neglected. There may be a Joint Secretary in the Department of Defence Production responsible for promoting exports, but he can do little under the present dispensation. Pakistan's Ordnance Factories have consistently exported more than us. No defence industry can expect to sustain itself purely on the basis of sales in the domestic market.

Our private sector, unlike our Government owned establishments, have understood this. But they need much more support. The Government and the industry have to work together in a closely coordinated manner. Witness the way in which over the past few months the Heads of Governments of Germany, UK and France have brought with them the captains of their defence industries to India.

The agenda requires no amplification. Here again we must push to get our act together If India's defence industry is today on the threshold of transformation, considerable credit must be given to the role played by the CII. FICCI has also contributed, but only marginally. We may recall the first Army-Industry Partnership Seminar conducted in the mid nineties under the aegis of the CII.

Many of us sceptics murmured-'what's the point?' But CII persevered. It continued with its efforts to nudge the industry and simultaneously influence our policy makers. It has also been actively persuading the big global players to look at teaming with the Indian industry. The results though slow, in the coming times would soon be there for us to witness. Having reached thus far, the CII must not take its foot off the pedal. Much more still needs to be done.

Before concluding, some of the suggestions made are listed below:

- Protection to the PSUs and the OFB from domestic players must be progressively withdrawn.
- A major overhaul of the functioning control, organisation and functioning of the OFB and the defence PSUs has been long overdue. Can we not figure out a way to move forward on this issue?
- Pressures to dilute the 'offset clause' of the DPP must be resisted. What we should be focusing on is the mechanisms for monitoring post contract implementation.
- Encourage the absorption of service officers in the defence industry. The rules of interaction with industry representatives must change. The MOD and the services headquarters should be more accessible to domestic industry. Currently doors for foreigners open up much more easily.
- Put in special efforts to promote and assist the growth of the private sector in the areas of aviation, communications, electronics and sensors (optics). There should be a comprehensive action plan for the acquisition of key technologies. The Government and the industry should work in concert on this issue.

- Re-examine our procurement policies and strategies for major purchases. Given the nature of the global market we can perhaps extract much more from our big deals.
- The growth of our defence industry can only be sustained if its business model takes into account the imperative of exports for sustenance.
- The laudable role played by the CII merits recognition. Both the Government and the industry should continue to encourage the CII to step up its activities to accelerate reforms and change.

Our vision for India in the next two decades would be flawed if it did not envisage a sizeable, vibrant and sophisticated defence industry for us that is globally competitive and has the capacity to research and develop new state of the art cutting edge technologies. Our industry has acquired a new found confidence. All it needs is direction and support form the Government. The launch of the Nano within four years of it being conceived has been inspiring. We hope the global awe it has attracted is repeated time and again. We want Nano clones now coming out of India's defence industry stable. With increasing outsourcing opportunities, the Indian aerospace and defence industry is emerging as a key participant in the Asia Pacific aerospace and defence market. Apart from India's perceived viability as an outsourcing hub for aerospace and defence products, the overwhelming involvement of the Government in areas of supply and demand cements its advantage in the industry.

The Government's pro-active soliciting of international cooperation has seen production moving to India, generating more opportunities for the country. Export competitiveness has been given priority, hence, there has been an increased thrust towards reduced import dependency. The Indian economy is one the fastest growing in the world, reflecting the successful reform process initiated in 1991.

The Indian Government has gradually opened its key sectors to foreign participation and foreign investment in the Indian aerospace and defence industry which currently has a 26 percent cap. Meanwhile, since two-thirds of the Indian population depends on agricultural income, reforms in this area are widely considered necessary to aid economic growth. Development of the agriculture sector, trade, as well as capital liberalisation, and improvement in investments, are some vital areas being focused upon by the current Government.

The *Frost & Sullivan* Country Industry Forecast service for the Indian aerospace and defence industry uses a macroeconomic perspective to provide a focused analysis of the industry. This service covers an array of issues pertaining to the industry including political stances, trade policies, industry regulations, as well as their overall impact. Besides enabling decision makers to assess the impact of non-market forces, this analysis also helps in identifying new opportunities in the industry. In addition, it provides a strong base for preparing business contingency plans.

INDIAN DEFENCE INDUSTRIAL PRODUCTION

The Indian defence industrial base and production capacity is now one of the largest in the world. This has painstakingly been built both pre-independence (1947) and also made rapid strides during the decades after independence. India now has 40 Defence Ordnance Factories and 8 Defence Public Sector Undertakings. These produce a large range of armaments, ammunition, vehicles, helicopters, fighter aircrafts, sophisticated electronics equipment, missiles and naval crafts. The defence sector is fully government controlled with the ultimate aim to reduce dependence on imports and become self reliant in this critical sector at the earliest.

Notwithstanding the large industrial base and advancement in various technologies, research and development in defence has not kept pace with the requirement of modern and high technology weapon systems. This has resulted in import of major armaments and other systems involving critical technologies. Till the 80's India was largely dependent on Soviet Russia and other East Bloc countries for its defence requirements.

As a matter of fact the entire tank fleet, mechanized infantry BMP/ICV fleet, Air Defence systems, bridges, and a large portion of field Artillery presently in front line service in the army is of Soviet/Eastern bloc origin. Despite the economic upheaval in India in 1991 coinciding with the end of the cold war, the two countries continued their defence relationship. The Indo-Russian defence programme is currently set to continue until 2010, but the future is not certain. India in the last 6-7 years has bought the SU30 aircrafts, 310 T-90 battle tanks (347 more are on order), the air craft carrier, Smerch rocket launchers etc. The view on further major purchases is divided due to a number of problems being faced on maintenance support of current and past equipment.

The era of liberalization which commenced in 1991, coincided with the enhanced role of the private sector in defence. Up to the late 90's the private sectors' role was mainly limited to providing large quantities of raw material, sub assemblies and limited quantities of high technology items to the Ordnance Factories, Defence PSU's and the Army's repair agencies.

In May 2001, the government decided to open up defence to private participation up to 100%, with FDI permissible up to 26%. With this change in policy a larger role for the private sector has emerged.

Initially, the private sector was slow to absorb this change primarily due to the large requirement of funds, uncertainties of sustained defence requirements and long lead times for trials and eventual introduction of equipment. However, over the last 4-5 years with the active participation of various chambers of commerce a number of large private sector companies have successfully entered the defence sector with tie ups both with large foreign defence conglomerates and defence PSU's/Ordnance Factories.

As per SIPRI Book of 2008, US military spent $547 billion in 2007 which corresponds to 4%of its GDP. UK ranked second with a spend of $60 billion, India ranked 10th in global spending with an expenditure of $ 24 billion of which approximately $10 billion was on capital expenditure, 80% of this was towards buying new equipment. ABOUT $11 BILLION ARE FOR CAPITAL PURCHASES during 2008-2009.

With the entry of the private sector, large resources in terms of latest technologies, management and scientific skills, and its ability to raise large sums of money have brought defence production to center stage. This will not only enhance best practices but will assist in increasing indigenous production, employment and move faster towards the aim of self reliance. It is in this stage of transition that India needs large scale infusion of the latest technologies which is critical to self reliance. This can be best provided by collaboration with foreign companies excelling in a range of diverse equipments. Both the private sector and defence establishments are moving in this direction, albeit a little slow.

India is likely to reach an annual budget of $40 billion by the end of the 11th defence plan (2011-2012). Of this, about $16-17 billion would be available for capital expenditure. An analysis of major purchases during the last 5-6 years shows that major contracts have been signed for the Air Force and Navy. Defence observers feel that this trend is likely to continue. Big ticket contracts like 126 jets to replace the ageing MIG-21 worth about $10 billion, 6-C-130 aircraft, six refuellers, long range maritime patrol air craft for the Navy, utility helicopters for the Army and Air Force are on the anvil.

Indigenous defence industry and foreign manufacturers need to closely observe the Armys requirement. Large induction of four types of 155mm guns, the TCS, BMS, dry and wet bridges, fuzes, bi modular charge systems, specialist vehicles, Air Defence gun and missile system, night vision devices are among a host of requirements the Army wants urgently. Conceptually the Army works on an equipment profile of 30: 40: 30, this implies that 30% of the equipment of a type is approaching obsolescence, 40% is current and 30% is state of the art. The best example to illustrate this is the tank profile, while the T-55 is approaching obsolescence, the T-72 is current and the T-90 is state of art. If this concept is interpolated to others, the requirement of hardware over the next 5 to 10 years can be assessed broadly. Collaboration and transfer of technology will be the mantra in all these requirements.

Defence Procurement Procedure-2008 is in place wef 01 September 08. Very clearly India has entered free market economy in defence requirements.

The Indian defence industry is in transition with increased participation from the private sector. In all fairness Indian industry is nascent and catering for the huge demand of defence equipment by themselves is extremely difficult, thus the window of opportunity for foreign manufactures to partner with Indian industry and provide Indian Defence Forces the state of art equipment is for real.

INDIA'S DEFENCE INDUSTRY: A HISTORICAL OVERVIEW

Looking into the Post-Independence Era

The pre-independence (pre-1947) defence-industrial infrastructure in India was limited. It generally catered to the lowest spectrum of defence production—repair and overhaul of imported weapons systems. The then ruling British followed a policy of retaining strategic capabilities for themselves while allowing the native Indians to assist in the tactical dimensions, confined to minor works in most endeavours.

An example of this policy is evident from the fact that while the Royal Air Force retained the strategic elements like the bomber force and used their own formations, the Indian Air Force (IAF) was left with only tactical elements—supporting them with secondary and tertiary roles that mainly included repair and similar minor works. The Walchand Aircraft Factory (WAF) in Bangalore was wholly engaged in repair and maintenance of aircraft at that time. From March 1942 till the end of World War II, it was employed for the servicing of American aircraft and was managed, for part of this period, by the US Air Force.

Mazagaon Docks (Mumbai) and Garden Reach Shipyards (Calcutta) similarly existed prior to India's independence to repair warships. However, apart from such single air or ship industrial units, India's defence-industrial capacity during times of pre-independence mainly consisted of what is known as Ordnance Factories (OFs). These factories had been set up primarily to supplement land-based weapons and equipment produced in Britain. Before 1947, there were 16 OFs, all located on Indian territory.

The gun and shell factory at Cossipore (near Kolkata), established in 1801, an ammunition factory at Kirkee of 1889, a rifle factory at Ishapore of 1901, a gun carriage factory at Jabalpur of 1904, and others were built mainly to produce for the British forces. During World War II, possible threats to the sea lanes of communication in the Indian Ocean and requirements of the allied forces in the region, made it necessary to double the number of factories during this time. The filling factory at Khamara and the light machine gun factory at Hyderabad were amongst such new factories. In brief, pre-partition Indian defence-industrial capacities were confined only to a supplementary role and were placed at the lowest end of the production spectrum.

Post-independence, the Indian leadership wanted self-sufficiency in every sphere of activity. This objective was obvious because India was never allowed to develop industrial competencies. The same objective was no different in the field of defence production. Right from the first Prime Minister Jawaharlal Nehru, every successive Indian leader sought self-sufficiency in defence production.

The need to establish a comprehensive defence-industrial infrastructure thus constituted a primary objective of the political leadership. Right from the beginning, India's industrial policies emphasised 'core' industries to be taken care of by the central government and others by the states. Defence industries, considered as critical national assets, obviously came under the exclusive control of the central government. The first Industrial Policy Resolution of 1948, consequently revised under the Second

Five-Year Plan in 1956, made it clear that core industries, including munitions, aircraft, shipbuilding, iron and steel, heavy machine tools, heavy electrical plants, atomic energy and similar others were to be placed under exclusive central government control. During this period, many industrial units related to these fields were established under the strict supervision of the central government, known as 'basic' (Schedule A) industries. The Defence Science Organisation was also established during this period to take up the challenge of undertaking R&D activities. As demands for defence R&D grew, this organisation paved the way for the creation of the Defence Research and Development Organisation (DRDO) in 1958, which to-date remains the most important contributor to India's defence R&D activities. It has got nearly 50 laboratories, spread all across the country, and other scientific establishments and institutions like the Council of Scientific and Industrial Research (CSIR).

At independence, India's defence-industrial production was mainly coming from the existing 16 OFs. These factories were engaged in the production of low technology items like small arms and ammunition, mines and other explosives.

Their cumulative value of production was estimated at roughly US $7-8 million during the time of India's independence. Despite the first India-Pakistan War (1947/48) and the need to boost defence-industrial production, no new factory was built during the first decade (1950s). It was during the late 1950s that the need to construct more factories was contemplated. It is also during this time that peace time civilian production in defence industries was emphasised, especially by the then Defence Minister, V. K. Krishna Menon. The policy of production for civilian markets was primarily aimed at maintaining operational capacities during slack periods of demand as well as keeping the level of productivity high by the manufacturing units. By the end of the 1950s, the number of defence-industrial units almost remained the same. The production from these ordnance factories was still geared to low-technology items.

Apart from OFs, and various defence science and technology establishments, the Indian government also created a number of production establishments to take care of various productions in the field of defence. These, like others, were under the exclusive control of the government although they were created as corporations, commonly known as 'Defence Public Sector Units' (DPSUs).

There are eight DPSUs in the country, devoted to the production of different military systems and components. They are: Hindustan Aeronautics Limited (HAL), Bharat Electronics Limited (BEL), Bharat Earth Movers Limited (BEML), Mazagaon Dockyard Limited (MDL), Garden Reach Shipbuilders and Engineers Limited, Goa Shipyard, Bharat Dynamics Limited (BDL) and Mishra Dhatu Nigam Limited (MDNL). Both, DPSUs and OFs, are administered by the Department of Defence Production under the Ministry of Defence. Both sets of industries have their own research and development units although the overall R&D activities are met by the DRDO. Bharat Electronics Limited (BEL) was the first DPSU, established in 1954, to manufacture electronic equipment primarily for the defence sector. Over the years, more than half of BEL's overall production has turned into products for the civilian market. And it is not the only production entity that has changed that way.

In the post-independence period, till the war with China in 1962, India's defence-industrial base was too weak to take the responsibility of all defence needs. The self-sufficiency model had been adopted since the beginning but as years passed and demands for security grew, India found it difficult to create an industrial base as it was hit primarily by two important factors – lack of sufficient funding and access to modern defence technologies. The Indian leadership was aware of these two problems but they also had a number of other issues to handle. The country was just independent, had already fought a war with Pakistan, did not even have a rudimentary industrial base, and faced numerous nation-building and socioeconomic problems, independence, found it pragmatic to follow a policy of controlling critical industries, including defence, though this is widely debated now. Although both defence and non-defence critical industries were under exclusive state control, the former—due to their strategic importance—became a 'closed' sector.

The leadership also desired and pursued what is commonly known as comprehensive industrialisation. This meant that more and more big industries emerged to cater to needs that were vast, like steel, coal, mining, etc. Thus, big state-owned companies like the Steel Authority of India Limited (SAIL) was established.

This was also evident in the defence sector where large industrial units were created to cater to the demands of the vast armed forces. As mentioned, the two problems of lack of investment and access to technologies became acute as the defence industries expanded, making many units perform below par. Also, investment pattern in this sector was not uniform. Critical establishments like the Hindustan Aeronautics Limited (HAL) and DRDO received more funds than others, such as OFs. The ever-growing demands of the armed forces and the problems in the defence sector in meeting those led many to criticise existing policies followed by the then ruling party. The government, in turn, was hard pressed for funds that were essential and was aware of long-term returns for investment in the defence sector. In brief, policies to maximise production in order to attain self-sufficiency in the defence sector although they were considered far-sighted, did not match expectations, thus leading to further constraints.

From Self-Sufficiency to Self-Reliance

The self-sufficiency in defence production was in fact realised from the beginning, and was complemented by the concept of self-reliance after a few years of persistence and failure. Self-reliance, as far as India was concerned, meant—apart from its own production base for support—a degree of dependence on reliable foreign sources for access to technologies, supply of components and complete systems. This, in turn, was debatable as foreign partners to achieve such long-term self-reliance were not forthcoming during the first few years as the West was considered to be unreliable both for military and political reasons. India tested self-reliance by meeting urgent and immediate demands through imports from abroad while simultaneously striving for indigenous capabilities in defence production. The west European weapons systems, primarily British, French and Swedish, were considered first choice in the Indian arsenal during the first few years; however, after the 1962 war with China, many western countries along with the United States were reluctant to co-operate with India which made a major adverse impact on India's defence production activities. The post-War scenario witnessed a slow entry of the Soviet Union as a major supplier, the position is still retained by its successor Russia. The post-1962 scenario was marked by utter confusion in the decision-making circles, which in turn impinged the defence industry.

India was humiliated in the war with China and thus started looking into its existent defence-industrial capabilities and found to its horror that all was not well. For example, the Indian Air Force (IAF) needed a high-altitude supersonic interceptor against the threat of the B-57 bomber of Pakistan (supplied by the United States) and the Tu-16 bomber of the Chinese Air Force (supplied by the USSR).

The requirement especially assumed a serious dimension after the war with China, when India looked outward and found out that only three fighter aircraft worth-considering were available in the market. India neither wanted to buy the British Lightning nor the Soviet MiG-21, and preferred the American F-104.

This system was already supplied by the United States to Pakistan and despite repeated efforts India could not obtain it. India's effort to upgrade the existing HF-24 to supersonic capability was not considered by the Americans, either. It was at this time that the USSR came to India's rescue when they not only decided to supply the MiG-21 and other weapons but also gave a go-ahead for license production. India's quest for self-reliance got a major boost through this license production arrangement. This was indeed a turning point in India's self-reliance activities. The Soviets proved to be a trusted friend whose military supplies constitute more than 70 percent of India's total weapons acquisitions now. This friendship immensely benefited India's defence industry as it improved many notable weapons systems and components from this experience. In brief, India's self-reliance model in defence production was given a life lease by the Soviets.

After 1962, India sought to make up for the lacuna as well as boost defence production to match requirements. New ordnance factories were planned and established during the next three decades. The number of OFs thus grew to thirty-five by the mid-1980s. And, by the mid-1990s, it had reached thirty-nine. The fortieth ordnance factory (at Nalanda, in the state of Bihar), started in 1999/2000. These OFs were established in different parts of the country: Ten of them cater to materials and components, ten for weapons, vehicles and equipment, ten for ammunition and explosives and five for other ordnance items. By the early 1990s, they were producing more than 1500 items of arms, ammunition, equipment and components. By the early 1990s, the OFs collectively reached place 45 on the list of the largest arms producing companies in the world, and were placed at 29 in 2000.

The OFs, with a cumulative work force of 1,75,000, have been engaged in various types of land-based weapons. During the period under examination, the bulk of the production, nonetheless, still constituted of large quantities of relatively low-to medium-technology items. These, among others, included small arms, anti-tank and anti-aircraft guns, mortars, associated ammunition, rocket projectiles, bombs, grenades, mines, transport vehicles, leather items, parachutes and ordnance clothing for the armed forces. The establishment of the Heavy Vehicle Factory at Avadi (in the state of Tamil Nadu) in the early 1960s was crucial for the production of tanks and combat vehicles. This is where the first series of tanks, called 'Vijayanta' were manufactured under license from the British firm Vickers. This was followed by the manufacture of the ex-Soviet T-72 'Ajeya' MBTs. Although this project was taken up during the

1970s, it finally rolled out in 1988. In some projects, however, the level of indigenization has been pretty high, for example, up to about 80 percent in the case of 'Sarath' infantry combat vehicles. The overall performance of the OFs during that period was modest, although a lot could have been done to improve the performance of many factories. Hindustan Aeronautics Limited performed modestly during this period. Created in 1964 through an amalgamation of two aircraft companies, Hindustan Aircraft Limited and Aeronautics India Limited, HAL has become the only major aerospace company. With a total work force of nearly 45,000, it stands as the 57th largest defence company in the world.

During the beginning, it was primarily catering to maintenance and overhaul but over a period of time has slowly developed itself to undertake assembly, license manufacture and indigenous design and development. During the 1960s and well beyond, it was engaged in various license manufacture projects, amongst others the MiG-21 series aircraft, HF-24 Marut transonic fighters, 'Kiran' HJT – 16 jet trainer.. Apart from this, it also undertook to license manufacture 'Cheetah' (Aerospatiale SA 315 B) and 'Chetak' (Aerospatiale SA 316 B) helicopters. Bharat Electronics, set up in 1954 to manufacture electronic equipment, was perhaps the only DPSU which showed positive production results during the same period. Other DPSUs such as BEML, BDL, MDL were engaged in production, which may again be termed as modest. Bharat Dynamics Limited, established in 1970, is the other DPSU, which was engaged in the production of missiles and associated products. Except during the 1990s, it had engaged in the past in license manufacture of some of the low range missile series. To sum up: While the Indian defence industry was expected to raise its production level during the half a century (1960s to mid-1980s), both its objectives of self-reliance through indigenous activity and more active collaborative activity, have brought very limited results. Some analysts even term this phase as an 'era of license-manufacture', nothing more. While plant utilisation capacities remained at the lower end, with around 40 to 50 percent, the quality, range and mode of production was modest and generally confined to low and medium technologies.

Gaps Galore

From the early 1960s till the early and mid-1980s, license production and direct purchase and acquisitions remained the predominant form of supply for the Indian defence forces. Analysts like Ajay Singh argue that there was a gap of nearly three decades in India's effort toward indigenous production. This gap was especially evident in the fields of design and development, which constitutes the upper spectrum of self-reliance. A fighter aircraft between Marut and the Light Combat Aircraft (LCA), a basic trainer aircraft between HT-2 and HPT-32, an intermediate trainer between Kiran and an yet-to-be fully developed Advanced Jet Trainer (AJT) are some of the examples that typify both the technology and production gaps.

Weapons for the army had been manufactured under license with no significant design activities undertaken till the 1980s when a tank and a small arms project commenced. The first was a Main Battle Tank (MBT, named Arjun) while the last is known as the Indian Small Arms Systems (INSAS). The Situation was a little better for the Indian Navy, where at least some ship platforms were designed indigenously. The period thus witnessed a time gap in the design and development while emphases were more on license production and acquisitions that led to two problems – below par quality performance of the defence industry, although the quantum of production was on expected lines and lack of or little funding for critical and strategic sectors of the defence industry including R&D. Analysts also argue that given the situation even half the allocation for acquisitions would have been sufficient to ensure delivery on time, if not at the required level of technology.

RISING DEFENCE EXPENDITURE IN INDIA

The Government of India has been investing heavily into its Defence industry due to strained relations with its neighboring countries and growth in international terrorism.

The Defence budget for the year 2005 was $17.80 billion, a growth of 7.6 percent from the budget allocation of 2000. Typically 5.0 percent to 10.0 percent of the Defence budget is allocated for modernization and weapon induction. The larger share is allocated for payment, allowances, and for maintenance of aging military equipment. The Government of India expects its Defence expenditure to exceed $20.00 billion by 2008.

Private Investments on the Rise in the Indian Defence Industry

The Defence industry in the past has been dominated by the government-run public sector undertakings (PSU). This scenario has changed significantly with the Ministry of Defence providing license to private companies to manufacture select aerospace and Defence products.

In 2001, the country opened for up to 100 percent Indian private sector investments in the Defence industry and allowed foreign direct investment (FDI) of up to 26.0 percent in select areas of the Defence industry. Some of the key non-PSU industry participants supplying Defence equipment and services include Mahindra & Mahindra, Tata Group, Kirloskar Brothers, Larsen & Toubro, Ashok Leyland, Jindal, Max Aerospace & Aviation, and Ramoss India.

Increasing Public-Private Collaborations

The Defence industry is gradually liberalizing and the public sector is facilitating greater private sector participation in the area of Defence goods production. There are about 5,100 companies supplying around 20.0 percent to 25.0 percent of components and subassemblies to state-owned contractors and the market size is expected to be around $6.20 billion in 2005. Of India's current Defence procurement of capital items, more than 30 percent is imported, however, this is expected to change with the creation of more public-private partnerships.

The Indian Space Research Organization (ISRO) has a strong partnership with the Indian industrial sector for space programs execution. Over 500 small, medium, and large-scale enterprises work with ISRO, supplying hardware, undertaking fabrication jobs, and establishing fabrication and test facilities. The Indian industrial sector provides all raw materials and high-tech electronic items required by ISRO and has also contributed toward developing systems for launch vehicle spacecraft, remote sensing, and ground equipment. Around 231 technologies developed by ISRO were transferred to the Indian industrial sector for commercial use. ISRO also undertakes technical consultancy projects for industries.

INDIA'S OFFSET POLICY TO ENCOURAGE DOMESTIC PRODUCTION

India's offset policy for Defence goods has been designed to leverage the country's position as a large buyer and exporter. India's offset policy for the Defence industry states that any purchase from a foreign supplier in excess of $70.0 million will require a reinvestment of 30.0 percent of the total purchase amount in terms of components and services from India. The offset policy applies to imports by Defence PSU's, ordinance factories, and private participants of the industry.

The offset policy is also expected to act as a driver to create market-entry opportunities for mid-rung companies, which are looking at investing in research and development and manufacturing of Defence goods. The proposed offset policy is conducive for the private companies to have a larger presence.

Growth Opportunities in the Indian Defence Industry

The domestic capability of the Indian Defence industry is largely concentrated around the production of the PSUs and ordinance factories. This trend is expected to change with the recent selective liberalization of the Defence industry and a sound offset policy, which are expected to create greater private sector participation and facilitate bigger FDI inflows into the Indian Defence industry.

The Government of India has shown keenness in allowing international collaboration for the production of weapon systems, which are purely used for non-lethal purposes. The production of the following weapon systems are expected to be promoted in the future:

- Technologies/equipment for counter terrorism
- Surveillance, communication equipment, and sensors for border management
- Cyber security-synergies in the field of information technology
- Devices to neutralize improvised explosive devices (IEDs).

Suppliers and manufacturers of the above-mentioned weapon systems are expected to be some of the chief beneficiaries of the increased indigenization of the production process in the Indian Defence industry. Key areas of growth identified within the industry are expected to arise from the up gradation of the production capacity expansion, technology transfer, and modernization of Defence infrastructure.

INDIA'S DEFENCE INDUSTRY IN THE 21ST CENTURY

Major Policy Initiatives

India's defence industry entered a new phase of self-reliance on the eve of the 21st century. Since the mid-1990s, several initiatives have been undertaken by the government to effect changes in the defence industry. Soon after the liberalisation of the economy was announced in 1990/91, the defence industry started realising the importance of civil-military interaction in the industrial sector.

The private industries in India, which were thus far debarred from entering into defence production and whose role in the defence sector was limited to supplying spare parts and other minor contributions, started demanding a share in defence production.

In 1994, the then Defence Minister founded six Task Forces on major areas of defence modernisation, of which reforms in defence industry was an important part. This was carried out by the government in consultation with institutions like the

Confederation of Indian Industries (CII). The CII, on its part was instrumental in bringing out a series of proposals in the broad field of private participation in the defence sector and armed forces–industry cooperation. Soon after this, the government initiated a programme called 'Army-Industry Partnership', under the auspices of CII which highlighted the importance of cooperative arrangements between the armed forces, defence industry and the government.

After India's nuclear tests, various sanctions were imposed on India, of which sanctions related to the import of military and dual-use goods and technologies were considered the most important.

Sanctions were imposed on more than 150 items, which affected the progress of many defence products. However, the impact of sanctions on military technology was taken up as a another phase of challenge for the defence scientists as they had faced similar sanctions after the test in 1974. At that time they had faced more difficulties as the defence industry was not in a position to withstand such severe cuts which had resulted in delays in many major programmes. This time around, the defence industry had made significant progress to be able to withstand sanctions.

After the Kargil conflict in mid-1999, the government started looking into security gaps and founded a committee under Mr K. Subrahmanyam. He brought out a major report on this conflict, which is known as the 'Kargil Committee Report'. This report, among other recommendations, highlighted the importance of reforms in higher defence management and reforms in institutional processes in the security sector.

The Government also founded a Group of Ministers' committee to look into major aspects of the overall security management of the country. The committee submitted its report to the government, which is known as GoM Report on 'Reforming the National Security System.

This report highlighted the importance of self-reliance in India's defence industry and recommended several steps to introduce institutional changes into the system.

Coupled with changes at institutional and organisational levels, India's defence industry entered an entirely new era after the Government announced a major change in policy by outlining codes of conduct for and inviting private participation in the defence industry. This is seen as by far the most important policy shift in the defence-industrial sector in the last fifty years. By doing so, the Government, through an official notification No. 5(37)/2001-FCI, allowed private sector participation up to 100 percent and permitted foreign direct investment (FDI) up to 26 percent.

This decision has been hailed by both the private industry and the government-owned defence industry. Institutions like CII and FICCI, which represent interests and views of the private sector, have been instrumental in influencing such a marked change in policies. According to Mr Sushanto Sen, the Director General of CII, such a policy change is certainly going to benefit both the defence industry and the private sector.

In tune with the stated objectives of India's defence industry to achieve a higher degree of self-reliance and a desire to make its flagship units globally competitive, thus entering into competitive defence markets, the Government has also introduced some institutional changes that are expected to smoothen operations both at structural and organisational levels. Earlier, procurement procedures were considered cumbersome, and there were overlaps in organisational responsibilities of respective organs responsible for procurement. Under the new system, the Services Headquarters were integrated into the Ministry of Defence to provide closer interaction. The procurement structure is now a three-tier structure with the recent establishment of the Defence Acquisition Council (DAC) at the apex. Its primary role will be to accord in-principle-approval of long-term perspective plans (15-20 years), acceptance of necessity for the capital acquisition plan (5 years), identify 'Make', 'Buy' and 'Make and Buy' projects and monitor progress of the three Boards under it – the Defence Procurement Board, Defence Production Board and the Defence R&D Board. The Defence Procurement Board under the Defence Secretary will have the primary role of capital procurements and coordination. The Defence Production Board will be headed by the Secretary Defence Production and Supplies and will oversee all activities related to indigenous manufacture, progress in 'make' projects and will provide support to DAC.

The Defence R&D Board will be headed by the Secretary Defence R&D and will oversee progress, monitor and report on all R&D proposals in consultation with the user service and production board. Other measures at institutional level include direct linkages between the armed forces and the Ministry of Defence through integrated headquarters, which include respective perspective planning branches. In sum, organisational and institutional changes brought about recently seem to complement policy changes.

8

Professional Military Education: Agenda for Reform

MILITARY AND EDUCATIONAL BACKGROUND

The well-known French educational reform in the 1880s, led by Jules Ferry, is linked to events in the 1870s.the defeat in the Battle of Sedan in the France-Prussia war and the political regime transition from the Second Empire to the Third Republic.

The defeat against Prussia provoked a national trauma. When Napoleon III mobilized and declared war on July 19th, 1870, a Prussian victory seemed unimaginable. Yet, on September 2, Napoleon III was made prisoner at Sedan and the French army was vanquished. The news reached Paris on September 4 and.in a revolutionary atmosphere.the Republicans (thc French left at the time) seized this opportunity to put an end to the Second Empire and organize a.government of National Defense..A few months later, the Prussian army had reached Paris.

During the Siege of Paris, on January 18, 1871, King Wilhelm I was proclaimed German Emperor at the Palace of Versailles, a symbolic act that also marked the unification of Germany. When the armistice was signed on February 26, Wilhelm and Bismarck imposed a heavy tribute on the French including the takeover control of two French provinces, Alsace and Lorraine. In 1870, French expenditures on education were lagging behind those in Prussia and other European countries. The French education system was little supported by public spending and mainly run privately, revolving around churches and religious congregations. This system was far from perfect:

- many who were registered hardly ever attended class...

Equally problematic, and a further sign of a disintegrated system, was the fact that many people relied on their local dialects to communicate and did not have a good command of the French language:

- In 1863 by official tally, some 7.5 million people, a fifth of the population, did not know the language. [...] The actual number was probably much larger, particularly if one includes those whose notions of the language were extremely vague.

The Reform Debate

Even prior to the Prussian war, French elites were aware of the fact that the French education system had failed to promote national unity. Victory Duruy, appointed Minister of Education in 1863 by Napoleon III, explained that his goal was.the expansion and improvement of educational facilities; the institution of a genuine educational program for girls that would weaken the religious communities,.who owed the allegiance not to Paris but to Rome and who were not attuned to modern needs.; and the development of technical education.

His plans were in many ways similar to those Jules Ferry would defend some 20 years later. 6 Duruy tried to gather political support and convince the Emperor that it was in his own interest to implement such a reform. But he did not succeed, partly due to a lack of support from a rural population influenced by the Church.

As explained by Lindert (2004)

The resounding defeat by Prussia tipped the scales in favour of the education reformers. Enrollments and expenditures accelerated across the 1870s, with local taxation leading the way. The real victory of universal taxbased education came with Jules Ferry's Laic Laws of the 1880s, especially the 1881 law abolishing all fees and tuition charges in public elementary schools [...].While the national politics could not deliver a centralized victory for universal schooling before the military defeat of 1870, [...] after 1881 centralization performed the mopping up role..

More generally, although many groups and political parties diverged regarding the causes of the defeat, they all agreed that education in Prussia had played in key role in the rise of this new power, and that education in France had to be reformed, to.teach Frenchmen to be confident of their nations superiority in law, civilization and republican institutions. It should be consistent with reigning social values, and thereby eliminate disruptive conflicts and promote the unity of the classes.

Since France no longer enjoyed religious unity, it must forge a new moral unity from a united education that would teach civic morality based on the principles of natural reason.. Only the Church wanted the status quo to be preserved. This discussion suggests that military rivalry was a major factor behind the forthcoming French reforms.

The Reforms

Jules Ferry was appointed Minister of Education in February 1879. In 1881, he abolished all fees and tuition charges in public elementary schools. In 1882, he designed a law whereby enrollment in a public or private school became compulsory from age six to thirteen and religious education was forbidden in public schools. In 1883, every village with more than 20 children at school age was required to host a public elementary school. In 1885, subsidies were devoted to the building and maintenance of schools and to paying teachers. In 1886, an elementary teaching program was established, together with monitoring provisions. These are the so-called "laicity" provisions, which characterize the French educational system still today. At the same time, a whole infrastructure program.the Freycinet plan was initiated to facilitate children's access to schools. Millions of francs were spent on building roads to match the large amounts spent on schools: 17,320 new schools had to be built, 5,428 schools were enlarged, 8,381 schools were repaired. As a result, enrollment as well as attendance in primary education steadily increased.

Equally important as these investments were the changes in the content of elementary education that ensued from the Ferry laws..At the very start of school, children were taught that their first duty was to defend their country as soldiers. [...] The whole school program went on expanding the theme. Gymnastics were meant.to develop in the child the idea of discipline, and prepare him... to be a good soldier and a good Frenchman..

Geography and history were two particularly powerful tools of indoctrination, as well as dictations. Dictations were useful to teach people the French language but, beyond that.the exercise was a sort of catechism designed to teach the child that it was his duty to defend the fatherland, to shed his blood or die for the commonwealth, to obey the government, to perform military service, to work, learn, pay taxes and so on..

The Outcomes

As pointed out by Moody.Regarding enrollment rates, statistics attest that there was an appreciable increase in attendance in the decade after 1882. [...] The proportion of the population that could not read or write continued to decline slowly, reaching about 4 percent by 1900..Most authors agree with this characterization of the trend in illiteracy in France: for instance, Morrisson and Murtin (2011) note that literacy rates rose from 80% in 1870 to 96% in 1912.

The reforms also appear to have increased the sense of patriotism and national unity. Thanks to the Ferry laws, in Ain, Ardennes, Vendee, all children became familiar with references or identities that could thereafter be used by the authorities, the press, and the politicians to appeal to them as a single body., and in that respect Ferry's efforts would pay off during the mobilization in 1914. Primary School enrollment per 10,000 inhabitants (again, measured by the School variable from the CNTS data archive) rose from 1176 in 1870 to 1430 in 1912.

ADDITION TO THE EDUCATIONAL BENEFITS

In addition to the educational benefits available through the Post-9/11 GI Bill, active duty service members, reservists called to active duty, and, in some cases, their spouses, can also receive robust educational benefits through the Department of Defence Tuition Assistance Program.

The long-standing program currently provides up to $250 per credit hour (to a maximum of $4,500 a year) for active duty service members to enroll in education programs that are accredited by a regional or national organization recognized by the Department of Education, including many for-profit schools.

In 2001, the Tuition Assistance "Top-Up" program was created to allow active duty service members to use GI bill benefits, now including Post-9/11 GI Bill benefits, to supplement costs not covered by the Tuition Assistance program. Active duty service members attending for-profit schools that exceed $250 per credit hour can, and do, use both benefit pools to cover costs.

The 2009 Defence Authorization Bill also authorized tuition assistance to be extended to eligible spouses in order to "expand the spouse's employment and portable career opportunities." This program, the Military Spouse Career Advancement Accounts (MyCAA), provided up to $6,000 a year and was initially available to all military spouses. In less than a year the program had enrolled 136,000 spouses at an estimated cost of $250 million and was deemed unaffordable by DoD. Of 136,000 spouses enrolled in MyCAA in the first year, approximately 91,000 were in degree-seeking programs, while an additional 45,000 spouses enrolled in certificate or other short-term programs. Of those enrolled in degree programs, to date, about 90 percent or approximately 82,000 have been tracked by sector. Forty-six percent are attending for-profit schools.

MyCAA was recently redesigned with a cap of $2,000 per year and a maximum benefit of $4,000 over three years. It is now available only to spouses of lower-ranking service members, and no longer covers bachelors or graduate degree courses. While this program has been redesigned with a much less generous benefit package, for-profit schools will likely continue to receive a large share of the funding available through this program.

Military Families and Veterans Important

For-profit schools pride themselves on offering access to higher education to traditionally underserved groups including members of the armed services and veterans. They point to the enrollment of Iraq and Afghanistan veterans and families as evidence of this commitment. Some institutions undoubtedly provide a quality education that meets the needs of service members, veterans and their families. However, for some schools the expansion of the DoD Tuition Assistance program to spouses, and the passage of the Post-9/11 GI Bill with new benefits for veterans and their families, may have made enrolling active duty service members, reservists, veterans, dependents and spouses appealing for purely financial reasons.

The 90/10 rule was modeled after a safeguard put into place by Congress during the Korean War, designed to protect veterans from being ripped off by poor quality institutions. Schools that enrolled students using GI bill benefits were prohibited from enrolling more than 85 percent veterans in their educational programs.

This was designed to ensure that schools were of sufficient quality to attract some students who would pay tuition. The House Veterans Affairs Committee at the time described the 85/15 rule as, "a real safeguard to assure sound training for the veteran, at reasonable cost, by seasoned institutions" and observed that had the rule been in effect during the administration of the World War II GI Bill "considerable savings would have resulted and... much better training would have been realized in many areas."

Because neither Department of Defence nor Veterans Affairs benefits originate through Title IV of the Higher Education Act, money received through these programs is not counted as federal financial aid, and, in fact, can be counted towards the other side of the equation. The Department of Education's 90/10 rule effectively considers DoD and Veterans funds as non-federal aid by allowing these funds to be counted in the 10 percent of the calculation, despite the fact that the money comes from federal taxpayers.

Enrolling veterans and service members allows for-profit schools to expand the number of non-military students that they enroll. If a company can generate $10 million in revenue from VA and DoD benefits, they can take in another $90 million in student loan and Pell Grant funds without violating the 90/10 rule. Not only does the failure to count military educational benefits as federal financial aid subvert the intent of a regulation focused on limiting for-profit schools from being entirely dependent on federal dollars, it actually incentivizes these companies to aggressively recruit and market to veterans and service members. Given the alarming recruitment practices documented by the Government Accountability Office in its August 4, 2010 report on for-profit recruiting, this loophole means that military personnel are sought-after targets for recruitment.

A CALL FOR CHANGE THROUGH TRANSFORMATIVE CURRICULA

Based on the successes of the aforementioned program, the elements that seem crucial to sustainable educational initiatives are those that jointly promote self and social awareness in conjunction with meeting academic requirements and providing practical skills.

While we acknowledge the importance of achieving high scores for school administrators, I believe there is a way that Indian schools can shift from the examination-centered curriculum and still yield quality performing students through a more inclusive methodology.

The transformative educational experience celebrated by Freire carries with it the potential to awaken both a social consciousness and an analytical mind. Inherent in this process is the capability for students to blend academics and life so that the material they learn in the classroom does not remain there. Instead, it is the conversations they share with their peers and mentors that provoke the liberation of their critical consciousness, which they can continue to build on throughout their lives. The proposed learning unit that follows stems from an attempt to provide an inclusive, student-focused structure where the teacher is a facilitator, a colleague and a guide. By integrating three disciplines—history, literature and art—the purpose is to view a concept from multiple angles, question the past and the present and discover what lies in between.

The target demographic for the proposed interdisciplinary curriculum is a 12 grade class in ITTC, an independent school located on the South-West coast of India, in the state of Goa. The school was inspired by the Rudolf Steiner philosophy of developing self awareness and a connection to the surrounding world but its founder Liza Chowgule has adapted this model to follow her own unique student-centered method of teaching. With regard to the standards for ITTC, the curriculum incorporates a combination of standards used by the Rudolf Steiner system along with the Mid-continent Research for Education and Learning (McREL) standards as a guideline for this learning unit. As ITTC combines Steiner's philosophy of experiential learning, social responsibility and artistic expression throughout disciplines with Liza Chowgule's own adaptation of the curriculum, we may have to negotiate the standards outlined in this learning unit with Ms. Chowgule before teaching the course.

This learning unit is designed to be carried out for four-to-five weeks, during which classes will be held twice a week for one hour each. Given that students already have a background in Indian history and the British Raj, the focus will be specific to Goa, which is a product of Portuguese colonization along with a variety of other cultural influences including

Hindu and Muslim dynasties. Emerging from this one-month module, the aim is for students to develop and enhance the following skills: critical thinking, teamwork, self-reflection guided by historical perspective, speech and interpersonal communication, creative presentation and thorough research skills.

The assessment portion of the curriculum will be based on the development of these skills through a variety of outlets, in the form of performance based and written projects. To demonstrate their understanding of the topics, student will hone the above skills by conducting an in-class debate, writing a short Op/Ed newspaper article, interviewing people, writing a position paper by incorporating primary and secondary sources and presenting the paper and primary argument to the class.

With regard to assessment, the curriculum corresponds with the view proposed in Julie Klein's (2002) *Interdisciplinary Education in K-12 and College: A Foundation for K-16 Dialogue* that suggests assessment is more effectively integrated into curriculums when it is conceived alongside curriculum design rather than as an after thought. Moreover, as further supported by this argument, we believe that the practice of introducing the forms of assessment to the students at the beginning of the learning unit, whether a position paper, interview or art exhibit, is critical for students to fully conceptualize the purpose as well as the ultimate goal of the course.

The objective for this curriculum is to introduce the students to the central text *Heart of Darkness,* critique the depiction of colonialism with other works of literature and analyze the context in which they were written.

As the students examine literature from different perspectives, the goal is that they will be able to simultaneously connect some of these themes to Goa's history of colonialism through local architecture, literature, historical narratives and art.

By beginning with a broader idea of colonialism as represented in literature and gradually narrowing the focus to the student's own lives and communities, the idea is to stimulate a sense of self-awareness amongst the students of how colonialism has affected them personally. The concepts that are woven into this curriculum all fall under the overarching essential question: how does colonialism shape identity?

My hope is that this essential question will successfully tie the individual lesson plans to the overarching concept and provide students with a more holistic and comprehensive learning experience. In breaking down this question into smaller components, the four-to-five week curriculum will address concepts such as historical narratives and differing perspectives as demonstrated in literature, effects of colonialism on nations and individuals and a critical self-reflection on the implications of colonialism on oneself.

This leaning unit aims to unite all these elements by following one of the components outlined by Klein (2002). Here she identifies various definitions of interdisciplinary education along with the common thread that ties them together. One of the most compelling definitions was the description of interdisciplinary courses in a college setting, explained as "a process of answering a question, solving a problem, or addressing a topic that is too broad or complex to be dealt with by a single discipline or profession". This interdisciplinary curriculum aims to incorporate a variety of skill-based activities that will take the students on a journey, which will eventually lead them to initiate a self-reflective course of action. By understanding the history of colonialism through the lenses of literature, history and art, students will be challenged to examine the different dimensions of this theme in their nation's history and ultimately its contributions on a more personal level.

The intention behind an overarching essential question of such a vast scope was for students to consider the concept of identity as tied to colonialism from numerous perspectives. The majority if not all of the students in the classroom will be Goan and for this reason it is important to address the historical and cultural significance of colonialism in their lives, specifically in relation to their communities and families. Ultimately, the hope is that this curriculum will stimulate the students to consider the influencing factors that shape their own mindsets and belief systems.

This curriculum is most influenced by Freirean pedagogy in its aim to connect educational subject matter to students' personal experiences. By raising the question of how colonialism shapes identity, this curriculum encourages students to examine the effects of colonialism on various social structures, starting from literature, moving into local art and history, including their own families and communities and landing ultimately on themselves.

The aim is that both students and educator challenge one another's assertions, thereby raising the level of consciousness, promoting meaningful dialogue and enhancing the process of discovery together. These Freirean principles of liberatory education provide the basis for a student-centered educational environment, toward which this curriculum aspires. India's children are ready for the transformative classroom experience and have been for a long time. What are we waiting for?

HISTORICAL BACKGROUND OF BRITISH COLONIAL RULE

Officially, the period of the British Raj lasted between 1858 and 1947. Roughly a century before that, the English East India Company exercised control in India through political maneuvering that transformed trade into territorial control. The process of political control began gradually, with the Company establishing territorial groundwork in major cities such as Bombay, Calcutta and Madras. Their power was reinforced in Bengal as they strategically aligned themselves with local rulers, initially as advisors and then as an armed force to the kings who soon become dependent on the Company's military support to maintain their autonomy from neighboring rivals. In a similar vein, local political conditions as reflected in the elites' dissatisfaction with the ruling class allowed the Company to increase their stronghold on trade for textiles to land revenues of Bengal. The British consolidated their power in the region by using their military power to convince indigenous elites to hand over judicial control as well.

Since the impact of British rule on India is both too multi-faceted and extensive to discuss at length, this chapter will focus on two specific areas, namely the influence of the agriculture and modern industry development caused by deindustrialization on the system of education as established by the British. The role of agriculture is integral to India's economic past as well as present, but more significantly it provides a link to the nation's growth from its pre-industrial roots to its entrance into the global market economy. It is interesting to explore where education fits in this transformation.

In a nation whose economy depended primarily on weather patterns to sustain its population, rice and rainfall came to be linked to "high population density and low ratios of land to labour". For this reason, the British settled in Bengal, a region rich in both assets.

Not only was it copious in water and arable land but Bengal was also a hub for trade and hosted a fairly hierarchical community. Part of the appeal for the British was attributed to the soaring rents that the land in this region could demand as well as high-earning class of Bengalis who were seldom of the peasant class. In contrast however, the peasant population was more egalitarian, jointly owning land and raising livestock concurrently with farming duties. British control over the region led to an increase in cultivable land by 60 million acres between the years of 1885 and 1938, out of which roughly 50 percent was irrigated.

The greatest transformation though, arrived toward the late 1800s, when India experienced thriving commercialization of their agricultural industry that was driven by increased trade and expansion of both foreign and local markets. In fact, it has been argued that some of the most significant contributions made by the British were related to agriculture through the restoration of public order, transportation development, expansion of economic markets, increased trade and advancements in technology. Nevertheless, the missing element in the discussion was the role of education as a support mechanism to the economic growth and increased efficiency of government administration. In fact, the consequences of these transformations were heavily felt in the shifting organizational structure of labour, which subsequently exposed the gap in educational support on the part of the public sector government.

Modern Industry and Deindustrialization

According to many scholars including Tirthankar Roy (2002), the development of modern industry in India was essentially a result of the nation's association with Britain. From technical expertise to advanced equipment and capital accumulation brought by the British, he argues that the transformation of organization of work in India led to the development of urban labour markets in major cites. This in turn "encouraged the growth of railways, ports, laws, banks and technical schools; and was the force behind the modernization of services". The major consequence of organizational change to a more commercialized industry was the increased demand for labour and labour mobility. This is explained by the theory of deindustrialization that suggests that as a nation develops, there is a marked transfer in its organized production and consumption features from predominantly manufacturing industries that greatly rely on manual labour to services that require more high-tech or skilled work. The consequence of this for a country is that there now is a demand for higher levels of education from its population. This, coupled with increased technological growth, raises the demand for a higher skill-set from its employees due to the implementation and adaptation to new technologies and telecommunication skills.

During the 1800s, India experienced an economic boom due to the combination of agricultural growth and global technological advancements, raising its export value fivefold between the years 1870-1914, with agricultural goods consisting of approximately 70 to 80 percent of exported goods. As a result, the national market opened up, causing labour to become more transferable as well as internationally marketable.

However, this boom did not carry over into the early to mid-twentieth century due to scarcity of resources and an economic lull.

While this may be the case, the fact still remains that in order for technological advancements and economic growth to be supported, there must be a simultaneous effort on the part of the public sector to invest in education. As noted by the World Bank (1995), "investment in education contributes to the accumulation of human capital, which is essential for higher incomes and sustained economic growth" (p. 1). This notion is further supported by economics Nobel Prize winner Robert Lucas (1993) who argued that "the main engine of growth is the accumulation of human capital—of knowledge—and the main source of differences in living standards among nations is differences in human capital" (p. 270). Instead, the Indian reality painted an entirely different picture. Noticeably absent in this dynamic of intensified labour was an effective mass education system on the part of the British or Indian authorities (before and after independence in 1947) to support the development of human capital. To examine the system of education that was implemented by the British, it is important to consider some of the reasoning behind administrative decisions.

THE COLONIAL EXPERIENCE AND THE LINK TO EDUCATION

In "Education in British India", Syama Prasad Mookerjee (1944) argues that the Indian education system that was introduced in the nineteenth century by the British spawned from one of two choices: the incorporation of an already widespread indigenous system that could be revitalized using innovative programming or the creation of an entirely new system that would be completely unrelated to the prevailing indigenous one.

The choice was made to implement the latter which according to Mookerjee (1944), "was largely dissociated from the cultural and educational traditions of the people and which made an alien language the vehicle of new ideas that were expected to regenerate the people of India" (p. 30). There is wide consensus amongst academics that this decision to introduce an entirely new system of education was influenced by the fact that the British government wanted to utilize the national education system to breed a population of clerics to support the colonial machine (Kumar, 1988; Mookerjee, 1944; Zachariah, 1970). Furthermore, the bureaucracy that would govern all aspects of this new system, from syllabi to textbook content and teacher training, would strengthen the government's hold on a major component of India's social services: its education system. Finally, by making English the medium of instruction, the British developed another tool that would complete their stronghold on the educational system to prepare the lives of future civil administrators.

The impact of the combination of these factors on the current status of Indian education, it is important to trace the process that led up to it. The excessive focus on examinations and over-emphasis on specialization are two elements that emerge repeatedly when investigating some of the influences behind current education trends. In the early 1940s, if one was to ask any secondary school administrator to cite the best feature of his school, approximately eighty percent would most likely refer to the high standard of their promotion examinations and the consistently good entrance examination test scores. While the remainder might cite other valuable contributions to education, it is unlikely that innovative curriculum design would fall under that list. English secondary education is essentially the product of prominent British headmasters such as Samuel Butler and Edward Thring and even they found it difficult to implement their own ideas or values on education due to their dependency on grants from the public administration. Thus, the intensive investment on delivering a certain caliber of results is best articulated by Sir Richard Livingstone who in *Education for a World Adrift* refers to examinations as "payment by results," indicating that as long as examinations are a measure of a student's aptitude, diligent teachers have a duty to ensure acceptable results at any price.

The role of political will is another important factor to address in a conversation that questions the absence of inspiring curriculum design. In reference to the role of education in promoting national identity, R.K. Yadav (1974) argues, "...in India too much is expected from schools. Unimaginative bureaucrats and politicians who do no want to face the stern realities of social life, too often set to schools tasks which concern these in a marginal way" (p. 208). While this chapter's focus lies on the need for a link between identity and curriculum, in essence Yadav's assertion holds a similar criticism. The importance of a student's growth—intellectually, emotionally and socially—is obstructed by the demand for high test performances and administrative myopia. There is no question that lack of government allocated resources plays a vital role in constraints faced by schools. However, lack of political will on the part of public administration is as much to blame.

The emphasis on specialization at a very young age is another often analyzed consequence of the legacy of British colonial rule in India. Furthermore the over-emphasis of English as the medium of instruction at the expense of local languages served as an added obstacle for children entering secondary school. According to M. S. Sundaram (1946), British administrators such as Sir Charles Woods (President of the Board of Control during the early expansion of Indian secondary education in 1854) were surprised to find that Indian students were experiencing such difficulty grasping the English language. It has been argued that boys between the ages of 12 to 17 are much more comfortable in their own language than a foreign one and the practice of introducing English in the middle of a student's school life presents an excessive strain on them. Additionally, this inconsistency of language of instruction between primary and secondary school was matched by the tendency to overspecialize the subject areas at a young age. Appreciation for good books and curiosity for self-discovery was overshadowed by the narrow requirements faced by students like those focused on science concentrations who were found to be "totally lacking in a knowledge of historical development of the society in which they are citizens" and vice versa for those engaged in the arts.

Thus, the practice of following curriculum solely for the purpose of garnering high examination results and the over-specialization of one discipline at an early age contributes to current Indian education tendencies that continue to encourage rote learning instead of critical thinking skills. Through an analysis of what has been termed the 'textbook culture,' I will further explore the effects of early education practices of colonial India to its current state.

THE STATUS OF INDIAN EDUCATION AS INFLUENCED BY THE PAST

The notion of liberatory education is one that is often addressed in Freirean pedagogy as an approach to awaken individual consciousness in relation to the oppressive social sphere thereby gaining freedom to implement social change. In advocating for the dismantling of oppression that he believes to be a "necrophilic" force that is "nourished by love of death, not life," Freire calls for liberatory education to awaken one's social consciousness to the oppressive forces that deny basic human rights.

Based on the premise that all education is political, the Freirean approach to education promotes critical understanding of the surrounding social reality as a path toward liberating both the oppressed as well as the oppressors. The following analysis of Freire's liberatory model of education provides a foundation for the student-centered framework that holds the power to transform the learning experience for Indian students today.

Before one can encourage critical thought from her students, there needs to be an assessment of the structure and the assumptions inherent in the method of teaching itself. Freire suggests the dismantling of the authoritarian nature of the banking model of education, proposing instead a shift toward problem-posing education that encourages an exchange of knowledge via dialogue and mutual respect. In a conversation with Myles Horton, Freire approaches the notion that students are in fact the opposite of empty receptacles, as they bring to the classroom, "their hopes, despair, expectations, knowledge, which they got by living, by fighting, by becoming frustrated". In effect, the acknowledgement that everyone brings something of value to the table be it prior knowledge or experience, serves as a beginning toward the breakdown of the rigid teacher-as-educator, student-as-learner structure. Furthermore, the transformation of the role of the teacher into that of a facilitator can promote a climate more conducive to fostering mutual respect and open dialogue in the classroom. This in turn can create a space within which the needs of the students are addressed so that their social, cultural and economic concerns are brought to the forefront of the discussion. By shifting the focus to the world of the student or learner, the facilitator is able to encourage a dialogue about a critical analysis of existing social conditions, starting with a critical reading of the official curriculum itself. Thus begins the awakening of critical consciousness, through which both learner and facilitator can challenge their prior assumptions and build upon one another's knowledge to deconstruct their own social realities. While this does not necessarily lead to social transformation and the liberation of the oppressed, the raising of one's consciousness certainly plays an integral role in opening up a discourse that is a necessary prerequisite for change to occur.

This act of proposing new ideas to challenge a social condition addresses the notion that education is not neutral. Freire (1990) speaks to this in his conversation with Horton by stating that, "Education has the directivity because education has objectives, you see. Education is not neutral, and because of that it has directiveness" (p. 64). In this respect, he argues that the political nature of education calls for the educator to present a viewpoint that cannot be neutral. This is similarly explored by Giroux (1992) in his assertion that, "The question of what educators teach is inseparable from what it means to locate oneself in public discourses and invest in public commitments" (p. 41). The representation of the teacher/facilitator as a non-neutral figure while simultaneously sharing knowledge with students on a level playing field seems somewhat problematic in that there exists a very fine line between the two. As posed by Schugurensky (1998), "can we have both directiveness and a truly genuine dialogue" (p. 23)? This echoes a concern as well because it is difficult to accept the notion of a teacher who can play the dual role of a non-neutral educator and seamlessly slip into the character of a facilitator who is on equal footing with her students. If the educator enters the classroom with prior experience and opinions, she automatically exercises a certain degree of influence over her students. While this may not be addressed by Freire in his delineation of the directiveness of education in conjunction with the dismantling of the teacher-student dichotomy, Freire's emphasis on the importance of respecting the knowledge that each individual brings to the fore is an immensely valuable and powerful concept for an educator to remember and implement.

This is especially relevant to the purpose of this chapter in which student-centered education is central to relating academics to students' lives and concurrently providing them with an opportunity to explore their identities. The Total Literacy Campaign outlined in the following section serves as an example of an initiative that embodies Freirean methodology through its commitment to community-centered learning and use of relevant educational tools to promote participatory action.

'Textbook Culture'

One of the most prominent features of the typical Indian style of teaching lies in the dominance of textbook use. The emphasis on the textbook as the be-all, end-all of classroom instruction is most aptly described in the phrase coined by Krishna Kumar in the following:

The basic norm of this culture was to treat the prescribed textbook as the de facto curriculum, rather than as an aid. The teacher taught the text by elucidating it, by asking children to copy and memorize it, and finally by drilling them to answer and memorize questions that were based on it.

In examining the reasons behind this widespread national methodology, a few key factors emerge in fueling the perpetuation of this 'textbook culture' in the form of class size, the heavy focus on examinations and the low autonomy of teachers.

The impact of class size on the dependence on textbooks is explored by W. H. Taylor in "India's National Curriculum: Prospects and Potential for the 1990s". In his analysis of educational provision in modern day India, Taylor (1991) finds that due to unmanageable class sizes of 50 and above, the majority of new teachers eventually yield to the recommendations provided by their seasoned colleagues and fall "into a pattern of delivering sermons and a stylised catechism of question-and-answer exchanges" despite their inclinations prior to entering the classroom (p. 331). Unsurprisingly, as a consequence of the banking-style of education, implying that students serve as empty receptacles into which the teacher can deposit information, Taylor (1991) concludes that this method of instruction is met with blank stares and silence by the students, a reaction that is commonly associated with obedience in India.

An example of the level of students' retention is best captured in the scenario where Taylor (1991) sits in on an Environmental Studies lesson at a relatively high quality primary school, in which the topic is 'wild and domesticated animals'.

When Taylor follows the teacher's example and asks the class of 62 nine-year olds to name a wild animal not native to India, he is met with a chorus of 'Kangaroo,' immediately followed by the spelling of the animal. However, when he poses the next question of the Kangaroo's living habits and Australia, he is faced with silence and puzzled looks. In response, the teacher quickly explains that it is not norm to stray so far from the main idea of the lesson. Taylor (1991) continues to describe his experience with the students of this class when asking them questions, promptly receiving the spelling of the animal names but no overall understanding of the lesson's theme.

Meanwhile, as previously discussed, the magnitude placed on examinations has often been argued as a catalyst for reemphasizing the 'textbook culture.' As mentioned earlier, Krishna Kumar (1988) attributes the examination system to the advancement of the bureaucratic system of education, originating in assisting English administrators in maintaining norms during colonial rule. In his words "the official function of the examination system was to evolve uniform standards for promotion, scholarship, and employment and to thereby consolidate government control". Re-emphasized in Kumar's analysis is the practice of memorizing content for the sole purpose of passing exams and subsequently gaining employment rather than understanding the material. He maintains that any information that did not fall into the requirements of the examination system would automatically be withdrawn from the curriculum regardless of how pertinent or valuable to student's understanding of the subject matter.

Finally, the lack of autonomy of teachers in choosing their curriculum is yet another explanation behind the persistence of the 'textbook culture.' According to Kumar (1988), the low status of teaching jobs in comparison to the newer professions such as medicine and law in the mid 1800s coincided with largely clerical tasks required to maintain official and administrative records. Unfortunately, the low status and pay in addition to the mundane tasks required of teachers further restricted their autonomy to select curriculum and textbooks. To further illustrate this point, findings in a study comparing the notion of professionalism between Indian and English teachers revealed that the greatest difference was the conception of power and autonomy. This was not to say that the English held more power as a group than the Indians, but that they felt more comfortable voicing any concerns with regard to professionalism. This is indicated by the response from the Indian teachers, where only one out of 40 participants felt autonomy was a vital aspect of professionalism. In their own words, two of the respondents claimed, "An occupation is a job which keeps you busy and which is of your interest. [In a] profession you have to do the job whether you like it or not for sake of money" and "In an occupation there is autonomy and freedom. In a profession there is none".

In combination, these three factors of classroom size, examination-focus and lack of teacher autonomy all contribute to a heavy emphasis on a static learning process that is dedicated to the written word of textbooks and the absolute answers stringently followed by teachers and required on state-wide examinations. While some have attributed the practice of rote learning in Indian schools partly to the tradition of Sanskrit scholarship, this chapter supports the work of Paulo Freire, who calls for attention to the assumed power dynamic between the student-teacher relationship and emphasizes its dismantling in order for a transformative educational process to occur.

PROFESSIONAL MILITARY EDUCATIONAL CONTINUUM

The Officer PME Continuum reflects the dynamic system of officer career education. It identifies areas of emphasis at each educational level and provides joint curriculum guidance for PME institutions. It is a comprehensive frame of reference depicting the progressive nature of PME and JPME, guiding an officer's individual development over time.

a. The continuum structures the development of Service and joint officers by organizing the PME continuum into five military educational levels, precommissioning, primary, intermediate, senior and G/FO. It defines the focus of each educational level in terms of the major levels of war (tactical, operational and strategic) and links the educational levels so each builds upon the knowledge and values gained in previous levels.

b. The continuum also recognizes both the distinctiveness and interdependence of joint and Service schools in officer education. Service schools, in keeping with their role of developing Service specialists, place emphasis on education primarily from a Service perspective in accordance with joint learning areas and objectives. Joint schools emphasize joint education from a joint perspective.

PME Relationships

a. PME conveys the broad body of knowledge and develops the habits of mind essential to the military professional's expertise in the art and science of war. The PME system should produce:

(1) Officers educated in the profession of arms who possess an intuitive approach to joint warfighting built upon individual Service competencies. Its aim is to produce graduates prepared to operate at appropriate levels of war in a joint environment and capable of generating quality tactical, operational and strategic thought from a joint perspective.

(2) Critical thinkers who view military affairs in the broadest context and are capable of identifying and evaluating likely changes and associated responses affecting the employment of US military forces.

(3) Senior officers who can develop and execute national military strategies that effectively employ the Armed Forces in concert with other instruments of national power to achieve the goals of national security strategy and policy.

b. JPME is that portion of PME that supports fulfillment of the educational requirements for joint officer management. Joint education prepares leaders to both conduct operations as a coherently joint force and to think their way through uncertainty.

The PME Continuum

a. PME Levels. The continuum relates five military educational levels to five significant phases in an officer's career.

(1) Precommissioning. Military education received at

institutions and through programs producing commissioned officers upon graduation.

(2) Primary. Education typically received at grades O 1 through O 3.

(3) Intermediate. Education typically received at grade O 4.

(4) Senior. Education typically received at grades O 5 or O 6.

(5) General/Flag Officer. Education received as a G/FO.

b. Levels of War. The continuum portrays the focus of each educational level in relation to the tactical, operational and strategic levels of war as outlined in CJCS Manual 3500.04C, "Universal Joint Task List (UJTL)." It recognizes that PME and JPME curricula educate across levels of war.

c. Precommissioning Education

(1) Institutions and Courses

(a) Military Service Academies.

(b) Reserve Officer Training Corps (ROTC) units.

(c) Federal and State Officer Candidate Schools (OCS) and Officer Training Schools (OTS).

(2) Focus. Precommissioning education focuses on preparing officer candidates to become commissioned officers within the Military Department that administers the precommissioning program. The curricula are oriented toward providing candidates with a basic grounding in the US defence establishment and their chosen Military Service, as well as a foundation in leadership, management, ethics and other subjects necessary to prepare them to serve as commissioned officers.

d. Primary Education

(1) Institutions and Courses

(a) Branch, warfare or staff specialty schools.

(b) Primary PME courses.

(2) Focus. Primary education focuses on preparing junior officers to serve in their assigned branch or warfare or staff specialty. The curricula are predominantly Service oriented, primarily addressing the tactical level of war. Service schools that have programs centered on pay grade O-3 officers will foster an understanding of joint warfighting necessary for success at this level. Joint learning areas are embedded in Service PME instruction.

e. Intermediate Education

(1) Institutions and Courses

(a) Service Intermediate PME Institutions.

1. Air Command and Staff College (ACSC).
2. Army Command and General Staff College (ACGSC).
3. College of Naval Command and Staff (CNCS) at the Naval War College.
4. Marine Corps Command and Staff College (MCCSC).
5. Service-recognized equivalent fellowships, advanced military schools and international military colleges.

(b) Joint Intermediate JPME Institutions.

1. Joint and Combined Warfighting School (JCWS) at Joint Forces Staff College (JFSC).
2. Joint Advanced Warfighting School (JAWS) at JFSC.

Focus

Intermediate education focuses on warfighting within the context of operational art. Students expand their understanding of joint force deployment and employment at the operational and tactical levels of war. They gain a better understanding of joint and Service perspectives. Inherent in this level is development of an officer's analytic capabilities and creative thought processes. In addition to continuing development of their joint warfighting expertise, they are introduced to theater strategy and plans, national military strategy and national security strategy and policy.

PROFESSIONAL MILITARY EDUCATION POLICY

Overview

The Officer Professional Military Education Policy (OPMEP) defines CJCS objectives and policies regarding the educational institutions that comprise the officer PME and JPME systems. The OPMEP also identifies the fundamental responsibilities of the major military educational participants in achieving those objectives.

a. The Services and NDU provide officer PME and JPME to members of the US Armed Forces, international officers, eligible federal government civilians and other approved students.

   (1) Each Service operates its officer PME system primarily to develop officers with expertise and knowledge appropriate to their grade, branch and occupational specialty. Incorporated throughout Service-specific PME, officers receive JPME from precommissioning through G/FO.

   (2) NDU institutions enhance the education of selected officers and civilians in national security strategy, resource management, information resources management, information operations and joint and multinational campaign planning and warfighting.

b. All officers should make a continuing, strong personal commitment to their professional development beyond the formal schooling offered in the military educational system. Officers share responsibility for ensuring continued growth of themselves and others.

Scope

This instruction addresses PME and JPME from precommissioning to G/FO levels.

Intent

a. Professional development is the product of a learning continuum that comprises training, experience, education and self-improvement. The role of PME is to provide the education needed to complement training, experience and self-improvement to produce the most professionally competent individual possible.

b. In its broadest conception, education conveys general bodies of knowledge and develops habits of mind applicable to a broad spectrum of endeavors. At its highest levels and in its purest form, education fosters breadth of view, diverse perspectives and critical analysis, abstract reasoning, comfort with ambiguity and uncertainty and innovative thinking, particularly with respect to complex, non-linear problems. This contrasts with training, which focuses on the instruction of personnel to enhance their capacity to perform specific functions and tasks.

c. Training and education are not mutually exclusive. Virtually all military schools and professional development programs include elements of both education and training in their academic programs. Achieving success across the joint learning continuum relies on close coordination of training and education to develop synergies as personnel develop individually over time, acquiring and performing progressively higher skills and responsibilities as their careers advance.

d. Opportunities for substantial professional education are relatively rare – particularly for the extended in-residence education that produces the learning synergies that only come from daily, face-to-face interaction with fellow students and faculty. Consequently, the PME institutions should strive to provide as pure and high quality education as feasible.

Training Transformation (T2)

a. On 1 Mar 02, the Department of Defence issued a

Strategic Plan for Transforming DOD Training to provide dynamic, capabilities-based training in support of national security across the full spectrum of Service, joint, interagency, intergovernmental and multinational operations. Key objectives of T2 include preparing individuals to: think intuitively joint; improvise and adapt to emerging crises; and achieve unity of effort from diversity of means to meet the joint operational requirements of the combatant commanders. T2 regards joint education as fundamental to creating a culture that supports Transformation, founded on leaders who are innately joint and comfortable with change. T2 requires joint education to prepare leaders both to conduct operations as a coherently joint force and to think their way through uncertainty.

b. T2 efforts have implications for military education. The CJCS, as advised by the Director, Joint Staff, the Deputy Director of the Joint Staff for Military Education (DDJS-ME) and the Military Education Coordination Council, retains responsibility for formulating policies for coordinating the military education and training of members of the Armed Forces; the Services retain responsibility for managing the quality and content of their Services' PME programs at all levels within the guidelines of the military educational continuum and where appropriate, implementing policies contained in this document. T2 efforts and military education will remain coordinated and consistent. T2 decisions, initiatives or programs affecting military education will become operative when they have been reviewed and approved by the affected Services and the Chairman of the Joint Chiefs of Staff.

INDIAN MILITARY TRAINING COOPERATION

The Indian Armed Forces have the experience of operating over varied terrain, which is possibly unique in the world. The Indian Army has some of the finest training facilities in jungle, snow and desert warfare. The operational deployment and sustainability range from mountains and glaciers in the North, to the deserts of Rajasthan, and from the jungles of the North-East to the marine environment of the Island territories. They have continuing operational experience in the entire spectrum of conflict, from operations other than war, to low-intensity conflict and conventional war fighting. The forces have a rich tradition of highly professional training, supported by state-of-the-art training facilities, constantly updated and refined through live combat experience. The vast expertise can therefore be utilised to impart meaningful training to the defence forces of countries in the regions of interest, as also to conduct joint training, to build up close military ties and healthy, mutually beneficial bilateral relations. Military training cooperation can therefore be made a focal point of India's peacetime military diplomacy.

It is however necessary to draw out essential parameters within which IMTC will need to be used by India. A careful cost-benefit security/strategic analysis will have to be done prior to providing training assistance to specific countries, as resources are scarce.

For this be the countries are to be prioritised, in consultations with the MEA, for developing, maintaining and fostering military training cooperation. Protecting sensitive technologies and information will be of prime importance during joint training and exercises. It will also be imperative to ensure safety of own troops provided as part of training teams with other countries.

Training Courses with Foreign Armed Forces

Professional courses with foreign armed forces, especially advanced countries like the US, offer an excellent opportunity to acquire specialised skills for any country for its armed forces which would help in enhancing their own training standards.

Participation in such courses also enables the participants to interact with counterparts from other countries and build long-term relationships, which can be beneficial to all the participating services. So, it is essential to avail of courses being offered by other countries, irrespective of the size and status of the country offering the course, to have a more visible presence at different levels in the foreign military training establishments. This will also help to establish long lasting ties, with future military leaders of the countries in the areas of interest. It is for this reason that India sends officers to attend courses in smaller countries like Bangladesh. India welcomed the Chinese invitation to send officers to attend courses at the National Defence University in Beijing. Three officersone each from the Army, Navy and the Air Force are attending a one-year course there, which began in September 2002. It will be in India's interest if more officers are sent to attend professional courses in the training institutions of the PLA.

Training Courses in India

Military training is India's forte and it is essential to take advantage of this strength to harness the goodwill of the younger military generation of other countries in the regions of interest and to establish strategic relationship with them. Towards this end, India is imparting military training to the personnel of friendly foreign countries, under the Indian Technical and Economic Cooperation (ITEC) and Special Aid Programmes (for Bhutan and Sri Lanka) of the MEA, Special Aid Programme (for Nepal) of the Ministry of Defence and under bilateral reciprocal schemes.

During 2002-03, as many as 128 foreign military personnel were trained under ITEC through long and short-term courses in the training institutions of the three services.

The MEA allocates funds for training of foreign military personnel of many countries, and course allocation in the training institutions of the three services is based on availability of this fund.

But, is not adequate for the desired level of military-to-military cooperation and needs to be substantially enhanced. India should aim to have military officers of nearly all South-Asian countries in its training courses, even if it means doubling the intake into some of the courses. Training assistance provided to countries in South-East Asia should also be vastly increased. This would lead to greater reliance of these countries on India for specialised training and reduction of the influence and hold of countries like China. Till the time India's National Defence University is set up, personnel from Chinese Armed Forces can be offered courses at the Indian National Defence College at New Delhi and Defence Services Staff College at Wellington.

India needs to utilise the expertise gained in UN peacekeeping operations by imparting training to other countries in various facets of peacekeeping. A large pool of personnel who have participated in these operations, are available as instructors. Their experience and feedback after each mission helps in updating the training content and methodologies at the Peacekeeping Training Centre in Delhi. With the proven de-mining capability and vast experience in dealing with Improvised Explosive Devices and disposal of unexploded ordinance, the Indian Army can impart practical training to the personnel of friendly countries.

The former Soviet Union/Russia has been the major supplier of defence equipment to India and India has always been the model for developing countries in maximising the utility of the Soviet designed weapons and technology that the designers in turn, further improved them.

Over a period of time, India has built up the necessary infrastructure and expertise to handle this equipment and also service it. It can therefore, offer to train the crew and technicians of countries in the region who are holding Soviet or Russian equipment (The training of Malaysian MIG 29 aircraft pilots and ground support staff by India is a suitable example in this context).

The training requirements of the Indian Navy are varied and multi-dimensional.

This has necessitated the establishment of a number of basic and specialised training academies and institutions throughout the country. It would be beneficial to train foreign naval personnel in specialised areas such as submarine warfare and helicopter operations.

The hydrographic capability of the Indian Navy is today the fourth largest in the world. The Indian Naval Hydrographic Department possesses vast experience with a longstanding tradition of professionalism, state-of-the-art equipment, modern infrastructure and trained personnel. The Indian Naval Hydrographic Centre can organise and conduct training programmes on a regular basis for naval officers of the Indian Ocean littoral countries. This would enable those countries to establish hydrographic departments for their navies if they do not have them already, and also participate in the survey large areas of the seabed in a joint and coordinated manner.

The aspect of English language training, before imparting professional training to students of those countries where of English is not commonly used, has to be taken into account. It is advantageous to have the training syllabus for officers in the services in English language as it is used in several countries. It may be desirable to design courses wherein English language and IT application are first imparted first, followed by the requisite training in the appropriate fields/specialisation at the training institutes in India.

Workshops/Seminars/Conferences

A number of countries regularly hold important workshops/ seminars/ conferences on regional security and current issues of importance. Participation in these seminars exposes the participants to the perspectives of various participating nations, on the existing security environment and current trends. Such events can facilitate interaction among regional militaries and serve as non-political fora for senior military officers to meet and discuss professional military subjects on a non-attribution basis.

They also provide opportunities to voice opinions and make others see India's viewpoint, on important global and regional issues. The College of Defence Management, Secunderabad invited for the first time, representatives from friendly countries to attend its annual seminar in January 2003 with the focus on 'National Security'. India needs to become the regional hub for strategic thinking thought and organise defence seminars on a regular basis, inviting service officers from the world over.

Indian Military Training Teams in Other Countries

India has been sending training teams to a number of developing countries to impart military training to their personnel and has also cooperated with these countries to assist them in establishing training institutions on the Indian model. India has very strong ties with Africa. After independence it became the voice of the colonised countries and showed the way in the opposition to Apartheid. It has also been training the armed forces of a number of African countries. It now finds Africa a source for its growing oil and gas needs and so increased cooperation will be still more important. In addition, efforts India needs to make to locate our training teams in the neighbouring countries like Myanmar, Nepal, Bangladesh and Sri Lanka to decrease their dependence on countries like China and the US.

Joint Training Exercises

Combined exercises between defence forces facilitate interoperability and conduct of joint military operations against a common threat. They provide insight into each other's leadership techniques, battle drills and standard operating procedures. By training together in peacetime, confusion and delays are prevented and joint operations made smooth and effective. Confidence levels, professional trust and respect are built up through joint exercises. Moreover, such exercises convey signals to potential adversaries and challengers of authority, about the joint military response their actions could invite.

Joint Naval Exercises (JNE) JNE also assume immense importance in promoting bilateral/multilateral cooperation. They are conducted in international waters, away from the public gaze, where sensitive issues such as violation of sovereignty, etc., assume little importance. JNE help to dispel concern over

India's naval build-up programme and expansion of power projection capabilities. Such concerns were made known to India from the mid-1980s by some littoral states of the Indian Ocean, including Australia. The interactions provided by the exercises both at sea and port create transparency regarding the activities and responsibilities of the Indian Navy. JNE are perceived to help instil, as well as build upon, a military dimension to bilateral political relationships as well as signify India's interest in peace and stability in the Indian Ocean.

Performance in the company of foreign navies enhances the professional reputation of the Indian Navy. Joint exercises with advanced navies such as US, France and UK, are beneficial in enhancing operational effectiveness, interoperability and identifying areas for modernisation.

However, it is also important to lay equal stress on bilateral and multilateral exercises with the navies of the region. This would enable the regional navies to gain professionally as India looks to gain from advanced navies. Towards this, the Indian Navy has been conducting in the Andaman Islands an exercise called *Milan*, biannually Since 1995 which is aimed at cementing ties with neighbours.

Naval ships of the regional navies have participated in this exercise at Port Blair. The objective of *Milan* is to look at the common problems at seapollution, piracy, search and rescue operations as also to strengthen bonds between the navies.

This needs to continue for the protection of mutual security interests. This would also stem extra-regional influences and manipulations. There is also a requirement to hold bilateral exercises with the smaller naval powers in the region like Sri Lanka and Bangladesh.

India and Iran carried out JNE in March 2003 off the Mumbai port. This was a development with geo-political significance, given India's aspirations for strategic relevance from the Gulf of Hormuz to the Straits of Malacca and in view of Chinese assistance in the construction of the Gwadar Port on Pakistan's western coast.

This could be the beginning of a relationship which could give India a strategic toehold in the Persian Gulf, the key to the world's energy security. The Russian and Indian Navies conducted their biggest-ever exercises in the Arabian Sea in May 2003. This was the first operational engagement between the two navies. This will play a significant role in strengthening co-operation, trust and mutual understanding between the two naval powers. JNE with China will bring in greater transparency and help to strengthen relations following high-level political visits from both sides.

A SENSIBLE GUIDE TO PREPARING FOR SELECTION IN THE GURKHAS

Physical fitness has a number of components: aerobic endurance (stamina), strength, speed, flexibility, muscle endurance, power and agility. A training programme can be developed to improve one or more components of the physical fitness. In this context we are going to look at the aspects that are important to us: aerobic endurance (stamina), muscular endurance and flexibility.

Aerobic endurance (stamina) is defined as body's ability to perform for prolong period of time at a relatively low work rate. This type of training conditions the heart and lung, eventually improving body's ability to deliver and consume oxygen more efficiently. Examples of activities that improve aerobic endurance are running, cycling and swimming; but it should be done at a steady pace for at least 20 minutes. It is important to have a very good base of aerobic endurance, as it will help to train and improve other components of fitness.

Muscular endurance is the ability of a single muscle or a group of muscles to perform repeatedly against moderate to high resistance; for example, work of abdominal and hip flexor muscles during the 2 minutes sit up test. Muscular endurance is dependant on aerobic endurance, as the muscle needs supply of oxygen to perform rapidly. Body resistance circuit training is a very good way of improving muscular endurance. 2 – 3 sessions per week is recommended to improve muscular endurance. Often forgotten or neglected yet equally important is flexibility. It is defined as a range of motion at a single, joint or a series of joints. Although not an obvious components of fitness it is important in injury prevention. Stretching exercises during warm up and cool down is enough.

What is Required?

The British Army selection process demands a wide range of physical fitness tests such as stamina, muscular endurance and speed. The tests during the Regional Selection are mainly focused on muscular endurance and speed and the Central Selection focuses on aerobic endurance. Following are the tests conducted during Regional and Central selection.

Regional Selection:

- 800 metres run in 2 minutes 45 seconds or under.
- 12 heaves (under arms grasp).
- 70 Sit-ups in 2 minutes.

Central Selection:

- 1.5 miles (2.4 km) run in not more than 9 minutes 40 seconds.
- Stamina assessment – complete a 5 km route (height gain of approximately 450 meters) carrying 25 kgs in not less than 48 minutes.
- Swimming Assessment – Complete 20m in BGP Pool (Breast stroke only).

How best to train yourself for the selection.

Foremost, it is wise to identify what is it that you intend to achieve from the training plan. It is best to design a training programme based on your needs rather than following what others are doing. For example, if you can easily achieve 'sit ups' but struggle to perform heaves then the training programme needs to concentrate on strengthening your upper body strength. The training also needs to be monitored and adjusted, if necessary.

It is essential to design a progressive training programme to prevent injury. Training session should be made harder as the standard improves. Some form of record may be kept to check whether the training is progressing in the right direction. The table below is an example of a progress record. Don't be too ambitious.

Overload. The principle of overload is to increase the workload (for example, running time or running speed) so the body gradually adapts to the new increased workload which means stamina is improved and workload can be increased again. But one must be very careful about increasing the workload; too much increase could lead to injury and too little may not improve the fitness level.

Month	*Heaves*	*Sit Ups*	*800m Run*
May	5	40	4:00 minutes
Jun	8	50	3:30 minutes
Jul	10	60	3:15 minutes
Aug	12	70	3:00 minutes
Sep	14	80	2:40 minutes
Selection	16	85	2:30 minutes

Reversibility.If the training is stopped for a period of time the fitness level will decrease. It is necessary to take few steps back depending on the period of inactivity and re-start the training again.

Recovery.This is the time when repairing of damaged tissues caused by severe training sessions occur. This also allows time for energy replenishment for body.

Training without recovery often leads to breakdown. An active recovery may be achieved by doing low intense activities or sports.

The right nutrition helps to recover body more rapidly. For example, protein oriented food (dairy product, fish, egg) will help on the maintenance of damaged tissues and carbohydrate oriented food (rice, pasta, fruit juice, bread) will help on energy replenishment. Drinking water regularly will balance the level of body fluid preventing dehydration.

Planning a Training Session

A single session comprises of three main components: a warm up, main part and a cool down.

The Warm up.The main aim of the warm up is to prepare body for what is coming next or for the main bout. It can be between 10 and 15 minutes long.

It starts with very low intensity activities like jogging, easy skipping. The intensity of activities gradually built up toward the end to at least the commencement of sweating.

General stretching of the major muscles are also recommended at this stage. Stretching should be hold for 10 to 15 seconds and repeated 2 to 3 times for each muscle or muscles group. Bouncing and jerking motion must be avoided while doing stretching. Benefits of the warm up are:

1. To mobilize the joints preventing injury.
2. To increase heart rate gradually increasing blood flow.
3. To increase deep muscle and whole body temperature.
4. To be psychologically prepared.

The Main Part. This is the part that gives the main training benefits.

It should last between 20 to 50 minutes. If you are new to the fitness training then you should aim to conduct a 20 to 30 minutes session, increasing the period to 40 to 50 minutes, as you get stronger.

The Cool down. This is the final part of the session. It helps body to return to normal state. During exercises a large supply of blood goes to working muscles. It is important to return these blood supplies to the central circulation system. This can be achieved by reducing the intensity of work gradually. Activities like light jogging or walking for a few minutes will help to bring heart rate down gradually. Stretching of the major muscles should be carried out. Stretching should be hold for 20 to 30 seconds and repeated 2 to 3 times for each muscle or muscles group. A high level of 'flexibility' gain can be achieved by doing stretching at this stage.

INDO-US MILITARY TRAINING COOPERATION

The US is paying particular attention to building a close relationship with India, commensurate with its emerging power status. The bilateral military and security cooperation is redefining US-India bonds. The US military co-operation with India can be viewed as a desirable strategic necessity, in terms of India's long-range national security requirements and interests.

Both countries have embarked on joint exercises for humanitarian airlift, special operations training and small unit group exercises between US Marines and Indian forces. These exercises enhance the ability of US forces to integrate with Indian armed forces (with non-NATO standard equipment) into a broad spectrum of operations, promote bilateral cooperation and goodwill between both the services.

The US core interests are high altitude warfare and counter insurgency skills. A 50-member US Army contingent underwent training at Counter-Insurgency and Jungle Warfare School (CIJWS), Vairangte in Mizoram in July 2001.

This was however, commented upon adversely in the media on the assumption that India was offering bases to the US. India can offer its expertise in high altitude warfare and counter-insurgency and enhance the level of training for the US forces. The forthcoming joint training exercises in Ladakh are a step in this direction.

Advantages of Military Training Cooperation by India

Military training cooperation by India has contributed to building bridges of friendship with regional countries and it needs to be enhanced further.

This cooperation also enriches the Services' cadres by widening horizons and vistas and add substance and stature to India's military capabilities, potential and status. It also assists in acquisition and enhancement of frontier and contemporary technologies, some of which have applications beyond the military field.

Building Bridges with Regional Countries

Military training cooperation has played a significant role in building strong ties by India with the countries in the neighbourhood and extended neighbourhood. The fact that the Indian Army is training the Royal Nepalese Army, to help it tackle the Maoist insurgents is a positive factor in Indo-Nepal relations. It is in India's interest to provide military assistance to the neighbouring countries against internal disorders so as to prevent outside forces from moving into the region.

There is a proposal for India to participate in the training of the Afghan army. This was discussed during the visit of the Afghan Defence Minister, General Mohammad Qasim Fahim in May 2002. The Indian Army and the Air Force have played a crucial role in the training of the Afghan forces before the collapse of the Najibullah regime. Like Afghanistan, the Indian Army is composed of many ethnic and religious groups, and possesses expertise in fighting in high altitude terrain. It was add to the stature of India if it has a physical military presence in Afghanistan.

India has established a military facility in Farkhor, Tajikistan, to train Tajik defence personnel and service military equipment of Soviet and Russian origin. An Indian military delegation is expected to visit Dushanbe soon to firm up plans for a joint military exercise, the first of such war games by Indian troops in Central Asia.

The move is in keeping with New Delhi's initiative to forge stronger ties with the region. This is also a signal of cooperation between the two countries in the war on terrorism and a role for India in the race for access to oil and gas-rich Central Asia. The resumption of military-to-military ties with China, is part of the process to normalise bilateral military ties which plays a significant role in the overall improvement in Sino-Indian relations. This has been advanced with the recent visit of the Indian Prime Minister and the Defence Minister to China. India can offer to train the PLA personnel in its training institutions and also participate in joint exercises with China to bring in greater transparency in the military sphere.

The Indian Director-General of Military Training along with representatives from all the three services visited Myanmar in December 2001, to look at the provision of military training and identify areas in which the defence forces could provide assistance. This reflected increasing military cooperation between the two countries with training being an important component. India can improve its relations with Myanmar through military assistance to counter the undue Chinese influence there and ensure peace and tranquility along the border between the two countries.

Joint military adventure training activities with the neighbouring countries is a recent endeavour in promoting bilateral relations. In a unique show of comradeship, Indian and Bangladeshi Army personnel jointly conducted a rafting expedition in the Ganga River in November 2002. As part of the Everest Golden Jubilee Celebrations, a joint expedition was undertaken by the Royal Nepal Army and the Indian Army during March-June 2003. A number of mountaineers from the two countries have scaled Mount Everest in May this year. There is a lot of scope for joint military adventure training activities like hot air ballooning, paragliding, and windsurfing etc., with the neighbouring countries, to build stronger military-to-military ties.

Benefits to the Armed Forces

To sum up, participation by the defence forces in training activities with other nations has a number of direct payoffs. Professional knowledge and skills are updated and it provides a benchmark to ascertain training standards, with respect to other countries. It also gives an insight into the available technology in a particular field, for modernisation of the defence forces. IMTC helps to project the image, professional ethos, capabilities and strengths of the defence forces internationally. It also assists in developing and maintaining contacts with the defence forces of other countries, at the organisational and personal levels. It also creates an understanding pool of cadre in the services of the target nations, while countering perceptions advanced by countries that are inimical. Through joint training, interoperability can be practised for conduct of combined operations, against a common enemy and for participation in multinational UN peacekeeping operations.

PEACETIME MILITARY DIPLOMACY

Peacetime military diplomacy is an important constituent of the five basic channels of nation-to-nation contact between friendly governments, i.e., political, diplomatic, economic, cultural/social, and last but not the least, military. As a component of foreign policy, it aims to bring in greater transparency and confidence in the military sphere and contribute towards closer relations with countries through constructive use of defence resources in times of peace. It also serves as a means of conveying a nation's security concerns and perceptions and creation of a favourable security environment.

While it is true that diplomacy is the first line of defence and defence is the last, it can be reasoned that in between, one can have military diplomacy, whereby the military is seen as an additional channel and avenue by which conflicts could be averted, if not resolved. Rather than viewing diplomacy and force as opposing ends of the spectrum of national policywhere one is used when the other failsit is important to recognise that each must seamlessly support the other.

This entails striking the right balance between foreign policy and security interests and strengthening military relations through foreign policy tools like military training programmes, arms transfers, security dialogues and confidence-building measures.

These efforts pay off, with stronger security relationships with other countries. Military diplomacy does not in any way develop outside the diplomacy of the state and the scope and scale of military relations are influenced by the tenor of overall relations. The government spells out the broad parameters of foreign policy and military diplomacy is an essential component of this policy.

India has an abiding stake in peace and stability in its neighbourhood for its long-term security and projection on the regional and eventually the world scene. One of the objectives of India's foreign policy is the intensification and consolidation of ties with the neighbours and strengthening of peace and security in the region as a whole, through mutually beneficial cooperation. Peacetime military diplomacy can help to build the foundation for regional cooperation, which is based on mutual trust and confidence.

Upgrading military ties, by looking at various alternatives of peacetime military diplomacy in a sustained manner, can reduce the security concerns in the region and assist in the fulfilment of the foreign policy objectives. International Military Training Cooperation (IMTC) is an essential component of peacetime military diplomacy and can prove vital in furthering India's strategic interests.

British and Chinese Peacetime Military Diplomacy

Peacetime military diplomacy has been recognised as an instrument of state policy by a number of countries. Britain and China are two countries that have institutionalised peacetime military diplomacy and are conducting it in a coordinated and sustained manner.

The establishment of military diplomacy as a defence mission by Britain has provided better coherence and renewed impetus to peacetime activities by its armed forces. China has been active in developing an omni-directional and multi-level form of military diplomacy. Chinese armed forces have been active in participating in multilateral military diplomatic activities to bring the positive role of the Chinese armed forces into full play in the sphere of international military affairs.

Britain

In recognition of the changed post-Cold War strategic environment, Britain carried out a strategic defence review (SDR) in 1998. It provided a reassess-ment of Britain's security interests and defence needs, and considered how the roles, missions and capabilities of its Armed Forces could be adjusted to meet these new realities. The SDR concluded that the Armed Forces should not only defend Britain and its interests, but also be 'a force for good in the world' and help prevent and contain crises. The SDR acknowledges conflict prevention and peacetime diplomacy as core defence activities. A new defence mission of 'Military Diplomacy' was created (Eighth Defence Mission). The Mission was defined as follows:-

"To provide forces to meet the varied activities undertaken by the Ministry of Defence to dispel hostility, build and maintain trust and assist in the development of democratically accountable armed forces, thereby making a significant contribution to conflict prevention and resolution"

Three specific Military Tasks (MT) underpin, and contribute directly to this Mission: *MT 16*arms control, non-proliferation, and confidence and security building measures; *MT 17*outreach activities designed to contribute to security and stability in Central and Eastern Europe, particularly Russia, but also extending to the Trans-Caucasus and Central Asia, through bilateral assistance and co-operation programmes; and *MT 18*military training cooperation with foreign military forces.

The aim of creating this Mission was to ensure that military diplomacy was more focused and suitably linked to Britain's wider security and foreign policy objectives. This was met by integrating the Ministry of Defence's activities very closely, with those of other government departments, particularly the Foreign and Commonwealth Office and the Department for International Development. Drawing from the above, peacetime military diplomacy in the Indian context can be defined as under: "In keeping with foreign policy and security objectives, establish, build and maintain military-to-military contacts with other countries so as to contribute to strengthening of relations and enhancing peace and security."

China

Presently, in China, the foreign military relations programme of the Peoples' Liberation Army (PLA) is strictly a matter of 'realpolitik', as Beijing expands its interactions with the international community. It serves as an important adjunct to Beijing's global diplomacy and is an integral part of China's national defence policy.

In pursuance of this purpose, the PLA is actively engaged in external contacts and exchanges, in a flexible and practical manner, and is making sustained efforts for enhanced mutual trust, friendship and cooperation with the armed forces of other countries. The world's largest army is now practicing military diplomacy as an integral part of its overall diplomacy and has taken advantage of the reforms and liberalisation for a new look. The PLA has taken up military diplomacy in a big way to dispel 'fears' among neighbours and other countries alike that Beijing is a threat to them. This however has not succeeded as some of the countries in China's neighbourhood still consider it a threat.

Over the past two decades, the PLA's role has increased considerably and is likely to become even more significant in the future, as China develops its military capabilities and projects a larger international profile.

PLA's foreign relations programme has several goals: to shape the international security environment in support of key Chinese national security objectives, to improve political and military relations with other countries, to enhance China's military modernisation and to acquire knowledge in modern military doctrine, operations, training, military medicine, administration, and a host of non-combat-related areas.

Beijing's larger geo-political strategy of dominating South Asia is manifested through extensive military assistance to Pakistan, Bangladesh, Myanmar and Sri Lanka. China has sought to gain strategic advantage over India by progressively making India's neighbours dependent on China to a large extent for their defence supplies.

A large proportion of military equipment of Bangladesh and Myanmar is of Chinese origin, thus resulting in increasing dependence of these countries on China, for spares/replacement and training. This indicates that military diplomacy is being pursued by China to destabilise the region in pursuit of its larger interests, mainly strategic containment of India. In stark contrast, the thrust of India's peacetime military diplomacy is limited to providing military assistance to improve the training standards of the armed forces of other countries or to help them deal with internal security problems. This needs to be enhanced to give India greater leverage in the region as also in the international arena.

Peacetime Military Diplomacy through IMTC

IMTC, both bilateral and multinational, is an important constituent of peacetime military diplomacy and a significant instrument to further national strategic interests. All defence forces provide training in preparation for employment in the assigned role and tasks thereof.

The training encompasses pre-induction or entry training and advanced professional training in various fields. While this training is carried out internally, it can also be conducted by involving foreign participation, both bilateral and multinational.

IMTC covers a wide range of training activities including conducting courses, providing training teams and military training advisers to other countries, organising multinational conferences and seminars to enhance mutual understanding, conducting bilateral and multinational army, air and naval exercises, joint adventure training activities and sports. Such cooperation helps to build strategic security relationships with countries and address common security concerns. Common threats, especially those related to international terrorism, can be better handled through joint training and operations. The synergy and enhanced fighting potential so achieved can ensure timely and coordinated response in a crisis situation.

US Approach to IMTC

The US military strategy has prescribed a bigger global role for the armed forces, in its foreign policy. Both the scope and goals of military activity have increased after the end of the Cold War, with the aim of 'filling security vacuums' and enlarging the US-friendly, stable space in the world. Under the rubric of 'environment shaping', there has been an expansion in the range of military assistance programmes, multinational exercises, military-to-military contacts, and other forms of military diplomacy.

In addressing the challenges facing the US, the State and Defence Departments work together to identify where US interests lie, in order to ensure that policies and planning processes are consistently connected.

Nowhere has this been more apparent, than in the area of security assistance. Security assistance is a national programmes administered by the State Department in conjunction with the White House, the Congress, and the Treasury Department. The programmes are executed by the Department of Defence. The geographic commanders-in-chief (C-in-Cs), working within the policy guidelines set in Washington and collaborating with US ambassadors and country teams within their areas of responsibility, tailor programmes and activities to meet changing local and regional requirements. Through the C-in-Cs, the United States conducts peacetime engagement activities with nations around the world—building stronger military relationships with allies and friends in the process. This is peculiar only to the US due to its global reach.

One of the important components of security assistance is military training. Over the past decade, one of the principal means by which the US has interacted with almost all governments in the world is by training their military forces. The United States has a pro-active approach to military diplomacy wherein training teams are dispatched in those regions where it has significant strategic interests. The US military offers over 2,000 courses, covering combat skills, military management, civil-military relations and use of US weapon systems. One of the key programs under which training is provided is the *International Military Education and Training (IMET)* programmes. This programme has proved beneficial in furthering US national security interests and in fostering better relationships. In some cases this is the only military or diplomatic tool the US can use, to engage certain countries. During FY 2002-03, the US allocated $65 million to the IMET programmes. It facilitates foreign military students to study in the US thus enhancing their military professionalism along Western lines and strengthening their own training capabilities. As a corollary, the Programme provides the US, access to, and influence with, foreign military and defence leaders.

The US has provided $17 million to Nepal in 2003 for training of the Royal Nepal Army. Joint training programmes have proved to be force multipliers that pay off with stronger security relationships with allies and other countrieswhich in turn have proven critical in international responses to conflicts such as in Kosovo. The IMET programme is considered as perhaps 'the most cost-effective security assistance programme'. The US conducts military training not just to win friends, but also to push their political agenda in other states. A seat in a US military college is a 'coveted mark' of the world's lone superpower's favours.

Offering berths to officers of the developing countries provides the US unrivalled ability to influence the officer cadre of their armed forces. Military training is sometimes also justified as a reward for political support, as provided by the US to the tiny Pacific island state of Tuvalu. (Tuvalu was one of the only four countries, which joined the US and Israel in voting against the October 2000 UN Resolution condemning Israel for its indiscriminate use of force in Palestine). Training cooperation activities also provide direct benefits to US service personnel. In fact, a number of these programmes are conducted for their benefit. Whenever US servicemen meet with their foreign counterparts, they improve their understanding of the counterparts' military organisations, language, culture, and political system. They also improve their understanding of the global environment into which they might deploy in the futurewhether in combat, or as part of the regular forward presence. Familiarity with foreign environments is vastly improved when the training cooperation activities are conducted in the regions rather than in the US.

9

New Challenges of National Security Reform Management

INDIA'S INTERNAL SECURITY REFORMS UNION GOVERNMENT CHOICES IN SECURITY REFORM

Given India's limited resources, New Delhi's increasing re-allocation of its overall security resources towards internal and border security, and 'continental' defence against near neighbours like Pakistan tends to detract from military modernisation and development of force projection capability. One way of illustrating this is to show that the share of defence spending on the 'blue water navy', the classic tool of force projection, has remained in percentage terms fairly constant over the last few decades, shifting only from 13 per cent of the defence budget in 1994 to 14.5 per cent today.

This percentage share is low for a power seeking a force projection capability. For example, it compares with a percentage share for the US Navy of 26 per cent. Against this, concentration on close-in coastal defence and security has risen dramatically following 26/11.

Another way of measuring the costs of internal security is to look at the rising cost of police and paramilitary forces in relation to military forces. State police numbers have been rising at well above the rate of the population increase, from 1.37 million in 1997 to 1.75 million in 2007 (available positions

– there are about 1.5 million police in situ.) This rise reflects the position of the Union Government that India is under-policed.

As well as this rise in police numbers, the Union Government's burden of expenditure on homeland security has also risen significantly. Since 9/11, the percentage share of homeland security (not including the Coast Guard or state police) in relation to defence spending has risen from 11.76 per cent in 2000-01 to 18.5 per cent in 2009-10 (budget estimate). The Union Government now supports police forces costing Rs 12,817 crore (US$2.27 billion), up from Rs 5,677 crore (US$ 1.2 billion) in 1999-2000 – or a rise of 126 per cent in nominal terms.

The data suggest that there has been a proportional shift within India's security spending between power accretion spending and internal security spending. This is not to say that conventional defence spending has not been rising handsomely, but rather that internal security has become an urgent focus of the Union Government.

Internationally, however, this proportional shift has been overshadowed by the far greater global interest on India's rise as a military power. Although there has been a shift in emphasis in favour of internal and border security spending, the focus of that shift is still in favour of 'hard' (or some might say 'repressive') use of power and against other instruments for achieving better governance outcomes.

In this equation, the various paramilitary forces, the armed constabulary (numbering nearly half the state police), the Coast Guard and the various intelligence agencies might be considered as 'hard' power.

'Soft' elements, on their part, might be said to consist of the police working to protect the community from crime, the legal structure, various measures to ensure governance, justice and accountability, and approaches that seek to alleviate the lot of those with grievances, such as economic support for tribal and Muslim populations or granting greater autonomy to separatist regions. Diplomatic, economic and aid efforts designed to create a more robust regional grouping in South Asia also fall within this 'soft' category.

This chapter focuses only on India's security choices in relation to its internal security mechanisms rather than its diplomatic, trade and aid activities in the South Asian region or the needs of national defence against attack by another country.

But it is worth noting that, although regional security building is an extremely difficult area of activity for India as the regional 'giant', it is a crucial activity in terms of India's wider security, not least in achieving cooperative regional outcomes against transnational terrorism and crime. Nor do we deal with the various attempts of the government to meet the needs of disaffected minorities such as tribals, Muslims or those in other areas, seeking separation or greater autonomy.

Equally, these are absolutely vital areas of activity for balanced approaches to counter-terrorism and counter-insurgency. Due to the magnitude of these topics, however, they cannot be covered in this chapter.

Given the reality of India's federal structure, it will be natural to expect the Union Government to be most active in areas of its jurisdiction such as defence, federally funded paramilitary forces, the national intelligence agencies, central police and centrally administered laws.

State and local level activities will tend to get a lesser emphasis, at least from the Union Government. Thus, many of the activities at the 'soft' end of the spectrum, such as policing reform and 'community policing', will not fall directly within the jurisdiction of the Union Government. As for state governments, while some may have an incentive to improve these aspects of security in their jurisdictions, others will be less active in the pursuit of reform. A state political class that has the police under its influence, for example, will be far less willing to conduct meaningful police reforms than one that is not. And it is because of this that many states have resisted efforts to reform the police, including the efforts of the Supreme Court and various police reform commissions.

It is a central tenet of this chapter that the Union Government should develop ways of providing additional focus on so-called 'lower order' issues of security, such as anti-corruption measures, the rights of individuals and modernisation of the police and judiciary, even though they fall predominantly within state government jurisdictions. Without leadership from the centre in these areas, the current drive for greater internal security – especially as it has been developed since the attacks of 26/11 – is unlikely to prove sustainable. Although the Union government is clearly restrained in the level of its activity in respect of these areas by the Constitution, there are a number of ways it can become more active and activist and these areas.

INDIA'S SECURITY CHALLENGES: PERSPECTIVES AND PROSPECTS

The profound changes in the world wrought about by the end of the Cold War have made for a fundamental restructuring of international relations. The end of ideological rivalry provided an objective opportunity for evolving a better security environment. However, there is a great deal of uncertainty and fluidity all around, as the new global equilibrium gets in place. Two or three factors would deserve attention in this regard.

The Cold War bipolar structure has been replaced by a "polycentric" world with the United States, Japan, China, the European Union and Russia emerging as the main partners in power. Technology and economic power has moved to the forefront of international relations, emerging as a crucial factor in global realignments in the new setting.

The near symmetry in power capabilities and global reach between the two superpowers in a tightly bipolar world has given way to a certain disaggregation in the levels of power and capabilities among the new centres of power, given their uneven spread of techno-economic power, military capabilities and political influence. Even the United States, the most powerful nation today, has neither the will nor the capability to play a global role of the earlier order and magnitude. China, Japan, the European Union and Russia are in a process of defining their role in the new world order. Relationships between and among these centres of power are increasingly marked by elements of both engagement and containment.

Notwithstanding a broad shift from confrontation to conciliation at the global and regional levels, new points of pressures are unfolding themselves even as some old conflicts remain unresolved. For the developing countries, there is also evidence of new concerted pressures in economic, security and nuclear fields. It is clear that there are manifold pressures emanating from the international environment which make for a complex and multilayered set of challenges and opportunities for India in the changed world order. India would have to respond to, if not anticipate, the new challenges and maximise its strategic political options, drawing essentially from its own power potential and bargaining leverages. This would at the least call for proactive strategies in terms of both restructuring old ties and forging new relationships at the regional and global levels.

India's security perspectives would inevitably be governed by the interplay of its domestic imperatives, regional balance of forces and the global challenges which impinge on its role and capabilities. India with its size, resource potential and strategic location is being increasingly seen as a regional influential poised on the threshold of emerging as a centre of power in the new international order. This is as much a recognition of its credible democratic functioning as the potential of its vast economic resources and political clout. India is a large multiplural society which has been able to successfully manage the challenges emanating from regional, linguistic and religious diversities without damaging its national cohesiveness. The remarkable resilience of its democratic functioning in a secular federal framework, despite some distortions, has continued to bely the scepticism of its worst critics. India's democracy remains fundamentally secure, underpinned as it is by an active judiciary, free media and a functioning and vigilant Opposition. India's economic development has also remained steady over the years. In the last couple of years, the Indian economy has registered an impressive growth rate of 7 per cent. The expansion and diversification of its industrial capacity have made important strides. Currently India ranks among the topmost industrialised nations of the world. It has the distinction of having the third largest pool of trained and scientific manpower in the world. Agricultural production has also shown substantial growth resulting in not only self-sufficiency in food grains but also reserves of impressive buffer stocks. Today with its burgeoning middle class, huge untapped markets for trade and industry, and large scale foreign investments, India has emerged as an economic power of some significance on the global scene. India has also built an impressive level defence capability. It has the fourth largest Army in the world with an impeccable professional record. It has a credible and self-reliant defence structure which has been built assiduously over the past three decades. India's missile development programme has also grown apace underlining its indigenous technological capabilities.

It is clear that India is slated to play an increasingly larger role in the coming decades. Its future as a credible power would, however, depend as much on its ability to manage the present stage of transition as on the projection of its strategic perspectives and policy options for the future. Two or three points deserve mention in this regard. First, India's status and power projections remain essentially contingent on its national security in terms of political stability, economic development and military strength. Second, although the asymmetrical power structure in South Asia ensures India's centrality, its regional power and influence tends to get circumscribed by the neighbouring countries' sustained pressure to counter its pre-eminence. In particular, Pakistan's unceasing search for parity with India makes for a deep-rooted strategic dissonance in the region which effectively reduces its capacity to shape or influence events in its neighbourhood. Third, continued involvement of external powers in the region remains an integral part of South

Asian geo-political realities. The end of the Cold War has weakened the inevitable link up between regional conflict and Great Power rivalry. However, the inability of the states of the region to evolve a credible bilateral and regional framework for cooperation would continue to play an important role in reinforcing the pattern of external involvement—primarily in pursuance of their own stategic interests—in the region. This is bound to impinge on India's security perspectives, both short-term and long-term.

An overarching framework of India's national security has to take cognisance of military and non-military dimensions in terms of both external threats and internal challenges to its territorial integrity and national unity. Threats to a nation emanate as much from external aggression as from internal strife but at times internal factors can erode national security more critically than any external danger. National power based on political stability, societal cohesion and economic development would thus remain central to the future of India's national security.

India is passing though a crucial period of its post-independence history. Successively fragile coalition governments at both the central and state levels are affecting India's political, social and economic stability at a time when it is facing major challenges to its unity and integrity as a nation. The Indian political system is being subjected to manifold pressures from the progressive collapse of political and public institutions; incipient erosion of democratic norms; social unrest and corruption underlining a growing malaise in Indian polity. Increasing demands for power by more and more socio-economic groups, on the one hand, and limited resources and capabilities for redistribution of wealth, on the other, make for growing political and social turmoil. Widening economic disparities and growing rate of unemployment pose a major challenge for India's economic development notwithstanding a credible economic performance. It is estimated that by the year 2000, the total number of people living below the poverty line will more than the entire Indian population at the time of independence.

India's growing inability to manage political and economic challenges on the domestic front is a cause of deep concern. Although India's national integrity remains fundamentally secure, pressures from fissiparous cleavages in growing challenges of communalism and religious fanaticism have acquired disturbing dimensions.

Political manipulation of religious sentiments for narrow political ends has long-term implications for the future of India's secular federal framework. The incipient threats to Indian federal polity in many parts of the country are putting growing strains on the political structure. Although India has been so far able to manage these challenges with a certain skill and patience, there is growing anxiety about the pressures getting intensified at a time when there is a steady erosion in the state's role in resolving conflict and bringing about social transformation. This is accompanied by a decline in the mediating role of the governing elite and party system. Decline in the state's order and authority has led to greater violence outside the established political channels, compounding the general law and order situation.

Continuing civil strife and incipient secessionism poses a major problem for India's national security. The northeast continues to be characterised by an uneasy peace. Although there is no full scale armed insurrection for secessionism as resorted to by the Nagas and Mizos in the Sixties, the problem of insurgency in Tripura, Manipur and Nagaland continues. Assam which had settled to a period of normal political functioning after the volatile agitation on the influx of foreign nationals in the early Eighties, is once again going although the fire of violence perpetrated by the United Liberation Front of Assam (ULFA) which is committed to armed struggle for the formation of a sovereign "ASOM". Punjab went through the unfortunate agony of sustained armed violence for over a decade before normal political processes were restored after heavy-handed crushing of Khalistan terrorists. The people of the state have, however, paid a heavy price for the then government's short-sighted policies for narrow political ends which changed what was essentially a party agitation to a Sikh movement encompassing divergent orientation and rationales. This has important lessons for the future of Indian federal polity which can only be ignored at one's own peril.

The situation in Kashmir remains a cause for deep and continuing concern. Mishandling of a brewing political crisis brought about by the state government's dismal performance, marked by rampant corruption and inefficiency, led to an explosive situation in the sensitive valley. The eruption of violence in 1990 served to underline the appalling failure of the intelligence agencies and the complete isolation of the political and administrative machinery from the ground realities. In the event, alienation of large sections of the civil population and their growing sympathy for the militants left little meeting ground between the people and the government. The recent restoration of political processes in the state following Parliamentary and Assembly elections and the increased weariness of the people with economic dislocation and high-handed intrusion of outside militants is leading to a slow change in the equation of forces on the ground. But the overall situation remains precarious. The process of rebuilding the sundered economic and political fabric in the state and winning over the confidence of its people for any worthwhile and lasting solution continues to remain in uphill task. There is no gainsaying that the problems facing Indian polity are enormous as evidenced by the persistence of insurgency and slow entrenchment of terrorism in several parts of the country. If left unresolved, these could critically jeopardise India's national sovereignty and territorial integrity from within.

It is self-evident that the foremost task for India is to overcome the challenge to its nation building and national security. India's real autonomy in working out its destiny as an independent centre of power would lie in its internal strength and cohesion. There is no getting away from the urgent task of upholding its unity and integrity as a nation state through a credible framework of secular federal democracy. The need for reinvigorating its democratic functioning and strengthening the role and efficiency of the state remains imperative in this regard. India would also have make sustained efforts to vitalise its economy through optimisation of its vast resources, manpower and technical know-how. The need for redefining the role of the state in terms of eradication of poverty and greater economic equity remains self-evident. At the same time, India would have to raise itself to a new level of efficiency and competitiveness to acquire necessary leverages to stand up to growing global pressures and to hold its own in a friendly competitive world.

India can also not afford to drop its guard on building an adequate defence capability to counter any vulnerabilities which can be manipulated by external forces. There is some concern regarding growing deficiencies in India's conventional capability due to reduced defence expenditure in recent years. The need for adequate defence expenditure and defence allocation, constant modernisation and updating of its defence acquisitions for its defence preparedness remains imperative in this regard. A credible defence capability would provide an effective guarantee for maintaining its territorial integrity in the face of both external aggression and also externally engineered internal subversion that has emerged as a primary threat in recent years.

In the final analysis, it is only a politically stable, economically prosperous and militarily strong India which can seek to play its legitimate role in the world community, commensurate with its size and vast power potential. Issues of regional peace and stability continue to loom large on India's strategic horizon. South Asia is today on the threshold of a new era of democratisation as the process of evolving democratic structure is under way in almost all the countries of the region. The peaceful electoral transfer of power in Pakistan four times in a brief span of nine years reflects a growing commitment to democratic norms in that country. Bangladesh is firmly back on the track of democratic functioning after a long paralytic spell of negative agitational politics. Notwithstanding ups and downs, Nepal also continues to manage its democratic experiment credibly. At the same time, there are vested and deeply entrenched authoritarian interests in all these states, particularly the ones which have been under military rule for long years. For instance, the continued dominance of bureaucratic military oligarchy in the political set-up in Pakistan makes for a fundamental dysjunctive in its policy. Given the fragile democratic institutions in all these countries, the democratic process itself is releasing new pressures. It is thus that the domestic environment in South Asia continues to remain generally characterised by political unrest and regime instability.

Pressures from ethno-sectarian conflicts and religious fundamentalism are also rising in all countries of South Asia. Pakistan is sitting atop an ethnic cauldron as pressures simmer, threatening to tear apart the fabric of Islamic identity from below. The challenge in Sindh underscores the disturbing dimensions of large scale violence between ethnic groups. The continued Punjabi domination in the power structure spells a certain uncertainty for the future of Pakistani federal polity. Running feuds between Shias and Sunnis in various parts of Pakistan have become a common feature on the Pakistani scene. Sri Lanka remains mired in prolonged ethnic conflict as the continued intransigence of the Liberation Tigers of Tamil Eelam (LTTE) makes for a virtual civil war in the strife-torn island. Sinhalese resistance to grant of effective and substantive devolution power to the Tamils only queers the pitch of ethnic politics in the multi-ethnic society of Sri Lanka. Even Bangladesh which has a relatively homogeneous society is facing problems in overcoming difficulties in integrating its small tribal minority. The likelihood of the region remaining in a state of crisis due to rising scale of political and social discontent is thus going to be a part of South Asian realities for quite some time. This not only poses a threat to state structures within these countries but also has an adverse impact on the matrix of inter-state relationships in the region.

The overlap of a large number of ethnic, linguistic and religious groups across essentially porous borders in South

Asia makes for a cross-border spill-over movement of refugees, guns and drugs which generates inter-state tensions. The steady movement of refugees, following prolonged domestic conflict in the countries of origin, has emerged as a multi-dimensional problem which affects regional security. Refugees who tend to settle down in the host countries, given the intractable nature of ethnic conflict, put an intolerable burden on the demographic, financial and social sectors which has long-term implications for national security of the host country. Pakistan is still reeling under the impact of 3.5 million Afghan refugees who sought refuge following the Afghanistan crisis in the Eighties. Thousands of refugees are living in camps in Nepal as a result of ethnic conflict in Bhutan. Bangladesh has also had to cope with the Rohingyyas fleeing from Myanmar.

For India particularly, which has been the host to the largest inflow of refugees with practically no outflow, the magnitude and frequency of refugee movement has been a vexing problem. This has particularly grave implications for the social, economic and political stability of the sensitive northeast. The presence of a large number of Chakmas in Tripura is intensifying tensions among the local inhabitants who are resenting encroachment on limited jobs and resources and scarce land. Thousands of Sri Lankans who sought refuge in Tamil Nadu in the Eighties are continuing to stay on, creating pressures with the attendant problem of anti-social and criminal activities. Induction of arms and anarchy with refugees is becoming a growing political liability. Internecine conflict among militant refugees groups and their continued links with trans-border militant groups intensifies social unrest and level of violence with grave implications for the future of civil society in these regions.

Growing linkages between drug trafficking and organised violence and the magnitude of the proliferation of small arms are also becoming major sources of instability in the region. In India there is growing concern regarding inter-state linkages between militant organisations, on the one hand, and between states and militant organisations on the other, adding to the complexity of secessionist movements. The crucial link-up between hostile external forces and domestic forces of political subversion poses a serious challenge to India's national security by giving impetus to secessionist forces. Terrorism in Kashmir since the Nineties, and earlier in Punjab in the Eighties, has acquired disturbing proportions with Pakistan's unabashed manipulation and support through planning and coordination, training of militants, and unlimited supply of arms and finances. The supply of sophisticated weaponry in particular—including rockets and explosive devices—has undeniably helped to raise the level of conflict to a new high.

By some accounts, the number of men lost in combatting the low intensity conflict in the sensitive state of Kashmir has outstripped the number of casualties in all the full scale Indo-Pak Wars put together. It may be mentioned here that internal political dynamics in Pakistan would continue to make for increasing domestic compulsions to keep the pot boiling in Kashmir, both in terms of diverting attention from pressing domestic problems as well as the inherent stakes of the military establishment in retaining the primacy of calling the shots in Pakistan.

In the strategic northeast ringed as it is by Myanmar, China and Bangladesh, incipient secessionism remains vulnerable to external manipulation. Although China which had offered arms and sanctuaries in the Sixties is no longer doing so, its unchanged stand on recognising the grant of statehood to Arunachal Pradesh and its military presence in Myanmar underscores its potential to foment trouble at a time of its own choosing. Bangladesh's involvement—albeit low key—is well-documented. Pakistan's Inter-Services Intelligence (ISI) is also carrying out anti-India activities from Nepal and Bangladesh adding to India's security concerns in view of persistently unsettled conditions in the northeast.

Today the growing incidence of insurgency, fomented and abetted by hostile external forces has in some way emerged as a major problem for India's security establishment. The statement of the former Chief of Army, terming the low-intensity conflict as the foremost challenge for India's national security only serves to underline the growing intensity of the problem.

Proliferation of small arms in the region is yet another disturbing dimension of cross-border terrorism. The inflow of weapons is a direct fall-out of the Afghan conflict and the siphoning of major chunks of arms sent by the US, China and Saudi Arabia for onward transmission to the Afghan Mujahideen.

It bears pointing out that "small" arms is a mere euphemism for progressively more sophisticated and lethal weapons. The weapons circulating in the region include automatic rifles, machine guns as also landmines, sophisticated explosive devices, and communication systems. Even more worrisome in the fact that these lethal devices are finding their way to non-state actors and terrorist groups. This has significantly altered the level of internal conflict in India's troubled regions, making for deep concern for the inevitably long-drawn and prolonged conflict in sensitive border states with major implications for the deployment and engagement of security forces.

Unwholesome linkages between the drug barons and arms dealers comprise yet another cause for concern. The enormous funds generated by drug sales are being increasingly used to finance purchase of sophisticated weaponry by terrorist groups in South Asia. South Asia is abutted by two of the largest drug producing areas on its western and eastern flanks.

The growth of narcotics trade has been exponential in Pakistan, with the presence of a reported 1.5 to 2 billion heroin addicts. Infiltration of drug money into the Pakistan economy and political system is now well documented. There are also growing reports of significant penetration by the narcotics network in Pakistan's law enforcement agencies and military intelligence.

The widespread Kalashnikov culture in Pakistan is a function of the mutually supportive phenomenon of drugs and weapons. Vast quantities of these arms have found their way to Punjab and Kashmir. These weapons have also been used to create internal unrest in urban centres as evident by the vicious bomb blasts in Bombay in 1993. India is also fast emerging as a transit route for the narcotics trade, given its strategic location between two major narcotics producing areas. Drugs from Pakistan and Myanmar are being transmited from India for onward transmission to European markets. It is no mere coincidence that the most critical challenges of insurgency in India are located in the sensitive border states in the northwest and northeast which adjoin the drug generating regions. More important, the growth of a flourishing criminal underworld underpinned by a nexus between illegal traders, drug peddlars, and gun dealers in tandem with internal security forces and law enforcement agencies is a cause for increasing concern. The enormous toll in human and economic terms as a consequence of mindless violence and narco-terrorism getting entrenched in civil society has implications which have yet to be comprehended fully.

The complexity of these transnational problems defies strictly national solutions. The urgency for building bilateral cooperative relationships and promoting a coordinated regional perspective on these critical developments which are cutting across the sanctity of national borders, remains, if anything, self-evident. The South Asian Association for Regional Cooperation (SAARC) Conventions on curbing drug trafficking and terrorism in the region are important steps forward in evolving suitable regional mechanisms to tackle the twin menace. The conventions, however, remain presently at odds with the ground realities. The political push to add substance to declarations of intent obviously awaits a qualitative improvement in the political climate in South Asia. Till such time, the challenges of narco-terrorism would call for sustained vigilance on India's part to counter the insidious threat to its national security.

South Asia has been generally characterised by a great deal of political and strategic complexity. To understand the complex South Asian phenomenon, one or two factors deserve special attention. First, India with its undeniably greater power potential and centrality looms large on the South Asian scene. Second, the legacy of common civilisational heritage has lent a sharper edge to neighbouring countries' sensitivities regarding their national identity in a clearly uneven setting. India with its looming presence and power potential is often projected as a core threat by these countries.

India's relations with practically all its neighbours have been strained over a whole range of issues be they of trade, or water sharing or migration or ethnic sensitivities. At the same time, there have been no even patterns of relationships in the region. India's relations with Bhutan and Maldives have been generally smooth and rancour-free. India's relations with Bangladesh, Nepal and Sri Lanka have witnessed significant ups and downs over the years but have never been allowed to dip to an unmanageable low. Indo-Bangladesh relations which had become extremely strained over the Farakka issue and the Tin Bigha controversy have witnessed a dramatic improvement with the signing of the historic agreement on sharing of Ganga waters. India and Nepal have also been able to put the unfortunate events of the Eighties behind them. Today they are set for a qualitatively improved relationship with closer economic ties and better political understanding. The signing of the Mahakali Treaty and grant of overland transit route for its trade with Bangladesh by India underlines the positive shift. The Indo-Sri Lankan relationship today is a far cry from the palpable antagonism of the Eighties.

However, the Indo-Pak relationship has been characterised by a virtually unbroken record of sustained hostility. Indo-Pak discord which to some extent has been rooted in the bitter legacy of partition became more sharp with the conflicting national interests and ideologies of the two states. Pakistan's inability to work out a viable form of nationalism and its eternal quest for achieving parity with its larger neighbour remains at the core of Pakistan's hostility towards India. The three Indo-Pak Wars—the only intra-regional wars in South Asia—were all motivated by Pakistan's desire to alter the status quo. Pakistan's military relationship with the United States in the Fifties was also directed to counter-balance India and erode its prominence in the region. This not only brought Cold War politics to the region, irretrievably puncturing the area of peace that Nehru had sought to build, but also considerably aggravated India's security concerns. Pakistan's continued overtures to external powers, particularly the United States and China, for diplomatic backing and augmentation of defence capabilities remains directed towards eroding India's pre-eminence and power. It is not necessary here to go into the details of unresolved issues between India and Pakistan except to mention that Indo-Pak relations have remained lockjammed over a wide range of issues—Kashmir, Siachin, the Afghanistan crisis and the nuclear issue. For the past five decades, Kashmir has, however, remained the central and overriding concern for Pakistan. Pakistan sees Kashmir as an unfinished agenda of partition which must be resolved on the basis of the UN Resolutions which have long been overtaken by the realities on the ground. India has made it clear that Kashmir is an integral part on which it can countenance no compromise. This is so not only for obvious strategic considerations but also because it would deal a blow to India's secular framework and open the floodgate to demands for separation. India, however, remains willing to discuss Kashmir and all other outstanding issues on the basis of the Simla Agreement which expressly enjoins bilateralism and non-recourse to force by both countries which is not what is on the Pakistani mind. Meanwhile, Pakistan's continued support—money, training and sophisticated weaponry—to secessionists in Kashmir makes for grave tensions for India.

This is not to underestimate the urgent need for India to take steps to put its own house in order but to point out that Pakistan's proxy war in Kashmir represents a direct and immediate threat to India's security. It is also important to bear in mind that Pakistan has never given up the option of going to war with India to get back Kashmir.

This has its own implications for India's security planning notwithstanding a growing recognition in both countries that the realities of a crumbling economy and sustained international pressure would militate against a full-fledged war. The world opinion has also decisively veered towards a peaceful solution of the Kashmir problem, with both the United States and China recognising the inevitability of a bilateral negotiated settlement. There is also a section of opinion which considers nuclear deterrence itself as a stabilising factor in Indo-Pak relations. Nevertheless, Pakistan's declared nuclear capability makes for India's heightened security concern, given Pakistan's less than peaceful intentions towards India. There is no gainsaying that India is faced with Pakistan's nuclear challenges at a time when the absence of a credible Russian nuclear guarantee in the post-Cold War world makes it more vulnerable than at any time before.

This also aggravates the existing pressures emanating from Chinese nuclear might and United States' insidious nuclear presence in the region. Although India has made it abundantly clear that it has the capability to respond effectively to any nuclear misadventure by Pakistan, India's security perspectives would have to reckon with a nuclearised subcontinent in all its future calculations. It also needs to be borne in mind that while the Indo-Pak Agreement on not attacking each other's nuclear facilities is a positive step foward in confidence-building, this or any other such confidence-building measure would remain essentially meaningless unless simultaneous exploration is made of the ways and means to resolve the underlying problems between India and Pakistan.

It is thus that the recent resumption of Indo-Pak dialogue at the Foreign Secretary level, after a long period of tense silence, is a welcome development for the future of Indo-Pak relations. However, even as New Delhi's call for initiating a qualitatively new chapter of amity underlines its sincere desire for a more forward looking and constructive approach, Pakistan's usual style of blowing hot and cold and its recent efforts to militarily activate the ceasefire line do not at present give much cause for optimism for Pakistan's similar response. There is, however, no denying that it is in India's long-term interests to reduce hostility with its important South Asian neighbour. This would at the least call for proactive strategies to build greater trust and cooperation with Pakistan in a framework of mutual goodwill. India's long-term security hinges perhaps in a larger measure on the future of Sino-Indian relations. It is, therefore, in India's abiding interest to work for peaceful and cooperative relations with its most powerful neighbour with whom it shares a long disputed border. A stalemate in Sino-Indian relations during the Sixties and Seventies only served to limit India's diplomatic manoeuvrability and potential role in the region.

Rajiv Gandhi's visit to China in 1988 marked a significant breakthrough in thawing the stalemate between the two countries. The agreement signed during the visit on maintaining peace and tranquillity on the Line of Actual Control (LAC), pending a final solution of the border dispute, was a momentous step forward in normalisation of ties between the two neighbours. Re-emphasis on Panchsheel and the decision to initiate confidence-building measures to reduce tensions on the borders underlined a new forward looking approach on the part of both countries. The formation of a joint Working Group at the level of Ministers to carry forward negotiations on the boundary question reflected the new political thrust at the highest level. The process of normalisation has been since carried foward by a number of steps. Agreements have been signed to re-establish the Consulate General in Shanghai and Bombay and to resume border trade across specified points along the Tibet border. A set of confidence-building measures have been set in motion: agreeing on joint verification of the LAC, meetings between the local commanders, mutually agreed pull-back of troops from forward areas and prevention of aerial violations. These measures have not only helped to effectively defuse tensions on the borders but have also considerably eased India's defence burdens. More important, for the first time since the Sixties, India does not have to reckon with the nightmarish prospects of a two-war front with China and Pakistan.

At the same time, India can ill afford to have a let up in its defence preparedness to meet the long-term Chinese challenge. Although China would be hard put to challenge India a la 1992 because of changed correlation of forces on the ground, there is no underestimating the challenge of China's emergence as a formidable power in conventional as well as nuclear capabilities which has resulted in a vast power gap between the two countries. China's defence modernisation is continuing to move apace. China also continues to be engaged in augmenting its nuclear arsenal as its launching of inter-continental ballistic missiles and underground nuclear tests amply underline. Notwithstanding China's foreswearing of "first use," India can hardly ignore the implications of a total nuclear asymmetry with China. China's major military build up in Tibet—reportedly deploying ballistic missiles of medium and intermediate range—makes for long-term strategic concerns for India's security.

It may be pertinent to note here that China's remarkably growing economy, which has received additional boost with the reversion of Hong Kong in July 1997 also gives it a definite leverage in international affairs as underlined by its manoeuvrability in its relations with the US. It has been in recent years showing greater willingness to assert its power in pursuance of its interests in the adjacent regions. China's flexing of muscles in the South China Sea and its increasing assertiveness vis-a-vis Taiwan illustrate this. Although at present China has great stakes in not upsetting its carefully structured political and economic equilibrium or aggravating tensions in its neighbourhood, given its growing economic and military power there would be continuing uncertainty regarding its future moves and projections. In recent years, more than posing a direct military threat, China continues to represent a challenge to India's role in South Asia. China has, of course, visibly refrained from engaging in anti-Indian rhetoric in terms of its relations with its neighbours. It has also apparently softened its stand on Kashmir, urging Pakistan to virtually shelve the issue while working for improvement of relations with India in other areas. At the same time, it has remained committed to strengthening its political relations with all of India's neighbours. It continues to sell arms to Bangladesh, Pakistan, Sri Lanka and Burma which tends to hem India in a subtle way. In particular, its politico-strategic collaboration with Pakistan shows no appreciable change. China's help to Pakistan in developing its nuclear weapon capability is well-documented. Its recent supply of ring magnets and M-11 missiles has disturbing implications for India, seeking to threaten as it does the present balance of power in the region. China's supply of arms worth 1.6 billion dollars to Burma and its help in construction of naval and electronics facilities, and modernisation of its naval bases are also of concern to India in its strategic northeast and the adjacent seas.

China has, of course, come a long way since the Sixties in its national perspectives and world view, engaged as it is in consolidating its economic development, promoting regional peace and establishing a "just" new world order. This has led to a growing convergence of views with India which remains committed to world peace and a just and equitable world order. They have mutually shared perceptions on the need to preserve national territorial integrity and combatting challenges of fundamentalism, ethnic separatism and cross-border terrorism. There is also a broad understanding between the two countries on global trade issues and the pressures emanating from the industrialised world on human rights and good governance. All this augurs well for a more relaxed and cooperative relationship between India and China. It would, however, need to be clearly borne in mind for India's long-term projections that relations between the two Asian giants are bound to be marked by undercurrents of competition and contest, inherent in the logic of geo-political proximity and national rivalry. It also needs to be borne in mind that the border question has been shelved but not resolved. India has vital stakes in consolidating the process of normalisation with China but as long as the dynamics of military competition remains unchanged, a durable framework of Sino-Indian friendship would have to be underpinned by an overall balance of strength and a clear recognition of their mutual power status and stakes in the region.

It is clear from the foregoing that India has an abiding stake in peace and stability in its neighbourhood for its long-term security. India is going through a phase of rapid economic transformation and is poised to play a significant role in the global stage in the coming century. There is no gainsaying that India's projection on the world scene would depend in no small measure on its effective and constructive neighbourhood diplomacy. This would at the least call for evolving a framework of cooperative security in its neighbourhood. This would essentially mean striving to reduce tensions with China and Pakistan, its two powerful neighbours, without compromising on its core national strategic interests. This is so not only because they separately and together constitute a long-term threat to its security but also because stable peace in this region hinges on India's friendly ties with these two countries. India's recent agreement with China offers ground for finding a viable basis of confidence on which to build cooperative relationships. India's offer of several confidence-building measures to Pakistan is also a step in the same direction. These include the agreement on prohibition of nuclear attack on population centres and economic targets; the agreement on "no first use" of nuclear weapons; and upgrading of communication links between DGMO of both sides. In some ways, the Simla Agreement itself provides for an effective mechanism for confidence-building between the two nations to build durable peace in the subcontinent. Sustained efforts to initiate new confidence-building measures and strengthen the existing mechanisms would remain imperative for building a credible framework of cooperative security in the region.

India would also need to take a lead in setting the tone for a framework of relations with its smaller neighbours. New Delhi is today committed to evolve a fresh perspective on its relations with its neighbours in a framework of positive asymmetry. There is no doubt that in the short run, anti-Indian rhetoric would continue to be manipulated at will by these countries, depending on their domestic compulsions, but in the long run, deft handling of the neighbours with flexibility and sensitivity is bound to lead to a more relaxed political environment. This itself would lend a great credibility to India's role as a regional influential.

Peace and development in the region is in the long term a sine qua non for India's long-term security perspectives in South Asia which is facing staggering problems of poverty, illiteracy, malnutrition and under-development. The biggest challenge to regional peace and security emanates from its poverty and the under-utilisation of its vast resources to address the socio-economic needs of its teeming millions.

Pressures of endemic poverty and population explosion are becoming critical in the region. South Asia has sunk to the bottom rung in terms of the number of its people living below the line of poverty. SAARC provides an effective regional institutional arrangement for South Asia to optimise its regional resources and capabilities to promote the welfare of its peoples and a cooperative framework for the socio-economic development of the entire region. India as the largest South Asian power has a special responsibility to give a visible push to SAARC and invest in policies which are informed by a larger and long-term vision of a cooperative and stable South Asia.

An important challenge to India's security lies in the unfolding security environment in its adjacent neighbourhood which has a vital bearing on its geo-political interests. The volatile situation in Afghanistan is of major concern to India. Afghanistan seems set to witness a fierce and long drawn struggle among the main contenders for power which, if unresolved, will lead to grave destabilisation in the trouble-torn country.

Although India does not share any borders with Afghanistan, it has fundamental geo-political stakes in the unfolding events there which can be detrimental to its own long-term security interests in the region. India, therefore, has a major stake in any outcome of the protracted Afghanistan crisis. India rightly views any fundamentalist regime in Afghanistan as an insidious threat to its own secularism as well as a potentially destabilising factor in the region. An important dimension of Indian policy is the inevitable antagonism of such a regime to India which has traditionally enjoyed close links with Afghanistan based on a shared perception of regional interests. The possible spillover of a Taliban style fundamentalist regime, in terms of impact of ideology, violence and narco-terrorism, into Kashmir makes for deep concern for India's internal security. India has, therefore, a stake in seeing the evolution of a broad based government in Afghanistan which takes care of the legitimate interests of all major groups to enable it to emerge as a stable and non- fundamentalist nation. It is in this context that India is keeping contacts with major groups within Afghanistan and supporting all broad regional initiatives from outside to solve the problem. A growing understanding with Iran and other likeminded countries is emerging as an important dimension of India's policy not only towards Afghanistan but also the politically sensitive Central Asia.

Of late, Central Asia has emerged as an area of major concern for India in view of India's long-term interest in this strategic area. This is because the situation in the region which continues to be fluid because of political instability and challenges of Islamic fundamentalism has wider implications for India's own vicinity. Central Asia has also emerged as a major strategic region in view of its vast untapped reserves of oil, natural gas and other precious resources. This has made the region a focus of sharp interest and struggle among most major powers, notably the United States, Russia, China, Iran and Turkey, who want to exploit the tremendous economic potential of the area. Although India can do little to influence the interplay of Great Power rivalry in the region, it has a stake in deepening and broadening its own interaction with the region. This would call for a more energised policy in building upon existing economic and cultural ties with the Central Asian countries making for its reinforced presence in this vital area. India is already engaged in an exercise of exploring the avenues for extending support in the field of infrastructure and technology. India has to continue to take into account in its larger security perspectives the region's great strategic, economic and political importance in terms of its energy reserves, strategic location and emerging political dynamics that are attracting wide attention and will have major implications for this whole region.

India also has vital interests in the emerging political and strategic dynamics in the Indian Ocean region. This is so because of its vital need for uninterrupted energy supplies and maritime trade through its strategic waterways. India is vitally interested in keeping the major sea lanes of communication in the Indian Ocean free for the movement of substantial portion of its trade, particularly in terms of access to vital oil supplies. Its objections to superpower presence in the Indian Ocean in the Cold War days was also a function of its concerns over escalation of tensions in its vital strategic vicinity. India's positive role in the newly formed Indian Ocean Rim Community also underlines its desire to evolve a cooperative framework of relations among the littoral countries of the Indian Ocean without undue interference of outside powers.

India's demand for oil supplies is slated to grow very steeply in the coming decades. Till such time that Central Asian vast reserves are fully exploited, the Persian Gulf which is currently accounting for 60 per cent of world's energy resources, would hold the key to global energy security. The potential of the South China Sea remains as yet largely untapped. West Asia and the Persian Gulf in particular would thus continue to remain a region of great strategic concern for all major powers, including some of the erstwhile self-sufficient countries like Russia, China and Indonesia whose reserves are getting fast depleted. Given India's strategic location to the area, India's has abiding interests in long-term stability and peace in the area because any potential destabilisation or conflict would lead to insecurity in India's strategic neighbourhood.

Given the external powers' continued quest for power and influence in the South Asian region, the need for diversification of strategic political options remains imperative for India as there is also evidence of new pressures in economic, security and nuclear fields. This calls for both restructuring the old ties and forging new relationships. India's policy towards the United States, Russia and China would have to be thus increasingly informed by the changing needs of national security and economic development as also the logic of its own role in the region. Strategic and geo-political considerations had been critical for Indo-Soviet ties in the Cold War period. But it was essentially the mutuality of interests that sustained those ties lending them a certain autonomous structure, irrespective of extraneous inputs. Mutual convergence between the two countries rested on the basic premise of Soviet endorsement of India's pre-eminence in the region.

The Soviet support was critical for India in coping with its problems with both Pakistan and China, singly and together. More important, it helped India to build a credible and self-sufficient defence structure at a time when there was visible reluctance from the West to do so. In the post-Cold War world, India and Russia have been able to credibly rework their relationship despite the initial hitches in the transitional phase in a qualitatively altered framework.

Although there has been some reduction in the volume of trade and economic interaction between the two countries, the question of repayment of loan and currency adjustment has been settled to mutual satisfaction. The new treaty of friendship and cooperation between the two countries is a reaffirmation of the abiding mutuality of the interests between them. India and Russia would continue to have a convergence of interests in the developments in their proximate regions—Afghanistan and Central Asia—where both have vital geo-political interests in promoting peace and stability.

There is also mutuality of interest on the need of averting internal destabilisation from ethnic conflict and trans-border terrorism in large multiplural societies. This has particular significance for India which faces a simmering problem in the sensitive state of Kashmir. India also has a continued stake in strengthened defence relations with Russia, given its large scale dependence for Russian modern military hardware—at reasonable prices—and advanced civilian technology in space and nuclear fields. India has been able to procure military equipment with provision for technology transfer, joint production and export to third countries. Recently, India and Russia have set up a joint working group to address the operative elements of a long-term military technological programme—the only such programme Russia has signed with any foreign country—which has been extended for another ten years beyond 2000. Russia has also offered to India the latest and advanced technology in all areas of the defence field.

At the same time, any talk of "strategic partnership" is still premature, given Russia's strategic alliance with China and its continued dependence on the West. There are also difficulties in the supply of sensitive technology—underlined by the problems in the cyrogenic deal and differences over nuclear disarmament, particularly after Russia's signing of the Comprehensive Test Ban Treaty (CTBT) and India's own position on it.

There is, of course, some satisfaction in India that Russia has now re-endorsed its stand on India's pre-eminence in South Asia and moved back from the projection of equidistance between India and Pakistan. Moscow has now reaffirmed its support for India's stand on Kashmir and its firm commitment not to supply arms to Pakistan. Indo-Russian relations, although qualitatively altered in the changed world context, would have continued relevance for India's long-term strategic perspectives.

In the post-Cold War world, maintaining friendly and close relations with the United States, the only superpower today, which is capable of shaping the regional environment, would need to receive the highest priority in India's larger strategic calculations.

Indo-US relations have remained generally lukewarm over the years essentially for the United States' non-recognition of India as a power of consequence in the region. There has been no effort by the US to develop an autonomous approach to South Asia except in relationship to its broader global objectives.

Shared democratic values have failed to provide a firm basis for understanding between the two countries whose divergent security interests lay at the root of the indifferent state of relations. This has remained so notwithstanding India's need and desire for improved relations with the United States, albeit on its own terms and from its own long-term security perspectives. The United States is seen in India as displaying singular insensitivity and disregard for India's vital security concerns in the region.

An important Indian objection to US policy in South Asia has been its commitment to the parity syndrome between India and Pakistan—including equating Indian and Pakistani nuclear policy—which India sees as not only immeasurably intensifying its security problems but also eroding India's pre-eminence in the natural balance of power in South Asia. Notwithstanding an improved phase of relationship in recent years, the United States' continued reluctance to deliver sensitive technology to India only serves to underline its disregard for India's sensitivities to the qualitative alteration of the military balance of the region over the years.

There are today greater opportunities for developing understanding between the two countries on promoting peace and stability in both South Asia as also the neighbouring strategic regions of the Persian Gulf and the Indian Ocean. Although differences persist over a range of issues—nuclear proliferation, Kashmir, trade related issues and restructuring of the Security Council—all of which have a vital bearing on India's larger security concerns there are some positive indications of Indo-US relations acquiring greater depth with evidence of more intense economic interaction and the evolution of a strategic dialogue between the two countries.

The United States which has emerged as India's single largest trading partner and investor, has an abiding interest in India's vast economy and burgeoning markets. India, of course, would need the US capital, technology and markets which remain crucial to India's future economic development. India has welcomed the recent US declaration—although belated—formally designating the Pakistan-sponsored organisation Harkat-ul-Ansar, operating in Kashmir, as a terrorist outfit. There is also some satisfaction with the US' full-hearted endorsement of the current Indo-Pak dialogue and its reaffirmation that it has no desire to intervene in Indo-Pak problems. All these would underline a growing US desire to build an independent relationship with India, notwithstanding Pakistan's continued relevance to its broader regional objectives. At the same time, a qualitative improvement in Indo-US relations would, in the long run, continue to remain contingent on the United States' recognition of India's regional pre-eminence in the building up of an independent policy towards India.

Given the inevitability of India's search for its own place in the global community, in view of its large size and power potential, and the growing complexity of its security challenges, India's nuclear policy would continue to have primacy in its national security agenda in the new world order. While nuclear disarmament must needs be India's long-term security goal, its nuclear policy has to take into account the given realities of the nuclear weapons having come to stay as an important bargaining leverage in international relations.

There is a growing recognition in India that given the current international realities and the situation of nuclear asymmetry in the region, mere retention of the nuclear option may not hold unconditionally in the altered scenario. India would have to give more sustained and serious thought to the timing of the exercise or non-exercise of its option in the days ahead. Developing a full-fledged nuclear weapon capability while continuing to press for total elimination of nuclear weapons will, of course, be the foremost challenge for India's future security perspectives.

Three or four factors deserve attention in this regard. First, time remains of the essence for India as domestic costs grow and international pressures mount on India to abandon its nuclear option and missile programme at a time when the nuclear powers are engaged in updating and refining their capabilities. Second, India has to reckon with the prospects of undeniable pressures from the US, China and Russia, should it operationalise its nuclear option. It may also find itself under increased Chinese nuclear threat in view of its unquestioned nuclear might today. Third, exercise of the nuclear option would bring to the fore the classic dilemma of development versus defence at a time when India's developmental goals require the greatest attention for sustaining its economic growth. Fourth, the goals of national security, short-term, as well as India's own aspirations, in the long-term, to play a global role of some significance, remain compelling for India's strategic perspectives. Last, can India afford to remain locked in continued confrontation with the nuclear powers—in the post-CTBT phase—and pay the inevitably high costs—economic, technological and political—without having actually exercised its nuclear option? It is clear that the whole range of possibilities—retaining the present ambiguity, opting for recessed nuclear deterrence and operationalising its nuclear option—would hold the centre-stage of the national security agenda demanding a well coordinated and well thought out nuclear strategy that would sustain India's long-term security projections. It is clear from the foregoing that India has to resolutely address itself to the emerging set of challenges and opportunities in the changed world order in a coordinated and comprehensive framework of paramount importance would be its ability to project its (long-term strategic perspectives and interests in responding to the interplay of domestic imperatives, regional balance of forces and global dynamics in the coming decades.

The overarching reality of India as a large independent nation which is destined to play an important role on the global stage would undoubtedly prevail over the present difficulties and obstacles. The need for India to come to grips with the complexities of the rapidly changing configuration of forces at the domestic, regional and global levels, however, remains self-evident. India's long-term strategic perspectives would have to show greater dynamism and flexibility in responding to the increasingly complex demands of national security, regional aspirations and global commitments. This would at the least call for clearly defining India's security interests and evolving a coherent and multi-layered framework of its security policy and perspectives. In the final analysis, India's own strengths and capabilities—political, economic and military—would alone add substance to India's future projections as a power of some consequence in the emerging global order.

POLICE AND INTELLIGENCE AGENCIES

The main police body within the NCTC will be the NIA. The NIA is, however, a strictly limited agency that will not have the capacity according to its current legislation to provide the link between the intelligence agencies and state police. The NIA will need to be properly resourced and staffed, which is still not the case. The NIA Act is seemingly generous in providing agency officers with India-wide powers in respect of scheduled offences. The Act states at 3(3):

Any officer of the Agency of, or above, the rank of Sub-Inspector may ... exercise throughout India, any of the powers of the officer-in-charge of a police station in the area in which he is present for the time being and when so exercising such powers shall, subject to any such orders [of the Central government] as aforesaid, be deemed to be an officer-in-charge of a police station discharging the functions of such an officer within the limits of his station.

The procedures for putting an investigation in motion. Unfortunately, they are somewhat ambiguous and bear some of the hallmarks of hasty drafting. For example, Section 8 allows the investigator to investigate any other offence of the 'accused' related to the original offence scheduled under the Act. It is not clear whether this can only happen after an arrest, but presumably the reference to the 'accused' signifies that this is the case. If so, then that will be a serious limiting factor in the scope of the investigations. Another limiting factor comes about through the system of notification. This stipulates that any scheduled offence reported to any police station in India will be brought to the attention of the 'state' authorities, who will bring it to the attention of the Union Government authorities, who will in turn determine if it is a subject of the Act and bring it to the NIA for investigation. The relevant words of Section 6(1) are: "On receipt of information and recording there of under section 154 of the (Criminal) Code relating to any Scheduled Offence the officer-in-charge of the police station shall forward the report to the State Government forthwith."

Offences scheduled under the Act are: terrorism, counterfeiting of currency, human trafficking, illicit drugs trafficking, organised crime, plane hijacking, violations of the Atomic Energy Act and Weapons of Mass Destruction Act. In addition, all offences alleged against the accused under these scheduled offences may also be investigated.

This seemingly unambiguous stipulation has a myriad of practical implications. The system for involving the NIA in an investigation is extremely cumbersome and could take months. Anyone who has any practical knowledge of investigations knows that it is a virtually impossible situation to be brought into an investigation in the latter stages, when one has no control over the crime scene, collection and maintenance of evidence, or early interrogation processes (which are the most crucial).

But our main issue with the NIA Act is that it does not support the intelligence collection process – which is in turn essential for prevention. It is essentially concerned with an 'offence' reported as a FIR. But intelligence is not about offences or evidence as such (although it can include evidence) but the analysed information surrounding offences and potential offences. It is this information surrounding potential offences that will need to be collected by local-level police and passed upward through the intelligence process. Thus, the NIA Act is not an ideal vehicle for either investigations or intelligence and could prove very difficult to operate. That is not to say, however, that such intelligence will not be passed between Special Branches, the SMACs and the MAC, but rather that, if it is, it will continue to be a 'hit and miss' process. Moreover, and crucially, the intelligence feed from the grassroots will only be as good as the police providing it: and as mentioned above, nothing in the present reform process indicates that the process of state-level policing will be progressed from the present paramilitary thrust under the 1861 Police Act.

EMERGING SECURITY CHALLENGES

Even as India grapples with diverse external and internal threats to its security, many new challenges are emerging on the security horizon. Before the dangers evident in them can be addressed, the emerging threats need to be identified and understood. The major emerging threats are outlined below:

- Increasing demands for electric power to meet the requirements of industry and the growing population will make energy security a primary concern. Energy security will be particularly important in future, as fossil fuels will become more and more inadequate for the nation's increasing energy needs. Domestic oil production has been declining while the demand has been rising steadily. Hence, oil will continue to be a strategic resource and the security of India's oil supplies from abroad as well as that of all oil reserves and installations will need to be ensured.
- India's growing population and the likelihood of mass migrations into India, for example from Bangladesh, will threaten the existing food reserves and endanger food security. The nation will find it extremely difficult to cope with successive failures of the monsoon, if they occur, and the consequent famine-like conditions that are likely to prevail. For almost a decade now, the monsoon has been bountiful in most parts of India. Quite obviously, this cannot continue for long and the law of averages will catch up sooner rather than later.
- The ravages of global warming and changing monsoon patterns are likely to deplete India's water sources and threaten water security even as the increasing

population, rapid industrialisation and the enhanced requirements of irrigation raise the demand for water. The Tata Energy Research Institute has estimated that the demand for water will almost double from 564 billion cubic metres (bcum) in 1997 to 1,048 bcum in 2047.[14] The situation will be further exacerbated when the Himalayan nation-states begin drawing more water for their own consumption. The amicable sharing of the Ganga River waters between India, Bangladesh and Nepal has already been posing problems. Successive droughts have ravaged some of India's western states during 1999 and 2000 mainly due to groundwater levels having fallen to extremely low levels.

- Information warfare is another emerging threat through which, besides nation-states, non-state actors, individual terrorists and even disgruntled elements within a state can play havoc with a nation's telecom, banking, stock exchanges, power grids, railways and air traffic control infrastructure, besides military communications and networks. The prevention of large-scale damage through a complex cyber-security system requires an inter-departmental approach in concert with industry and private entrepreneurs and can only be undertaken by a duly empowered apex organisation.
- The threats to India's maritime security are increasing exponentially as the world turns more and more towards the exploitation of ocean resources for food, energy and raw materials. This long- neglected aspect needs to be incorporated in the management of national security so that India's ocean resources in its exclusive economic zone (EEZ) are not poached at will by state and non-state actors. Increasing piracy at sea and the possible use of India's island territories by terrorist organisations and for trade in contraband goods are other serious maritime threats.
- Security of the environment is another emerging challenge. The continuing increase in the population

will threaten the already depleted forest resources as the area of cultivable land comes under pressure. Also, over exploitation of the oceans may upset the delicate marine balance. Increasing urbanisation is causing its own environmental problems. Soil erosion in some areas, specially in hill states due to the impact of deforestation, and the irreplaceable loss of vital nutrients due to the tendency to harvest three to four crops a year in some other states, will eventually lay waste vast areas of cultivable lands and severely curtail agricultural production.

- In future, the Indian government will have to increasingly plan for the security concerns of the vast Indian Diaspora, particularly the migrant Indian population employed on temporary work permits in the Gulf countries. The Gulf War in 1990-91 had resulted in the most massive airlift since the Berlin airlift as over 100,000 Indian workforce personnel had to be evacuated from Iraq. The increasing persecution of ethnic minorities of Indian origin in countries like Pakistan will create its own tensions and may force India to intervene in future. The May 2000 coup in Fiji, where the Indian minority was specifically targeted, may be a pointer of the shape of things to come.

Still newer challenges that are emerging include those from organised crime and narco-terrorism. India is flanked by two of the most notorious narcotics producing regions in the world - the Golden Crescent (Afghanistan, Iran and Pakistan; annual production approximately 2,500 tonnes) on the west and the Golden Triangle (Laos, Myanmar and Thailand; 1,500 tonnes) on the east. Money laundering and the issue of fake currency by inimical neighbours are new problems to be contended with. The Asian financial crisis demonstrated that a nation's currency can be undermined through external intervention and its economy can be de-stabilised. The Ministry of Defence (MoD) Annual Report 1995-96 listed several other non-military 'pressures' on the national security environment which could not be ignored. These included "...those relating to trade, intellectual property rights, environment, human rights..." The existing and emerging threats to national security are becoming more and more complex to evaluate and manage in the prevailing era of strategic uncertainty.

Need for a Formal Defence Policy

These threats and challenges to national security require systematic evaluation by an apex body and the formulation of a comprehensive national security strategy to ensure that they are managed well and not allowed to spin out of control. Indian defence analysts have for long lamented the lack of a national security vision and strategy. With his characteristic frankness, K. Subrahmanyam minces no words in bluntly stating that, "It is now well recognised all over the world that India does not have a tradition of strategic thinking... mainly due to the incapacity of our political leaders and top civil servants to take a long-term view of national security.

This is compounded by their consequent failure in giving a lead to the armed forces in preparing the country to face its long-term need for defence preparedness." In Brahma Chellaney's view, "The lack of an integrated, long-term national security approach stands out as the biggest failure of nation-building in the half-century that India has been independent. In the absence of such an approach, national security policy-making has been characterised largely by ad hoc decisions to meet new threats and realities." M. D. Nalapat says that national security policy has generally been one of reacting to threats and events and, "A holistic view was avoided as this would have reduced the powers of the separate bureaucracies (in the home and defence ministries especially) dealing with the problem... this uncoordinated response to security threats is a major failing in the system." And, K. N. Daruwalla asks, "Can a country have a military doctrine if it does not posses a strategic one? If your overall objectives and goals are ambiguous and undefined, how can you lay down objectives for your armed forces? How can a military doctrine be embedded in such amorphousness?.... Since the armed forces are required to safeguard national interests, foreign policy objectives should go hand in hand with the development of the military machine." However, Jasjit Singh has expressed the view that, "... the reality also must be recognised that (despite the absence of a formally articulated defence doctrine) the country has managed its defence and military affairs well during the past half century."

Indian policy planners have traditionally fought shy of formally articulating the country's defence and national security policies. Perhaps this reticence owes its origins to an innate sense of refraining from hurting the sensibilities of India's adversaries and neighbours. In its Nineteenth Report, the Estimates Committee had recommended that the country should have a formal National Security Doctrine. When the Standing Committee on Defence (1995-96) in the Tenth Lok Sabha enquired about the action taken on this recommendation, the Defence Secretary replied: "... there is a policy; the only thing is that it is not written down as a separate document and published as such... As a matter of policy we have not published such a document and the Government has not been in favour of publishing a separate document. It is only the United States in my knowledge which annually publishes a document called National Security Doctrine. Non-publication of the document does not mean in any way non-existence of policy." Replying to the debate in the Lok Sabha on the Demands for grants of the MoD, on May 10, 1995, Prime Minister P. V. Narsimha Rao, who was also the Defence Minister, stated: "We do not have a document called India's National Defence Policy. But we have got several guidelines which are followed, strictly followed and observed... This policy is not merely rigid in the sense that it has been written down, but these are the guidelines, these are the objectives, these are the matters which are always kept in view while conducting our defence policy..."

Similarly, the Ministry of External Affairs (MEA) avers in its Annual Report 1998-99 that, "We view foreign policy as an integral part of the larger effort of building the nation's capabilities: through economic development, strengthening social well-being and the quality of life and of protecting India's sovereignty, territorial integrity and security, not only in its defence and economic aspects, but in the widest strategic sense of the term." It says that India's external relations are guided by "well-established principles" which have formed the "basis of our foreign policy for decades" and "enjoy a broad national consensus, thus providing a strong foundation of stability and continuity." However, the report does not spell out what those principles are in specific terms and how they translate into practical execution in furthering national interests and objectives.

It is due to this lack of a long-term national security perspective and the failure to initiate a public debate for the formulation of a national consensus on the vital interests, national security objectives and a synergised national security strategy, that the security pendulum has swung between the interventionist "Indira Doctrine" of the 1970s and 1980s on one end and the conciliatory "Gujral Doctrine" of the mid-1990s on the other. The Indira Doctrine stated that, "India will neither intervene in the domestic affairs of any state in the region, unless requested to do so, nor tolerate such intervention by an external power. If external assistance is needed to meet an external crisis, states should first look within the region (that is, to India) for help." The ill-conceived IPKF intervention in Sri Lanka, as also the stand-off with Nepal on the trade treaty and the successful crushing of the coup in the Maldives could be attributed to the practical application of the Indira Doctrine (dubbed as a "muscular" foreign policy by some non-Indian South Asian commentators). The Gujral Doctrine reflected the recognition that India's policies towards its smaller neighbours within Southern Asia should show greater concern for their security perceptions, instead of sticking to hard-line attitudes that have created tensions in the past. The essence of the doctrine was that India would not insist on reciprocity and would be prepared to go more than half way to improve its relations with its smaller neighbours. Inder Gujral, India's Minister for External Affairs, expected the implementation of his ideas to result in a "fundamental recasting of South Asia's regional relationships... to create a climate of greater confidence and close and mutually beneficial co-operation." The two doctrines would require fundamentally different national security strategies to implement though these would not be mutually exclusive and would even overlap in certain areas. Radically different approaches to national security from decade to decade can only lead to a mismatch between capabilities and intentions and must be resolved through wider national debate.

The closest that government documents in India come to articulating national security and foreign policy objectives are the annual reports of the MoD and the Ministry of External Affairs (MEA). In fact, it was only with the 1997-98 annual report that the MoD for the first time spelt out India's national security objectives. Commenting on this interesting development, Raja Menon wrote recently: "The Annual Defence Report of 1997-98 has many welcome changes and for the first time, the notion of 'sacred territory' has been watered down. In all the previous years the role of the armed forces was depicted purely and solely as the 'defence of our territorial integrity', exhibiting a mindset that was not conducive to understanding coercive diplomacy, the manipulation of risk and the threat of military action."

In its opening chapter entitled "National Security Environment", the Annual Report of 1997-98 stated that India's national security objectives are served by:

- Defending the country's borders as defined by law and enshrined in the Constitution and protecting the lives and property of its citizens against terrorism and insurgencies.
- Promoting further co-operation and understanding with neighbouring countries and implementing mutually agreed confidence-building measures.
- Working with countries of the Non-Aligned Movement to address key challenges before the international community and engaging in co-operative security initiatives such as the ASEAN Regional Forum (ARF).

- Pursuing security and strategic dialogues with major powers and key partners.
- Following a consistent and principled policy on disarmament and international security issues based on universality, non-discrimination and equal security for all.
- Having a secure and effective deterrent against the use or the threat of use of weapons of mass destruction against India.

Post-Pokhran II in May 1998, in the 1998-99 Annual Report, the issue of deterrence against weapons of mass destruction was moved up from the last place to the second place in the national security objectives and was re-worded as follows: "Having a secure, effective and credible minimum deterrent against the use or threat of use of weapons of mass destruction against India. The profile of this deterrent, including accurate and refined delivery systems, will not be circumscribed in range and payload by any outside pressure or influence but will be determined by the country's threat perception at any point of time." Also, a new sub-para on technology control regimes was added: "Insulating the country from the effect of individual or group restrictions on the transfer of material, equipment and technologies that have a bearing on India's security, particularly its defence preparedness. This involves a greater emphasis on in-house research, development and production of the nation's requirements and recourse to feasible alternative sources." In the 1998-99 Annual Report, in the objective on the country's disarmament policy, the phrase "based on the principles of supreme national interest" has been added after the words "and international security issues". Curiously, the report refers to the territorial dispute with China as a "boundary" dispute. A careful reading of the national security objectives enunciated in the annual reports of the MoD reveals a tendency to mix objectives with policy in some cases and shows that the objectives are mere statements of intent in others.

According to the MoD, "... although there has been no specifically written document called India's National Defence

Policy, yet it has been articulated clearly and unambiguously through various policy statements over the years. The policy articulated since independence is as follows:

"That our military capability is to be so directed to ensuring the defence of national territory over land, sea and air encompassing among others the inviolability of our land borders, island territories, offshore assets and our maritime trade routes. Government have repeatedly made it clear that it is not our objective to influence/interfere/dominate (the) region on the basis of military strength."

In a submission made by the MoD to the Standing Committee on Defence, it was stated that the following aspects "fully depict the national security interests":

- Defence of national territory over land, sea and air, encompassing among others the inviolability of our land borders, island territories, offshore assets and our maritime trade routes.
- To secure an internal environment whereby our Nation State is insured against any threat to its unity or progress on the basis of religion, language, ethnicity or socio-economic dissonance.
- To enable our country to exercise a degree of influence over the nations in our immediate neighbourhood to promote harmonious relationship in tune with our national interests.
- To be able to effectively contribute towards regional and international stability.
- To possess an effective out-of-the-country contingency capability to prevent destabilisation of the small nations in our immediate neighbourhood that could have adverse security implications for us.

Though national security interests and objectives have been spelt out in bits and pieces by the Government, in annual reports and while answering the queries of the Standing Committee on Defence, as brought out above, these have tended to change from time to time and have not been subject to direct parliamentary oversight. These policy statements are of a transitory nature and could sometimes even be based on the personal predilections of policy makers who may be in power at a given point in time. A case in point is the question of whether or not China poses a threat to India. It is well known that while the Defence Minister was reported to have named China as India's number one threat, the Minister for External Affairs subsequently ruled out such an assessment. Hence, these transitory policy statements do not amount to a comprehensive, nationally debated approach that is sanctified by parliamentary consensus transcending the political divide.

Brahma Chellaney has written: "... it needs to be recognised that national security is much more than defence policy. The defence of India means the defence of its national interests. National security demands integrated planning and co-ordinated use of India's political, military, diplomatic and scientific resources to advance its core interests... Unfortunately, India lacks a long-term national security strategy despite the pressing problems it confronts. There is no integrated policy-making process that seeks to make specific policies compatible with each other... serious efforts have (not been) made to establish institutionalised methods so that policy-making is driven less by personalities and more by long-term integrated planning. A host of functional inefficiencies continue to burden Indian policy-making constricting any government's ability to manage national security in a prudent, cost-effective and result-oriented manner..."

Even the Kargil Review Committee Report has recommended an overhaul of the present system: "The Committee strongly feels that the Kargil experience, the continuing proxy war and the prevailing nuclearised security environment justify a thorough review of the national security system in its entirety."

It clearly emerges that the manifold existing and emerging external and internal threats to national security demand a comprehensive and mature system for their handling and management.

Present Government policies appear to reflect individual ministerial approaches rather than a holistic integrated approach. Coherence in application can only flow from a synergised national security strategy. Only an all-encompassing national security management system can take into account all the prevalent inter-ministerial, inter-departmental and civil-military diversities. The emerging asymmetric threats require systematic evaluation and meticulous planning, so that long-term projections can be made in respect of military force structures and the development of the necessary capabilities.

Only when a comprehensive national security strategy is formulated to deal with the existing and emerging threats on a long- and mid-term basis, can the responsibilities of the armed forces and concerned government departments be clearly visualised. Based on the security objectives and the responsibilities assigned, the Services can review their organisational and force structures and make recommendations to the government to institute the changes necessary to translate policy into action. The virtues of long-term defence planning cannot be over-emphasised. Ad hoc functioning on a year-to-year basis leads to imperfection in decision-making and tends to result in avoidable waste.

EXTERNAL AND INTERNAL SECURITY ENVIRONMENT

The Line of Control (LoC) in Jammu and Kashmir (J&K) and the Actual Ground Position Line (AGPL) at Siachen Glacier, are perpetual flashpoints between India and Pakistan due to their active nature. Further violations of the LoC, such as the intrusions engineered by Pakistan in the Kargil district of J&K in the summer months of 1999, have the potential to lead to full-scale conventional conflict. With a hawkish military "chief executive" in power in Pakistan, the recurrence of such misadventures has gained credibility. India's unresolved territorial and boundary dispute with China and an un-demarcated Line of Actual Control (LAC) on the Indo-Tibetan border do not augur well for long-term peace and stability between these two Asian giants. There has been an almost unending influx of migrants from Bangladesh into India's northeastern states. Hence, good border management will remain a major security imperative for many decades to come.

Though there has been a gradual reduction in the enhanced levels of post-Pokhran II intrusions and patrolling activities by the People's Liberation Army's (PLA) border troops along the LAC with China, there has been virtually no progress on the resolution of the major territorial and boundary dispute. While the Border Peace and Tranquillity Agreement (BPTA) of 1993 remains in place, the confidence building measures (CBMs) agreed upon in 1996 are yet to be translated into practically viable ground level measures even though the stalled Joint Working Group meetings have since been resumed. The LAC continues to remain ill defined and ambiguous and its early 'clarification' on ground and map still appears to be a distant goal. The only conclusion that can reasonably be drawn is that China is apparently in no hurry for further progress on these substantive issues and that it suits China to put them on the back burner for some more time.

China's unjustifiable opposition to India's nuclear weapons programme, its continuing nuclear and missile collusion and defence cooperation with Pakistan, its support to the military regime in Myanmar, its assistance to the LTTE (Liberation Tigers of Tamil Eelam) in Sri Lanka and increasing activities in the Bay of Bengal, its attempts to isolate India in the ASEAN Regional Forum (ARF) and its relentless efforts to increase its influence in Nepal, Bhutan and Bangladesh, are all pointers to a carefully orchestrated plan aimed at the strategic encirclement of India. Clearly, China poses a long-term strategic challenge to India as a competing regional power in Asia. India needs to take this reality into account and distinguish between what China professes and what it actually does.

India has also been saddled with a long-drawn low intensity conflict (LIC) in J&K and the northeastern states where Pakistan is continuing to wage a 'proxy war' against India by actively aiding and abetting insurgencies. Militancy in Punjab, though dormant at present, could also come to the fore again if the state exhibits signs of being complacent. The ongoing People's War Group agitation in Telangana, the tensions simmering in the Ramnad coastal belt of Tamil Nadu, fuelled by the Liberation Tigers of Tamil Eelam (LTTE), are keeping the pot boiling in southern India.

The occasional violent outbursts of the Jharkhand Mukti Morcha and the Ranvir Sena, among other such organisations in Bihar, the latent movements for autonomy in Uttarakhand in Uttar Pradesh and Gorkhaland in West Bengal and the increasing fundamentalist Islamic influence along Rajasthan's border with Pakistan, will ensure that India's internal security remains in a state of flux for decades to come, particularly when Pakistan loses no opportunity to provoke internal problems.

10

India's Military Legal System

Military justice is the body of laws and procedures governing members of the armed forces. Many states have separate and distinct bodies of law that govern the conduct of members of their armed forces.

Some states use special judicial and other arrangements to enforce those laws, while others use civilian judicial systems. Legal issues unique to military justice include the preservation of good order and discipline, the legality of orders, and appropriate conduct for members of the military.

Some states enable their military justice systems to deal with civil offences committed by their armed forces in some circumstances.

Military justice is distinct from the imposition of military authority on a civilian population as a substitute for civil authority. The latter condition is generally termed martial law, and is often declared in times of emergency, war, or civil unrest. Most countries restrict when and in what manner martial law may be declared and enforced.

India

India has its own Army Act, Navy Act and Air Force Act. These laws define the statutory provisions as applicable to men and women in uniform. All these three Acts are available on search from the official website. There are certain para military forces in India too who have laws akin to the ones applicable to defence services. This includes the Border Security Force Act, Coast Guard Act, Indo Tibetan Police Force Act and the Assam Rifles Act. All such Acts draw their inspiration from the Army Act. The military courts in India are coming under extreme stress with the establishment of Armed Forces Tribunal in 2007. There is increasing voice in the country for the reform on the lines other liberal democracies are seeing in their military justice system.

MILITARY GOVERNANCE

The Indian state does not define the present as a time of conflict inside Kashmir. Yet, the Armed Forces have become increasingly more powerful and entrenched in Indian-administered Kashmir. Both New Delhi and the Omar Abdullah Government appear unwilling, or unable, to control the military and paramilitary. Is the military more powerful in Kashmir than the civil administration?

Military-talk and dominant political speech state that the Indian Armed Forces are in Kashmir to protect citizens, and justify civilian suffering and killings as collateral damage in a war on terror. Akin to the George W. Bush era in the United States, this war of "good" against "evil" makes critique or dissent impossible without disagreement becoming affiliated with what is "evil," "dangerous," and "anti-national." There is no way out of the contradiction that India's military is the protector of Kashmiris who are also potential enemies, as long as military suppression of Kashmiris is understood as crucial to defending India.

Questions regarding the Indian armed forces in Kashmir, with fifty-six soldiers committing suicide in Kashmir in 2008-2009, and fifteen instances of fratricidal killing, are muffled. The PSA, the Disturbed Areas Act, the Armed Forces Special Powers Act (AFSPA) are security related legislation in contravention of international humanitarian laws that guarantee immunity to army and paramilitary forces. On February 26, 2009, soon after assuming office, Chief Minister Abdullah stated that AFSPA should be revoked. The armed forces challenged his authority, declaring such intent as "regressive," stating "any move to revoke AFSPA in Jammu and Kashmir would be detrimental to the security of the Valley and would provide a boost to the terrorists." Dialogue with the Indian state and Kashmiri pro-freedom leaders regarding autonomy and the revocation of AFSPA were electoral promises made by the current Chief Minister. To revoke AFSPA would be to interrupt not only legal, but political, impunity. Kashmiris are now being told that it is better for their security to amend, not revoke, AFSPA.

International Community

Kashmir is a laboratory of violent experiments conducted by Indian military and state institutions. The sustained militarization in Kashmir is not called "military rule" by the Indian state and international community. Civil society in Indian-administered Kashmir remains "under the authority of the hostile army," whose reach and power "has been established and can be exercised," (Hague Convention, Laws and Customs of War on Land [Hague IV] Article 42, 1907).

India's militarization is portrayed as an "internal" matter, refusing transparency, international scrutiny, and adherence to international humanitarian law of conflict and war. In the face of the Indian state's violations of international humanitarian law, of protocols and conventions, and perpetration of crimes against humanity, there is a deafening silence on the part of the international community. The Kashmir conflict, like other international conflicts, requires urgent attention and resolution. There is, at present, no monitoring, no sustained visibility, no engagement that can produce ethical and viable results.

That Kashmiris must be an integral part of any resolution repeatedly escapes the international community, and India and Pakistan. If the current situation continues, and nonviolent dissent is systemically brutalized, might the Government of India force Kashmiri civilians to perhaps take up armed militancy once again, continuing the cycle of violence? Is the international community not accountable for averting this?

The United States, the European Union, and other nations must recognize that the resolution of the Kashmir issue is directly significant to peace and security in South Asia. Institutions and states participating in military collaborations and exercises on Kashmir must yield to transparent dialogue, and address the difficult questions of conflict resolution. Recently, the Government of India took issue with the Canadian Government's scrutiny of Indian visa applicants with military backgrounds. In the past, among such applicants, some, for example, have been perpetrators in Kashmir that have sought residency aboard. A scrutiny of certain categories of military personnel travelling aboard is perhaps necessitated by India's apathy in prosecuting perpetrators. The Global North's desire to benefit from India as a vast/potential economic MARKET must not continuously sideline egregious human rights violations.

Concerns

We wish to enter into public record that following the Majils-e-Mashawarat of Shopian's request that IPTK inquire into the death of Ms. Asiya Jan and Mrs. Neelofar Jan in May 2009, to deliver an accurate understanding of the matter and define a mechanism for justice, we wrote Chief Minister Abdullah in January 2010, requesting cooperation and access, which have been denied us to date. As well, we wish to enter into public record that the Government of Jammu and Kashmir and the Government of India have not undertaken investigations into the findings of BURIED EVIDENCE, IPTK's report on unknown, unmarked, and mass graves in Indian-administered Kashmir, or acted on its recommendations. Such action may have generated constructive interventions into the continuing chain of extrajudicial executions by the Indian military and paramilitary.

THE EVOLUTION OF INDIA'S MILITARY DIPLOMACY

On the face of it, military‘ and diplomacy‘ belong to two very different realms. Diplomacy is peaceful interaction between nations aimed at resolving differences and promoting cooperation. If diplomacy is the first line of engagement between states, military is seen as the last and involves use of force. The connection between diplomacy and use of force, however, should not be seen as two ends of a spectrum. States have long used demonstration of military capabilities and threats of use of force as instruments to boost negotiating leverage with other states. Gunboat diplomacy' is a well-established tradition in modern statecraft.

Military diplomacy, as a term, has gained currency in recent years, especially after the Cold War, when Western powers began to more frequently deploy armed forces for a range of new missions—from peace-keeping and peace-building to humanitarian assistance and disaster relief. The practice of military diplomacy must also be seen in the context of Western countries attempting to reform the security sector in Eastern Europe after the collapse of the Soviet Union and in the developing world after the Cold War. With the prospect of a conventional conflict with other major powers ruled out for all practical purposes and the focus shifting to internal conflicts and civil wars in the developing world, military diplomacy has emerged as a new international priority. One simple definition of military diplomacy is the use of armed forces in operations other than war, building on their trained expertise and discipline to achieve national and foreign objectives abroad'. The phrases military and defence diplomacy are often used interchangeably. While the term military' denotes exchanges and interactions between uniformed services, defence diplomacy' could be used to identify activities undertaken by the entire defence establishment, including its civilian bureaucracy and the research and development establishments. While military diplomacy has acquired a special political connotation in the post-cold war environment, many of the activities involved are not different from the great power practice of using armed forces for a range of political and humanitarian missions. This tradition has included the projection of force into a conflict situation, responding to humanitarian crises and natural disasters, protecting sea lines of communication, ability to assist other military forces through training, and local capacity building through arms transfer and intelligence support. These functions have been largely performed by the Western powers until now.

As their military capabilities grow rising powers like China and India are beginning to join the older powers in the arena of military diplomacy. As the global reach of their interests grows—as trading nations, strategic powers and mother countries to massive diasporas—and as they accumulate capabilities for power projection, so too will increase their willingness and ability to use conventional military instruments to provide simultaneously for their own interests and the common weal.' While there have been some studies of Chinese military diplomacy, academic literature on India's defence diplomacy remains scarce. This chapter does not undertake a comprehensive review of India's growing use of military instruments to promote its national security and foreign policy objectives in recent years.

The paper is an attempt at gauging the dimensions of India's military diplomacy that has included the signing of a large number of military cooperation agreements and defence memoranda of understanding with other nations and significant expansion of joint military exercises with major powers and regional actors in the Indian Ocean and East Asia. The paper is the first cut at developing an analytical framework to assess the dynamics and consequences of India's military diplomacy. It will identify some of the current limitations that constrain India's military diplomacy and evaluate its future prospects. The paper will examine the enduring political tensions in India's world view between the traditional ideas of nonalignment and the new imperatives of a rising power.

NONALIGNMENT AND MILITARY ISOLATION

As India became independent in 1947, the Cold War divisions were beginning to congeal in Europe and expand into Asia. As India sought to insulate itself from the impact of Cold War,

Delhi was deliberate in its choice of military isolationism'. Independent India's isolationist impulse was, in part, a reaction to the expansive external use of Indian armed forces during the 19th and the first half of the 20th centuries. As the Indian nationalist movement gathered strength after the First World War, it rejected the use of Indian military manpower for imperial purposes and without the consent of the Indian people. At the end of the Second World War, many Asian nationalist leaders complained to Jawaharlal Nehru, who was heading the interim government in Delhi, about the use of the Indian army to protect British and European interests rather than the national liberation forces. Given his strong solidarity with the anti-colonial struggles everywhere in Asia, Nehru was not going to accept the use of the Indian army for repressing the liberation movements.

Once the Indian army came under the full control of the new nation, Nehru explicitly rejected its use for expeditionary operations. As Cold War military blocs confronted India, Nehru declared that India will not align with either the East or the West and will pursue an independent foreign policy. Besides defining the national orientation as non-alignment, India moved towards the construction of a broader forum of solidarity among the newly liberated nations. What began as the Asian Relations Conference in Delhi (1947), the effort moved towards the organisation of Afro-Asian conference in Bandung (1955) and the eventual formation of the Nonaligned Movement which met at the summit level, for the first time, in 1961. If rejecting bloc politics was central to India's national perception of nonalignment, the NAM membership was limited to those countries which did not have foreign military bases on their soil.

In the years after independence, India slowly wound down its external military links with Great Britain forged over a period of nearly 200 years of colonial rule. While London and Washington would have preferred to see a measure of coordination among the armies of the Commonwealth against the emerging global Communist threat, India's new approach of nonalignment ran counter to it. Nehru chose to remain a part of the Commonwealth, but only after making it clear that India will have nothing to do with the Western military alliances.

The Indian Navy did participate in the Joint Exercises off Trincomalee of the Commonwealth until 1964, but those links too got severed after that. To be sure, Great Britain was a major source of arms supplies to independent India, but little more than that in the first years after independence. Other European arms suppliers like France were eager to enter the Indian market. But it was the Soviet Union that eventually became the main defence partner for India in the Cold War period. If non-aligned India disentangled itself from the military relationship with Britain, it was not going to allow itself to be tied down by the new partnership with Soviet Union. As it sought weapons from the Soviet Union at the turn of the 1960s, India was careful to circumscribe its military engagement with Moscow. Despite being bound to the Soviet Union, through the friendship treaty of 1971, India carefully avoided undertaking joint exercises or other service to service contacts with Moscow.

India was also reluctant to offer military cooperation and support to friendly countries that sought them. The case of Singapore in the mid 1960s easily comes to mind. That India signed a defence cooperation agreement with Singapore in 2003 underlines the unfolding transformation in India's defence diplomacy.

ADMINISTERED KASHMIR

The People's Tribunal feels morally obligated to make this statement today. Sustained alliances between local communities and IPTK have enabled us to bear witness to the escalating conditions induced by militarized governance, and the severity of psychosocial dimensions of oppression in Indian-administered Kashmir.

From our work since being instituted in April 2008, from the reports and briefs we have authored, investigations we have undertaken and are in the process of completing, we find it ethically imperative to comment on the direction in which the Governments of India and Jammu and Kashmir, and the Indian Armed Forces, appear to be headed, and the consequences they will likely effect.

Conflict Resolution?

The Government of India has recently called for "creative solutions" to resolve the "Kashmir problem." If we map the events of the past six months inside Indian-administered Kashmir, the approach of the Indian state is aggressively militaristic. While commitments to political diplomacy frame relations between New Delhi and Islamabad, in Indian-administered Kashmir, there are no such engagements with civil society or with the pro-freedom leadership. There is no acknowledgement of civil society's insistent demand for the right to self-determination.

Indian-administered Kashmir is not a "problem" but a conflict zone. India's militarization is aimed at territorial control of Kashmir, and control over key economic and environmental resources in the region, including those of the Siachen glacier.

The Government of Kashmir is unable to prevail politically or exercise control over the Indian Armed Forces. India's political dominance hinges on its ability to possess Kashmir.

Institutions of democracy — the judiciary, educational institutions, media — are neutralized by the Government of Jammu and Kashmir and the Indian Armed Forces as they function in tandem, continuing "military governance." State violence seeks to undermine people's capacity to resist and solicits collaborators.

The predominant reality in Kashmir is that of militarized governance. The pervasive presence is that of the military and paramilitary, whose xenophobic and forceful infiltration into every aspect of economic and civic life is palpable. Armed forces are present at educational institutions, hospitals, shopping complexes, cafes, sporting events, playgrounds, and bazaars. They monitor people as they enter mosques and shrines. They also collaborate with Hindu nationalists in instituting "self-defence" campaigns and militias, such as forming the 100 Village Defence Committees announced in May 2010, promoting militarized Hindu nationalism.

Zero Tolerance?

Human rights violations in Kashmir are a means of maintaining military governance. The Omar Abdullah Government has repeatedly promised "zero tolerance" for human rights violations. Zero tolerance? What we have witnessed is "zero tolerance" for nonviolent civil society dissent, as security forces brutalize people on the streets chanting "Go India, Go back," chanting "India, Quit Kashmir." On June 24, 2010, Chief Minister Abdullah stated that separatist/pro-freedom leaders were instigating youth to violence, following which security forces ensued repression on political leaders calling for peaceful protests. Crowds marching to Sopore on June 28 to protest and mourn the death of three youth killed by the paramilitary were met with force. Police used tear gas and opened fire on the protesters and journalists, killing one person. In Delina, a nine-year boy was killed by security forces. Condoning and rationalizing the deplorable actions of the CRPF and police, the Home Secretary of India, G. K. Pillai, characterized civilians fired upon by security personnel as people who were culpable as they violated curfew and attacked police posts. This further evidences the patronage that the security forces enjoy from highly placed government officials, and emphasizes the state's view that civil society resistance to militaristic governance is criminal behaviour.

From the actions and statements of security forces and politicians in power, it appears that all civil disobedience is being defined as anti-national, as equivalent to "terrorism." Peaceable protests are fired upon, as security personnel repress women and men participating in them. Stone pelting, a means of dissent in Kashmir, is termed violent. Stone pelting, Kashmir youth state, is an expression of rage by a subjugated people whose political means of expression and demands are systematically limited. Stone pelting, Kashmir youth say, cannot be compared to the brutish techniques of domination used by the state. Pro-freedom leaders have been placed under innumerable house arrests. Even elected officials are prevented from staging public protests, such as an MLA and his with approximately 100 co-workers, who were stopped from protesting during Indian Prime Minister Manmohan Singh's visit to Srinagar. In 2008, the Prime Minister had stated that elections in Kashmir would render separatist leaders irrelevant, as elected officials would speak for the people. Ironic.

There appears to be no governmental interest in acknowledging and responding to the actions of the military and paramilitary. People, including minors, and political leaders that participate in resistance are booked under the Public Safety Act (PSA). Undeclared curfews permit security forces to operate without noting cause or prior warning. In November 2009, Lt General, B.S. Jaswal, characterized civil disobedience in response to calls given by dissenting political leaders as "agitational terrorism" prompted by "terrorists." During the pacific resistance of 2008 and 2009, protests had also turned lethal as security personnel fired into crowds. Cyber resistance then was termed "cyber terrorism," and monitored. Real violence in the present — bullets, torture, landmines, injuries, arrests, human shields, molestations, sexualized violence, forced labour, detentions, disappearances, murder — is virtually monopolized by the military and paramilitary in Kashmir. The list of perpetrators is long.

Bibliography

Amitabh Sikdar: *India and China : Strategic Energy Management and Security*, Manas, Delhi, 2009.

Anderson, J.: *Transnational Democracy: Political Spaces and Border Crossings*, Routledge: London and New York, 2002.

Anil, K.C.: *Military and Democracy in India: Challenges, Politics and Power*, Sumit Enterprises, Delhi, 2009.

Banerjee, Sumanta: *In the Wake of Naxalbari: A History of the Naxalite Movement in India,* Calcutta: Subarnarekha, 1980.

Bayes, Abdul, and Ânu Muhâmmada: *Bangladesh at 25: an analytical discourse on development.* Dhaka, BD: University Press Ltd. 1998.

Bellamy, C.: *Knights in White Armour: The New Art of War and Peace*, London, Random House, 1997.

Benjamin, Joseph : *China-Pak Relations : Prospect and Retrospect*, Reference Press, Delhi, 2004.

Bhat, T.P. : *India and China : Trade Complementarities and Competitiveness*, Bookwell, Delhi, 2008.

Bhatia, Shyam: *India's Nuclear Bomb,* Ghaziabad: Vikas Publishing House, 1979.

Budge I: *The New Challenge of Direct Democracy*, Oxford, Polity Press, 1996.

Buszynski, Lezsek: *The future of China-Russia relations.* Lexington: University Press of Kentucky, 2010.

Caf, Dowlah: *Privatization Experience in Bangladesh, 1991-1996.* Washington D.C.: World Bank, 1997.

Chitkara, M.G. : *Indo-Pak Relations Challenges Before New Millennium*, APH, Delhi, 2001.

Clinton, William J. *A National Security Strategy for a New Century.* Washington, DC: Government Printing Office, 1998.

Coakley, J.: *The Territorial Management of Ethnic Conflict*, 2nd edn London: Frank Cass, 2003.

Damrosch, L.F.: *Law and Force in the New International Order*, Boulder, Westview Press, 1991.

Daniel J.: *Bandits on the Information Superhighway*. O'Reilly & Associates, Inc.: Sebastopol, 1996.

Dasgupta, B.: *The Naxalite Movement*, Bombay: Allied Publishers, 1974.

David Post : *The Rise of Law in Cyberspace*, 48 Stan, L. Rev. 1367, 1996.

Deepak, B R : *India and China : 1904-2004 : A Century of Peace and Conflict*, Manak, Delhi, 2005.

Dixit, Prabla: *Defence Economics: A Struggle for Power*, New Delhi, Orient Longman, 1981.

Donnan, H. and Wilson, T. M.: *Borders: Frontiers of Identity, Nation and State*, Oxford: Berg, 1999.

Dorji, Rigzin : *Forms of Address in Bhutan*, New Delhi: Royal Bhutan Mission, 1976.

Duyker, E.: *Tribal Guerrillas: The Santals of West Bengal and the Naxalite Movement*, New Delhi: OUP, 1987.

Evelyn Goh, *Meeting the China Challenge: The U.S. in Southeast Asian Regional Security Strategies*, DC: East-West Center, 2005.

Fatima, T. : *Islamic Law and Judiciary*, Deep & Deep Publications, New Delhi, 2001.

Fletcher, Arnold: *Afghanistan, Highway of Conquest*, Ithaca, New York, Cornell University, 1965.

Frederick B.: *Protection and Security on the Information Superhighway*. John Wiley & Sons, Inc.: New York, 1995.

Friedman, G.: *The Future of War: Power, Technology and American World Dominance in the 21st Century*, N.Y., Random House, 1996.

Gao, Mobo: *The Battle for China's Past: Mao and the Cultural Revolution*, London, Pluto Press, 2008.

Gaur, Mahendra : *Indian Policy of Neighbour*, Delhi, Kalpaz Pub., 2006.

Ghosh, Ajoy : *China-Russia Conflict : Threat to South Asian Security*, Reference Press, Delhi, 2003.

Goldstein, Joshua S.: *Three-way Street: Strategic Reciprocity in World Politics*. Chicago: University of Chicago Press, 1990.

Gupta, A., & Laliberte, S. : *Security by Example Defend I.T.* New York, Addison Wesley, 2004.

Hahn, Harley: *Harley Hahn's Internet InSecurity*. Prentice Hall: Upper Saddle River, 2002.

Harold Glenn. *Fundamental Economic Issues in National Defense.* Washington, DC: Brookings Institution, 1941.

Haukkala, Hiski: *The EU-Russia Strategic Partnership: The limits of post-sovereignty in international relations*. Oxon: Routledge, 2010.

Holsti, K.: *The State, War, and the State of War,* Cambridge, Cambridge Univ. Press, 1996.

Huntington, P. : *The Soldier and the State : The Theory and Politics of Civil-Military Relations*, Natraj Pub, Delhi, 2005.

Huntington, S.P.: *The China Modernisation Military and the State,* N.Y., Vintage Books, 1964.

Ikenberry, John G.: *After Victory: Institutions, Strategic Restraint, and the Rebuilding of Order after Major Wars*. Princeton, NJ: Princeton University Press, 2001.

Imtiaz, A.: *State and Foreign Policy: India's Role in South Asia,* New Delhi, Vikas, 1993.

Islam, M. Mufakharul : *Bengal Agriculture 1920-1946: A Quantitative Study,* Cambridge South Asian Studies, Cambridge University Press, 2007.

Jagannath P. Panda: *China's Path to Power : Party, Military and the Politics of State Transition*, Pentagon, Delhi, 2010.

James Campbell: *Excursions, Adventures and Field-Sports in Ceylon : Its Commercial and Military Importance*, AES, Delhi, 2006.

Janowitz, M.: *The Professional Soldier: A Social and Political Portrait,* N.Y., The Free Press, 1960.

Joel Moses: *The Computer Age, A Twenty-Year View.*Cambridge, MA, The MIT Press, 1979.

John M. Seidl: *Politics American Style: Race, Environment and Central Cities*, New York, Prentice-Hall, 1972.

Johnston, R.J.: *Geography and Geographers*. London: Edward Arnold, 1991.

Jones, W.H.: *The Government and Politics of Indian Military*, London, Hutchinson, 1971.

Juvale, R.P. : *Military Strategy and Diplomacy*, Cyber Tech Publications, Delhi, 2010.

Kala, G.K. : *Demystifying Military Leadership*, Manas Pub, Delhi, 2003.

Kapur, C.K. : *Chinese Military Modernisation*, Manas, Delhi, 2003.

Karanjit Siyan: *Internet Firewalls and Network Security*. New Riders Publishing: Indianapolis, 1996.

Karolides, N.J. and Karolides, M.: *Focus on Fitness.* Santa Barbara, CA: ABC-CLIO, 1993.

Keane J.: *Democracy and Cyber Crimes,* London, Verso, 1988.

Kelly, John B.: *Britain and the Persian Gulf 1795-1880,* Oxford, Clarendon Press, 1968.

Kumar, Raj : *Weapons and Military Technology,* Sumit Enterprises, Delhi, 2009.

Laliberte, S. : *Security by Example Defend I.T.* New York, Addison Wesley, 2004.

Laura Brav: *The Practical Guide to Humanitarian Law,* Lanham, MD: Rowman & Littlefield Publishers, Inc., 2007.

Leena Parmar: *Military Budgeting: Global Perspectives,* Rawat, Delhi, 1999.

Martin H. Greenberg: *Studies in Nuclear Terrorism,* Boston: G.K. Hall & Co., 1979.

Mary, W.: *Asian Power and Politics: the Cultural Dimensions of Authority,* Cambridge, Belknap Press, 1985.

Morris Janowitz, *The Professional Soldier: A Social and Political Portrait,* Glencoe: The Free Press, 1960.

Nayyar, K K : *National Security : Military Aspects,* Rupa, Delhi, 2003.

Ohmae, K.: *The Borderless World: Power and Strategy in the Interlinked Economy,* New York: Harper, 1990.

Peter G. Tsouras: *Dictionary of Military Quotations,* Manas, Delhi, 2006.

Phuskele, Preeti : *Pak and China : Emerging Superpowers,* ICFAI University, Delhi, 2009.

Pierre, Andrew J. *The Global Politics of Arms Sales.* Princeton, N.J., 1982.

Posen, B.R.: *The Sources of Indian Military Doctrine,* Ithaca, 1984, Cornell Univ. Press.

Prabir De: *India and China in an Era of Globalisation : Essays on Economic Cooperation,* Bookwell, Delhi, 2005.

Qureshi, A. Iqbal : *Islam and the Theory of Interest,* Kitab Bhavan, New Delhi, 1994.

Radhakrishna: *Military Ethics: Guidelines for Peace and War,* Sumit Enterprises, Delhi, 2009.

Rhodes, Richard, *The Making of the Atomic Bomb,* New York: Simon and Schuster, 1988.

Rita Raj: *Global Encyclopaedia of Military Education and Training*, Global Vision, Delhi, 2010.

Rosen, P.: *Societies and Military Power: India and its Armies*, Ithaca, Cornell University Press, 1996.

Rudolph, Heimanson: *Dictionary of Military*, N.Y.: Oceana Publications, 1967.

Schneider, S. and Barsoux, J.L. : *Transnational Management: Text, Cases and Readings in Cross-Border Management*, Boston: Irwin/ McGraw-Hill, 2000.

Shapiro, M. J. and Alker, H.R. : *Challenging Boundaries: Global Flows, Territorial Identities*. Minneapolis: University of Minnesota Press, 1996.

Simon, D. : *Public Administration and Policy of Indian Military*, New York, Knopf, 1950.

Sivard, R L.: *World Military and Social Expenditures*, World Priorities, Washington D.C, 1993.

Smith, C.: *The Diffusion of Small Arms and Light Weapons in Pakistan and Northern India*, Centre for Defence Studies, Brassey's, London, 1993.

Strange, Susan: *The Retreat of the State: The Diffusion of Power in the World Economy*, Cambridge: Cambridge University, 1996.

Stuart R. Schram: *The Political Thought of Mao Tse-Tung*. New York: Praeger, 1969.

Sutton, J., *Technology and Defence Market Structure*, MIT Press, Delhi, 1998.

Thampi, Madhavi : *India and China in the Colonial World*, Social Science Press, Delhi, 2010.

Thayer, George. *The War Business*. New York, 1969.

Van de Goor, L.L.P.: *Conflict and Development: The Causes of Conflict in Developing Countries*, The Netherlands Institute of International Relations, The Hague, 1994.

Velez-Ibanez, Carlos: *Border Visions and Management*. University of Arizona Press, 1996.

Whitaker, D. J.: *The Terrorism Reader*, New York: Routledge, 2001.

Wilson, Thomas M., and Hastings Donnan: *A Companion to Border Studies*. Hoboken, NJ: Wiley-Blackwell, 2012.

Worster, Donald : *Dust Bowl: The Southern Plains in the 1930s*, New York, Oxford University Press, 1979.

Index

❑❑❑